J.W. Boddam Whetham

Across Central America

J.W. Boddam Whetham

Across Central America

ISBN/EAN: 9783337255206

Printed in Europe, USA, Canada, Australia, Japan

Cover: Foto ©Andreas Hilbeck / pixelio.de

More available books at **www.hansebooks.com**

ACROSS CENTRAL AMERICA.

BY

J. W. BODDAM-WHETHAM,

AUTHOR OF
'PEARLS OF THE PACIFIC,' AND 'WESTERN WANDERINGS.'

FLORES, LAKE OF PETEN.

LONDON:
HURST AND BLACKETT, PUBLISHERS,
13 GREAT MARLBOROUGH STREET.
1877.

PREFACE.

N the following pages I wish to give the reader an insight to a country not often visited by travellers, and which on that account may perhaps afford some interest.

I arrived at the port of San José de Guatemala from San Francisco in October, 1875, proceeded to the city of Guatemala, and after some interesting trips, east and west, continued my journey northward. A good road took me as far as Coban in Alta Vera Paz, then by an Indian path over the mountain ranges I reached the Rio de la Pasion, which enabled me by canoe to land within a few leagues of what has been called "the mysterious Lake of Peten." From Peten a journey of six days through the forest brought me to the village of Tenosique, situated on the Rio de la Pasion, which here assumes the name of Usumacinta; thence by canoe to the island of Carmen in the Gulf of Mexico.

Preface.

Of the wonderful ruins—evidences of ancient Indian civilization—which are so profusely scattered over this part of the continent I visited Quiché, Copan, and Palenque. These have been so ably dealt with both by pen and pencil by historians and explorers, that I have only ventured to give a general idea of them for the information of those who have not read the important works on Central America. If my readers only know as little of the subjects of this volume before taking it up as I did before I started on my journey, I trust they will in some measure be repaid by its perusal.

J. W. B. W

CONTENTS.

CHAPTER I.

PACIFIC PORTS—MAZATLAN—PRONUNCIADOS—BRIGANDS—JESUIT INFLUENCE—ACAPULCO—HARBOUR SCENES—A LAZY TOWN—A MEXICAN FORT—COAST RANGE—VOLCANOES—PACIFIC GALES—SAN JOSÉ AND GUATEMALA—CUSTOM HOUSE—PAINFUL INTEREST—DEPARTURE 1

CHAPTER II.

EN ROUTE TO THE CAPITAL—SCENERY—GAZZA LADRA—BREAKFAST—OX-TEAMS—NATIVE PLOUGH—ESCUINTLA—CHANGE OF SCENE—A MACHETE—FALLS OF SAN PEDRO MARTIR—AMATITLAN—NOPAL PLANTATIONS—COCHINEAL—REFRESHMENT—LAKE OF AMATITLAN—HOT SPRINGS—ASCENT—PLAIN OF GUATEMALA——COURTESY—ARRIVAL IN CITY 10

CHAPTER III.

A MARKET SCENE—FRUITS AND VEGETABLES—A GENEROUS VENDOR — DRESS — A SUPERSTITION — NOON — BEGGARS — THE PLAZA—A USEFUL CLOCK — CATHEDRAL — FOUNTAIN — UNDER THE COLONNADES—MOSAIC—BATHING—AN ILLUSTRIOUS EXAMPLE—CLIMATE—ASPECT OF CITY — INDIAN PORTERS — BUSINESS-HOUSES — DINNER-HOUR — VIEW FROM THE CARMEN HILL 20

CHAPTER IV.

FEAST DAYS—LE JOUR DES MORTS—ENTRANCE TO CEMETERY—THE INTERIOR—A CONTRAST—PICKPOCKETS—EARLY HOURS—HOSPITALITY — SOCIETY — PRESIDENT BARRIOS—PRIESTS AND NUNS—EXAMINATION—PRESIDENTIAL CAPACITY—GOVERNMENT—IMPROVEMENTS—A NEW ROAD—PUBLIC INSTITUTIONS—THE THEATRE—A COINCIDENCE—PROGRESS—AMUSEMENTS—PICNICS—START FOR THE COAST 31

CHAPTER V.

INDIAN MOUNDS—AQUEDUCT—INDIANS GOING TO MARKET—MIXCO—COMPOSITION OF AN AVERAGE VILLAGE—BARRANCAS—SANTA MARIA EARTHQUAKE—CATTLE FAIR—CHIMALTENANGO—LOOKING BACK—TEMPERATE ZONE—A FLOUR MILL—TECPAN—CHURCH—INDIANS—GOITRE—INTERIOR OF CHURCH—MIRACLE STONE—IXINCHE—ASCENT TO LOS ALTOS—ATITLAN—A WEIRD SCENE—A MARIMBA—RAINSTORM — ENCUENTROS — MOUNTAIN VIEWS—SANTO TOMAS—RELIGIOUS FESTIVAL—A FRUGAL MEAL—SANTA CRUZ DEL QUICHE—THE CONVENT—HOSPITALITY—A NIGHT'S REST 43

CHAPTER VI.

RUINS OF QUICHE—IDOLS—THOUGHTS—ALPINE SCENERY—TOTO-
NICAPAN—INDIANS OF LOS ALTOS—CAPTURE OF TOTONICAPAN
—AN "ON DIT"—STRANGE ASPECT OF COUNTRY—WEALTHY
INDIANS—QUEZALTENANGO—ITS VOLCANOES—PLAZA—ANCIENT
DIET—CATHEDRAL—DEATH OF FLORES—A CENTRAL AMERICAN
DRAWING-ROOM—A NEW ROAD—ALMOLONGA—HOT SPRINGS—
POTTERY MANUFACTORY—INDIAN SUPERSTITIONS—AN INDIAN
GOVERNOR—ASCENT OF VOLCANO OF QUEZALTENANGO . 58

CHAPTER VII.

A MUD ROAD—MULES—BAD LANGUAGE—CHANGE OF VEGETATION
—TREE FERNS—VIEW OF COAST—BIRDS—ARISTOLOCHIA—A
FINCA—COFFEE ESTATES IN GUATEMALA—ADVANTAGES AND
DISADVANTAGES—IDEAS ON SELLING AND BUYING PLANTATIONS
—DESCRIPTION OF COFFEE RAISING—AVERAGE PRODUCTION—
PROCESS OF PREPARING THE BERRY—LABOUR SYSTEM—COFFEE
CULTURE OF SERVICE TO THE COUNTRY—ESTIMATE OF COST
AND PRODUCTION OF A NEW COFFEE PLANTATION . 71

CHAPTER VIII.

A FINCA—COFFEE TREE—ANTS—HAMMOCK BRIDGE—GRAVE
INDIANS—COSTA CUCA AND COSTA GRANDE—RETALULEN—AN
INN—A FOREST KING—SAPOTE TREE—BIRDS—BUTTERFLIES—
INDIAN WOMEN—A SPORTSMAN—PARROTS—CHITALON—VOL-
CANOES—WASHERWOMEN—A KNOWING MULE—WIFE BEATING
—PACING—COCOA PLANTATION—VAMPYRES–GOITRES—AN ANI-
MATED FLOWER-BED—CUESTA D'ATITLAN—ASCENT—VIEW—A
CURIOUS TREE—INDIAN SUPERSTITION—CABILDS—LIGHTNING
EFFECTS 83

CHAPTER IX.

LAKE OF ATITLAN—INDIAN LEGENDS—CERRO DE ORO—GEM OF ATITLAN — CUESTA — NORVAL —VIEW OF LAKE — GODINES — NAMES IN GUATEMALA—STEEP PRECIPICE—EXCHANGE OF CIVILITIES—ASCENT TO TABLE LAND—PATZUN—FEAST DAY—TO ANTIGUA—ACCOUNT OF THE DESTRUCTION OF THE TWO OLD CAPITALS—ENTRANCE TO CITY 102

CHAPTER X.

A SANATORIUM—A RUINED TEMPLE—THE PLAZA—SANTA MARIA —CONVENT QUARTERS—A CONCERT—MIDNIGHT—START FOR VOLCANO—A SHORT CUT—HEIGHTS OF VOLCANOES—A NAP IN THE CRATER—INSCRIPTIONS—VIEW FROM SUMMIT—MANO DEL MICO—FLOR DE MADERA—RARE PHEASANT—DRUNKEN INDIANS —AZTEC LAW—RETURN TO GUATEMALA . . . 113

CHAPTER XI.

POT-POURRI—VOLCANIC FIRE—A STRANGE THEORY—SUN'S RAYS— NACIMIENTO—FEAST OF GUADALUPE—ITS ORIGIN—JOCOTENANGO—SAN DOMINGO — ZOPILOTE — STARLING — TOUCANS — A MESON—EL CARABAN—WHO GOES THERE?—WAR—PASSPORTS— START FOR COPAN AND ESQUIPULAS 126

CHAPTER XII.

A PILGRIMAGE—A· BLACK SAINT—CERRO REDONDO—PASCUAL— ARPINO—A TORTILLA—THE ROAD-RUNNER—SWALLOW-TAILED FLY-CATCHER — CUAJINIQUILAPA — ESCLAVOS—AZAGUALPA—JUTIAPA—ORGAN-CACTUS—AGUA BLANCA—SAN ANTONIO—VOLCANO OF SUCHITAN—SANTA CATARINA—EL RIO—AMATILLO—SILVER MINES OF ALOTEPEQUE 146

CHAPTER XIII.

MOUNTAIN SCENERY—PILGRIMS' GRAVES—PIEDRAS GORDAS—MERINO SHEEP—A RESTAURANT—A DELIGHTFUL VALLEY—A MUD HUT—THE CROSS—A NIGHT WITH THE PILGRIMS—TILLANDSIA—FIRST VIEW OF ESQUIPULAS—A DOUANE—THE CALLE REAL—BRIDGE AND STONE FIGURES—A FAIR—CHURCH OF ESQUIPULAS—THE BLACK CHRIST—STRANGE OFFERINGS—LAST VIEW OF ESQUIPULAS 161

CHAPTER XIV.

PIEDRA DE AMOLAR—JUPILINGO—SAN JOSÉ—ORIOLES—OSTINOPS MONTEZUMA—TETERIA VIRIDIS—SWAN ORCHID—COPAN RIVER—DON PEDRO ARELLANOS—THE MYSTERY OF COPAN—THE IDOLS—HIEROGLYPHICS—CEIBAS—ANCIENT SEPULCHRE—EL CERRO DE LAS VENTANAS—CARVED ALTAR—HUMAN SACRIFICE—STONE HAMMOCK—GARRAPATAS—NIGUAS 172

CHAPTER XV.

HACIENDA—TIERRA CALIENTE—PASCUAL IN DIFFICULTIES—AZTEC MYTHOLOGY—HAT-BRUSH PLANT—JOCOTAN—SAN JUAN ERMITA—PLAIN OF CHIQUIMULA—RUINED CHURCHES—CHIQUIMULA—VISIT TO THE JEFE POLITICO—GIOTE—CHIMALAPA—SAN AGOSTIN—GUASTATOYA—MOTMOTS—A SPANISH DISH—LAGUNA—EL PUENTE—PONTE AGUELA—SAN JOSÉ—A SLIPPERY DESCENT—A CATARACT—ORIOLES AND THEIR NESTS—PLAIN OF GUATEMALA 186

CHAPTER XVI.

MILITARY SERVICE—STRENGTH OF ARMY—EQUIPMENT—FOREIGN OFFICERS—EL POLITECNICO—CONGRESS—A FEDERAL UNION—JUSTICE—FALSE WITNESSES—JUSTICE IN SALVADOR—RIGHTS OF FOREIGNERS—INHABITANTS OF CENTRAL AMERICA—A PROBABLE FUTURE—PETEN AN UNKNOWN LAND—DEPARTURE FROM THE CITY. 205

CHAPTER XVII.

SPIRITUAL RELATIONS—CARRIZAL—VUELTA GRANDE—THE RIVER MOTAGNA—HOT SPRINGS—LLANO GRANDE—A SUGAR PLANTATION—MOUNTAINS OF CHOACUS—AN INVALID CARRIAGE—SAN GERONIMO—SALAMA — FLOWERING YUCCAS — MOUNTAINS OF QUILILA—SANTA ROSA—VALLEY OF PURULA—CABILDO . 214

CHAPTER XVIII.

GROTTO OF PURULA—STALAGMITES—SANTA CRUZ—VALLEY OF COBAN—CAJABON RIVER—CURASSOWS—PACAYA—THE QUESAL—NEST OF TROGON—SAN CRISTOVAL—CROSSES IN WOODS—A "MILPA"—INDIAN LABOUR—MOZOS—COBAN COFFEE—PASION RIVER—DEPARTURE OF MOZOS—AN ANCIENT CITY UNDISCOVERED 226

CHAPTER XIX.

LIQUID AMBER TREES—SAN PEDRO CARCHAH—BARRICADES— A CENSER—ARRIVAL OF MOZOS—EUPHORBIA—A BEAUTIFUL RIVER—LA TINTA—MATCHES—ACCIDENT TO MULE—NIGHT SOUNDS—A DESCENT—STRELITZIA REGINA—ANTHURIUM—BROAD LEAFED PLANTS—ESPIRITU SANTO—THE CABILDO . . 244

CHAPTER XX.

A VILLAGE SCHOOL—STRANGE NOCTURNAL VISITORS—A SWAMP— FOREST PLEASURES—CANDELARIA—A DESERTER—INDIAN VOICES —A NIGHT JAR—CHACHAS—INDIAN POST-MAN—A RIVER CAVERN —LOST IN THE FOREST—SAN DOMINGO—PALM GROVES—SAN ANTONIO—INDIAN FREEMASONRY—TALPEMIX—CONCUEN—DON RAMON 257

CHAPTER XXI.

EL RIO DE LA PASION—DON CARLOS—WILD COCOA—TREES—DYE WOODS—BIRDS—A CANOE—START FOR EL PASO—IGUANAS—A USEFUL FIRE-ARM—JAGUAR—CURASSOW—HANGING NESTS—FISHING BY TORCHLIGHT—SCORPION AND COCKCHAFER—INDIAN ENCAMPMENT — LACANDONES — ARRIVAL AT EL PASO DE SACLUK 271

CHAPTER XXII.

MAHOGANY CUTTERS—RAINY NIGHT—A TAPIR—A FEARFUL SPECTACLE—PASO NUEVO—TOUCAN—A BEAUTIFUL PIGEON—THE SAVANNAS—ARRIVAL AT SACLUK—NARANJA COTTAGE—SACLUK—OCCUPATION—NIGHT—EL REY ZOPILOTE—EN ROUTE TO FLORES A SAVANNA VILLAGE—SAN BENITO—PETEN-ITZA—CONQUEST OF THE ITZACS. 282

CHAPTER XXIII.

LAKE OF PETEN—FLORES—ISOLATION—GLAZED POTTERY—DRESS—GEOGRAPHICAL KNOWLEDGE—CAVE OF JOBITZINAL—INTERIOR OF CAVE—A CURIOUS BIRD—SHELLS—CORTES' HORSE—PETEN BY MOONLIGHT—RUINS OF TICKAL—RETURN TO SACLUK—HIEROGLYPHICS—DESERTED CITIES 293

CHAPTER XXIV.

COMMUNICATION WITH FLORES—SAVANA—SAN PABLO—SHEDS FOR TRAVELLERS—SAN DIEGO—NEST OF PAVO—BIRD CRY—MAHOGANY TREE—RONDELETTA—PALMETTO—GANAPATAS—THE PETEN TURKEY—JAGUAR STORIES—ENTER MEXICO—NO WATER—STORM IN FOREST—RIVER SAJAB—LAKE COPAR—HOLY GHOST ORCHID —ARRIVAL AT TENOSIQUE 303

CHAPTER XXV.

THE USUMACINTA—TENOSIQUE—PRETENSIONS—SOCIETY—ADVANTAGE OF POVERTY OVER RICHES—SPITE—TO-MORROW—A TWISTING STREAM—ANECDOTE OF SPANISH INDOLENCE—DEPARTURE FROM TENOSIQUE—PHILODENDRONS—CROSSING THE RIVER—RARE SWALLOWS—RIVER CHACAMAS—LOST IN THE PRAIRIE—A WET NIGHT—A LAKE SCENE—ARRIVAL AT MONTECRISTO . 313

CHAPTER XXVI.

TO-MORROW—MONTE CRISTO—START FOR PALENQUE—HORSE-FLIES—SAN MIGUEL—DON DAVID—CUEVA DE DON JUAN—GHOST STORIES—SANTO DOMINGO DEL PALENQUE—START FOR RUINS—THICK FOREST—THE PALACE—ANCIENT NAME OF PALENQUE—GENERAL ASPECT—ANCIENT INHABITANTS—HIGH TOWER—RELICS—CROSSES—PYRAMIDS—EXTENT OF RUINS . . 325

CHAPTER XXVII.

BANKS OF THE USUMACINTA—INGA PODS—LAGARTOS—RIO CHICO—LAS PLAYAS—ROUTE TO PALENQUE—SAN GERONIMO—GUACO—DYE WOODS—PALIZADO—MODERN CIVILIZATION—TOWN LIMITS—LOGWOOD—ON THE RIVER—LAS CRUCES—BOCA CHICA—LAGUNA DE TERMINOS . . - . . 337

CHAPTER XXVIII.

ISLAND OF CARMEN—ITS DISCOVERY—DEPARTMENT OF CARMEN—TOWN—LIGHTHOUSE—MALINCHE—TRAFFIC BY WATER—SHIPPING—A TRAVELLING COMPANION—SOCIETY—WAITING FOR A BREEZE—A STAB IN THE DARK—LEAVE CARMEN—FRONTERA—A COLONY OF ALLIGATORS—THE MANATEE—THE BAR—WRECKERS—AT SEA 345

ACROSS CENTRAL AMERICA.

CHAPTER I.

PACIFIC PORTS—MAZATLAN—PRONUNCIADOS—BRIGANDS—JESUIT INFLUENCE—ACAPULCO—HARBOUR SCENES—A LAZY TOWN—A MEXICAN FORT—COAST RANGE—VOLCANOES—PACIFIC GALES—SAN JOSÉ AND GUATEMALA—CUSTOM HOUSE—PAINFUL INTEREST —DEPARTURE.

RIGHT cheery weather and light breezes accompanied us as we sped along in one of the Pacific mail steamers bound south from San Francisco.

Most of the passengers were for Panama, but a few, chiefly Mexicans, disembarked at each of the little ports at which we touched. Pretty enough at a distance were the villages belonging to these ports. Mazatlan, San Blas, and Manzanilla; but on closer acquaintance the poverty-stricken aspect of the streets and houses, which is so characteristic of Spanish-American towns, gave a tinge of gloom to the otherwise bright scene.

B

Mazatlan has the reputation of enjoying a good climate during the winter months for those troubled with lung disease; but much of the benefit derived therefrom must be counteracted by the depression caused by the unkempt streets and plaza, and last but not least, by the bad food which has rendered Mazatlan a by-word even in that country where good living is not a strong point.

Perhaps when we were there, much of the dullness was to be ascribed to the near approach of the "pronunciados," as of course Mexico was in a state of rebellion—one of those chronic affairs which form the principal amusement in the Spanish American Republics—and the inhabitants of Mazatlan, in great fear, were shipping off all their money and valuables to safer quarters. Two men-of-war, which the Mexican Government in a fit of extraordinary generosity had recently purchased from England, were daily expected, but it was a question whether they would not prove a curse instead of a blessing, as it was generally thought that the rebels would seize them at the first opportunity.

How suggestive of Mexico is that one word—rebel! Ever since she stepped forth into the family of independent nations, revolutions, rebellions, and assassinations have swept over the land, destroying her wealth, paralyzing her industry, and reducing her population.

Throughout the country the laziest and most unprincipled join leaders who, in the name of politics, unite to plunder their neighbours, " pronounce" against the government, and under the name of war or " pronunciamentos" become a terror to the country as great as that inspired by the brigands.

Of the latter, strange stories were rife, and when we arrived at Acapulco, so uninviting were the reports that the male members of a Spanish family, who had intended to proceed from that port overland to the city of Mexico to look after their property, were so discouraged that they preferred to continue their journey by Panama.

On the road to the capital these bandits had actually posted placards to the effect that no one was to travel with less than twenty dollars under pain of death, and there is no doubt that the threat was not an idle one.

It is only fair to the Government to say that it was taking strong measures to put down the banditti. A band of fifty under the leadership of a notorious villain, named Ruiz, had lately been almost totally destroyed, and the celebrated Rosalio Mendez had been taken and shot. The chief delight of this ruffian had been to flay the soles of the feet of his prisoners, and then drive them before him over the flinty road. The death of this merciless bandit caused more rejoicing in Mexico than that of all the other brigands put together.

At San Juanico a strong force of brigands had perpetrated some dreadful crimes, amid enthusiastic cries of " Long live the Sisters of Charity." A Paulist priest who was supposed to be implicated in the affair was arrested, but on account of want of evidence was allowed to leave the country.

It had been generally supposed that friars, monks, and Jesuits were things of the past; but after the expulsion of the Sisters of Charity and the uprising of the Church party, many of them who were hidden away came boldly to the front. These men work strenuously to arouse the lower classes against the Liberal Administration, and by spreading pernicious doctrines among their blind adherents sow the seeds of constant strife and civil war.

The enmity between the religious and political elements is manifested by the bitter and relentless attacks upon the Government by the Church papers, whilst those of the administration in their turn denounce by name the priests and bishops who are endeavouring to overthrow the established order of things by sword and flame. The Church party invariably place themselves in opposition to whatever government is in power, in order thereby to create a revolution, and thus endeavour to prove that liberal institutions are a failure and that a strong centralized power, backed by the mitre and the musket, can alone prevent Civil wars.

That the views of the Government were correct was demonstrated by the terrible massacre in the church of Acapulco, at the instigation of a Jesuit bishop, only a few weeks before our arrival.

The harbour of Acapulco is very picturesque; entirely land-locked, and shut out from the sea by green slopes and wooded islands. The small town, with its white houses and thatched roofs, is effectively finished off at one end by groups of palm trees, and at the other by an old fort. At some distance behind, a low range of hills closes in the view. The rain which occasionally falls in its purple gorges looks like a coloured mist when the sun shines on it, and as the shades melt and blend into one another the varied background lights up the scene with marvellous effect. Canoes glide over the water, freighted with eggs, shells, limes, pine-apples, hammocks, and curious little pieces of pottery of quaint forms. Birds and squirrels and various other objects of beautiful form and colour, so often met with in tropical ports to entice the voyager, were not wanting, and one wtetched parrot that had been taught to say " good morning" in English, in a moment of excitement at having its tail pulled by a small monkey, fluttered off its perch, fell into the water, and before its owner could rescue it, was seized by a shark, between whose formidable jaws it disappeared, screaming its familiar salutation as an appropriate farewell.

On landing, the charm of the scene vanished. The town was found to consist only of a few rag-littered lanes bordered with low houses, whose cracked white walls reflected the hot glare of the sun, and under whose piazzas were strown the most untempting articles for sale. Through the open doorways, the monotonous swing of hammocks showed us that most of the population were occupied in their usual business, and the only signs of life were the hideous turkey-buzzards, Central American policemen, as they are called, and even they seemed impregnated with the atmosphere of laziness, and with a slight jerk of the head would merely hop on one side at our approach.

After crossing a gully through which a supply of water was conveyed to the town, but which at the time was almost dry, and amongst whose slimy stones pigs and buzzards were disputing for old boots and other delicacies of a like sort, we paid a visit to the fort. A grove of fine old trees led up to it, and after a short colloquy with the officer commanding the guard, who was at first evidently afraid that we had come to take possession of the place—there were four of us—or at least to discover its strength and spy out its weakness, we were permitted to enter.

The same air of repose pervaded the inside of the fort as we had observed on the outside. Sleeping forms were lying in the small casemated rooms. A cow, which had inadvertently strayed in through the neglected gateway, was endeavouring to obtain a little nourishment from the herb-grown wall, and a sentry half asleep, with a cigarette in his mouth, was stretched at full length on the dilapidated stone steps leading to the ramparts.

Lazily rising when he saw us, this watchful soldier went to fetch his musket, which was leaning against the wall at some distance off, and offered to accompany us; but we declined his obliging offer, and he gratefully resumed his recumbent position.

Negligence and decay still prevailed everywhere, guns which should have occupied places on the ramparts had fallen into the surrounding ditch, and lay half buried in weeds and undergrowth. In many places the stone masonry had given way, and what might have been a position of some advantage and considerable strength, was now simply a ridiculous spectacle of Mexican inefficiency.

When we left the fort the sentry was sound asleep on the steps, and as the one sergeant who had greeted us on our arrival was nowhere to be seen, we presumed that he also had fallen a victim to the general drowsiness.

The coast range after leaving Acapulco presented a softer outline and looked green and fertile to us, accustomed as we had been of late to the rugged bare mountain chain which, though doubtless full of mineral wealth, bore a wild and dreary aspect. On the following day we sighted the first of that wonderful series of volcanoes whose system is developed in its grandest form in Guatemala, and on the morning of the twelfth day out from San Francisco, we rode at anchor a long way from shore in the little surf port of San José.

Three great volcanoes, Agua, Fuego, and Pacaya, raise their huge forms seventy miles or so inland barring the way to the city of Guatemala, which lies on the other side.

"Mountains that like giants stand,
To sentinel enchanted land."

Between us and them was a flat stretch of country covered with a dense tropical growth of trees and shrubs.

This part of the Pacific coast is visited by strong gales at certain seasons; between September 20th and October the "cordonazo,"—equinoctial—blows; in the rainy season from June to September the "chubasco" sometimes rages with fury, and at odd intervals is felt the "chiflon jugadu," which is merely a puff, but frequently strong enough to capsize a badly balanced vessel.

We found it no easy matter to land on the jetty as a heavy swell was running, and it required some caution to approach and clamber up the narrow rope ladder, which at one moment was swinging above the water, and the next was immersed in it to its highest step. However, the feat was accomplished, and we were soon undergoing as severe an inspection of our baggage at the custom-house as if we were in some frontier station in Germany.

A more uninviting-looking spot than San José cannot well be imagined; a few tumble-down houses, in which live the limited number of officials who are obliged to pass their time here, face the sea; behind them is a swamp redolent of malaria, and abounding in mosquitoes, while a little farther on are the miserable huts of the native village. Intensely hot and very unhealthy, the place possesses no interest except the painful one of being the spot where a drunken commandante had the audacity to imprison and flog a British Consul a few years ago. Fortunately we had not to stop long at it, as my only companion, who was on his way to the city of Guatemala on business, had previously given notice of his expected arrival, and a comfortable waggon drawn by four mules was ready to proceed with us on our journey.

We were soon splashing through the swamp, and after passing the green plaza, where partial atonement for the afore-mentioned insult had been made by military salutation of the English flag, we quickly lost sight of the melancholy village in a cloud of dust.

CHAPTER II.

EN ROUTE TO THE CAPITAL—SCENERY—GAZZA LADRA—BREAKFAST
—OX-TEAMS—NATIVE PLOUGH—ESCUINTLA—CHANGE OF SCENE
—A MACHETE—FALLS OF SAN PEDRO MARTIR—AMATITLAN—
NOPAL PLANTATIONS—COCHINEAL—REFRESHMENT—LAKE OF
AMATITLAN—HOT SPRINGS—ASCENT—PLAIN OF GUATEMALA—
—COURTESY—ARRIVAL IN CITY.

T San José we had heard that an opera company, which the Government had engaged at an expense of about forty thousand dollars, was daily expected. How we wished that the money had been expended in improving the road on which we were travelling! At one moment our waggon was up to the axle-tree in deep ruts, at the next jolting over great rocks and stumps of trees. Still, in spite of heat, dust, and dislocation, there was a great charm in the novelty of the scene, at least to me, but my companion had traversed the road before and consequently was not so alive to its attraction.

The country around San José was mere jungle, but bright creepers ran over the tangled undergrowth;

Staple Dishes.

here and there a gnarled ceiba stretched out its shady branches, laden with mosses and giant arums, and occasionally some gay-coloured bird darted rapidly from side to side. Clouds of butterflies hovered over the half dried-up bed of the stream that filtered slowly across the dusty road, and as they settled on its moist banks resembled clusters of flowers; all the butterflies in the country appeared to be visiting these watering places.

A certain species of bird* appeared very glad to see us. One in particular was very sociable, flying after us from tree to tree, and looking very knowing with its pretty raised top-knot. In appearance, this bird is a sort of tropical magpie with light blue back and long tail-feathers of white and blue, a white breast and throat with black necklace. It is one of the commonest birds in the country, and the people say that it is more addicted to stealing than they are themselves, a charge rather hard on the magpie, which in fact is a veritable "gazza ladra."

Here and there an open thatched hut peeped out from a group of bananas and orange trees; picturesque enough by itself, but marred by the untidiness and unwashed appearance of its occupants. We stayed at one of these domiciles for luncheon, and were regaled with the staple dishes of the country—tortillas and frijoles; the latter, merely cooked beans, were palatable, but the former, the maize-flour fritters, were, I thought, the most detestable things I had ever tasted.

* Calocetta formosa.

To show how use will accustom us to anything almost, I must mention that before I left Central America I quite enjoyed tortillas; certainly there was often nothing else to eat, but I was surprised to find I really liked them.

Soon after leaving our resting place we met a number of ox teams, the express waggons of the country, wending their slow way to the coast; each small covered cart drawn by two oxen, whose noses almost touched the ground, so heavily were they yoked. Something under a week is the usual time taken by these vehicles to accomplish the journey from the port to the city, a distance of barely thirty leagues, *i.e.*, ninety miles.

In Central America, distances are always mentioned in leagues, one of which averages about three miles, but it is no easy matter to find out from a native the exact distance to any place; they have their short and their long league, which may vary from two to six or seven miles. They often measure by time only, and from that infer the space travelled over, so that distances greatly depend upon the qualities of the animal ridden or driven.

As we approached Escuintla, the half-way village where we were to pass the night, signs of civilization increased; there were patches of sugar-cane, little gardens with a few vegetables, and an occasional shed by the road-side with fruit and balls of lime for sale. In one small clearing there was a man actually at work ploughing, and this is how he ploughed and the im-

Escuintla. 13

plement he used. The curved branch of a tree, shod at the extreme point of the lower limb with a piece of iron and with a beam attached to the upright limb, formed the plough. To this beam two oxen were yoked, which the man directed with one hand by means of thongs attached to their horns, whilst with the other hand he guided the plough. And thus he scratched away at the ground, happy in the idea of owning an implement superior to the hoe and machete of his neighbour ; but never dreaming of economizing his resources by attending to the depth rather than to the extent of his furrows. There is an old saying that "no farmer owns any deeper than he can plough." What a little property my friend must possess !

It was growing dark when we entered Escuintla, but there was sufficient light to show off the straggling street, with its rows of unpromising-looking houses and still more forbidding inn, through the gateway of which we drove into a small courtyard which did duty for stables.

As the dining-room opened on to this court, or rather farm-yard, we did not linger long over the meal of strange meat and beans that was tardily prepared for us, but went out to inspect the village by moonlight.

The appearance of the old church, almost roofless, with its rent walls, told us that we were in the land of earthquakes, and the apparent proximity of the volcanoes suggested a greater catastrophe even than that which had already occurred.

The village presented no features of interest, with the exception of a picturesque stream, and we returned to the hotel only to pass a very hot and uncomfortable night. At 3 a.m. we were ready to start again, but as no driver appeared a search was instituted, and he was at last discovered fast asleep in the wagonette, where he had spent the night so as to have a close supervision over our luggage.

From Escuintla the road commences to climb successive plateaux, and we found the air cold enough to render it necessary for us to make use of our rugs and overcoats; but when the sun rose we appreciated the delightful freshness of the atmostphere after the sultriness of the coast region. With the cooler temperature had come a change in the vegetation; the character of the country was different, and the only part of the landscape that maintained its original features was the road.

The inhabitants too seemed to be infused with fresh life, and whether hastening to Escuintla with their market produce, or making their way to their maize fields and sugar-cane, all had a business aspect. Everyone carried his machete—a long knife without which to a native life would be insupportable, and which he uses on every possible occasion from cutting through a forest to eating frijoles.

As we ascended, the road grew more picturesque. On our left was a wall of rock covered with ferns, which grew luxuriantly in the moisture caused by the water that trickled down in every direction. Little ravines which cut through the hill sides here and there were full of wild plantains and arums. On our right, down below, was the river Michatoya, watering a fertile plain, and beyond were the mountains, rugged and bare in some places, wooded and gracefully sloping in others.

Near the hamlet of San Pedro Martir we passed a very beautiful cataract, about ninety feet in height, which rustled over the arching rocks in masses of foam, that lit up the broad under-leaf of the silvery plantains as if with flashes of fire, then after battling with the granite boulders that vainly strove to intercept its progress, and flowing with swift stillness through narrowing walls, emerged into more open space, and tranquilly flowed on as a peaceful river totally oblivious of its recent fury.

Less and less tropical grew the scenery, and no one who had been set down here unexpectedly would have imagined he was in Central America. The soft stretches of meadow through which flowed the river, its banks lined with osiers and willows, the fields of maize which might have been wheat, the mountain peaks and the undulating hills, clad with pines, were all reminiscences of home, as charming as they were unexpected. Certainly a close inspection of the scene revealed cane plantations and tropical shrubs, but they did not intrude themselves sufficiently to destroy the home illusion.

After some hours travelling we reached a lofty eminence, and looked down upon the village of Amatitlan.

This village appeared to me to present a very novel aspect. The long narrow streets, consisting of low red tiled cottages arranged symmetrically, and running at right angles to each other, lay in a deep valley surrounded by abrupt mountains. A curious appearance was caused by numerous high mud—adobe—walls carefully thatched, and enclosing a considerable extent of ground, which constituted the nursery gardens of cochineal. Fields of nopal—the variety of cactus on which the insect feeds—extended in every direction, each surrounded by a mud fence.

The afore-mentioned nursery gardens are used during the wet season; the thatched roofing over the wall forms a shed which is open on the sunny side, and in it the insects are preserved on nopal leaves and breed there.

The young are placed in little leaf-boxes, or bags, which are attached to the leaves of the cactus, and thus the plant is seeded. Rain is fatal to the young insect; and although it is said that, if it escapes injury during the first ten days after being attached to the plant, it has a fair chance of reaching perfection, yet many an owner of a nopal plantation has gone to his field after a heavy shower, only to be met at the gate by a red stream indicating the loss of his crop. In Amatitlan the female is left on the leaf long enough to produce a second crop annually; the second, which is much heavier than the first, is all clear profit, the first paying all expenses.

The insects when gathered are spread out on flat

trays, covered with thin cloth and put into stoves. When dried they are sifted, packed in bales and are ready for the market. The value of a nopal plantation is between three hundred and four hundred dollars per acre; the average yield of an acre being about one thousand eight hundred lbs. of insects in the two crops. Formerly this industry was a very extensive one in the district, but now it is comparatively insignificant owing to the introduction of patent dyes &c.

In other parts of Guatemala the manufacture of indigo is fast dying out for the same reason. Mr. Judson and others, I expect, would meet with a very cool reception in this country if they ventured to pay it a visit.

A cup of coffee and some oranges had formed our breakfast before we left Escuintla at three a m., and so we were glad to pull up at a little cottage just off the main street of Amatitlan, where we had been assured of refreshment. Our mules, too, evidently thought that it was time for them to feed, and had stubbornly stopped and looked into every doorway that we passed. Their wants were soon provided for, for in the more civilized parts of Guatemala the sight of a mule is sufficient to bring several offers of "sacate" *i.e.* provender.

The courtyard into which we stepped was full of most delicious roses, and a small parroquet bade us welcome in the prettiest manner possible. The hostess, who was equaly polite, showed us into a pleasant room, and we were soon discussing the repast she placed before us, which included some very excellent fish from the lake.

This lake is a fine expanse of water, about three leagues in length by one in breadth. On the far side from the village it is overhung by a precipitous mountain, which forms with the sloping hills on the near side a striking and romantic view. Hot springs, said to be very salutary in cutaneous disorders, issue close to the lake. In the valley boiling water is found only eight or nine feet below the surface of the ground, and, indeed, it is feared that the whole may ere long become a lake. The volcanic mountain which almost cuts the lake in two, and the appearance of the surrounding country, with its hot and cold springs, all point to some unusual phenomenon, which at some unknown period has changed the entire scene. The lake is situated nearly four thousand feet above the level of the sea.

As we ascended the steep road leading out of the valley, the view on looking back was superb; the wild garden of the great mountain, pierced with shadowy ravines and with bare crags falling sheer down to the water's edge, was in strange contrast to the rounded aspect of the hills and the cultivated gardens of the rest of the valley.

For about three leagues we wound our way slowly up the mountain, now passing through a narrow defile or crossing the bed of a fast drying up stream, and anon urging our animals to put forth a little additional effort when a few yards of tolerably level land lay before us.

At last the volcanoes were no longer in our front; we had passed them and soon reached the plateau on the other side of which lay the city of Guatemala, three leagues away.

This table-land, five thousand feet above sea level, is a vast green plain dotted with trees and plots of maize with an occasional small coffee plantation. Pretty white villages nestle in the surrounding hills and cattle wander over the pastures. Indian huts dot the road, and a few more pretentious farm-houses peeping out from their orange groves give a pleasant air of civilization and repose.

The kind-hearted Guatemaltecans have a custom of driving out to the plain to meet expected friends, and as my companion's arrival had been anticipated we soon exchanged our mule team for a barouche and pair that quickly carried us to the city. Entering under the shadow of an old fort we rattled over the cobble stones of a long narrow street, turned sharply out of a paved courtyard, and found ourselves in the hospitable precincts of the Gran Hotel.

CHAPTER III.

A MARKET SCENE—FRUITS AND VEGETABLES—A GENEROUS VENDOR — DRESS — A SUPERSTITION — NOON — BEGGARS — THE PLAZA—A USEFUL CLOCK — CATHEDRAL — FOUNTAIN — UNDER THE COLONNADES—MOSAIC—BATHING—AN ILLUSTRIOUS EXAMPLE—CLIMATE—ASPECT OF CITY—INDIAN PORTERS—BUSINESS-HOUSES—DINNER-HOUR—VIEW FROM THE CARMEN HILL.

SAID Socrates to himself in the market place, "How many things are here which I do not want!" With this idea I started out early next morning to visit that ever interesting and amusing part of a foreign town. The hotel was in the main street, a little farther on was the Plaza with a fine cathedral, behind which was the market. I soon discovered that I need not have risen so soon, as early marketing in Guatemala is unnecessary, business being lukewarm before ten o'clock.

The building itself is spacious and admirably constructed. Six large entrances lead into two quadrangles, the centre of the larger being occupied entirely by the fruit and vegetable vendors, whilst round the walls run a series of shops or stalls filled with native and foreign productions, such as baskets, cord, bird-cages, woollen and cotton goods, fancy articles, straw hats, mats, iron ware, saddlery, rebosos of silk and cotton, shoes, cigarettes, &c.

Fruit and vegetables abound in the greatest profusion; pine-apples lie in heaps under the long tables, on which are baskets of melting custard apples; anona, golden grenadillas, the crisp rind of one of them just open sufficiently to show its snow white lining and its jelly-like contents; rich brown sapotes shaped like ostrich eggs, and in whose red flesh is concealed a large stone with a bitter almond kernel; mangoes, plantains, bananas, lemons, limes, oranges, nine for a cuartillo—three cents—cocoa-nuts, jocotas, yams, beans, tomatoes, chilis, avocates, and aguacates or alligator pears. In shape and size this fruit resembles the sapote, but the pulp, which looks like fresh butter, is of a very delicate flavour. It is usually eaten more as a vegetable than a fruit, pepper and salt improving it greatly. We used always to invest in some of these in our marketing expeditions, and once were much amused at the apparent generosity of an old lady whose stall we were patronising for the first time, and who, would persist in selling the fruit at a lower rate than we knew was the proper one. Of course she did it with an eye to future dealings, but it reminded us of the Irishman who bought apples at eighteen pence a dozen and sold them at a penny a piece, and who on being asked how he could make anything in that way, replied "Only by doing a very large business."

The throng moving about is composed of Indians, Ladinos, and a few foreigners. Ladinos predominate both as sellers and as buyers, for they form the chief part of the population. The word "ladino" is understood to apply to descendants of whites and Indians; but few have Spanish blood, the majority being either aboriginal Indians or mixed with the various conquering races which have come from the north.

The dress of the men consists of pantaloons of cotton cloth, and a jacket of thick woollen cloth of native manufacture. The Indians generally envelop themselves in their striped serapes. The dress of the Indian women which somewhat resembles that of the Japanese, consists of a blue cotton skirt wrapped round and kept up by a broad coloured girdle, to which is added an embroidered chemise with loose sleeves. Sometimes they wear linen kerchiefs round their head after the manner of Italian peasants. The material of Indian clothes is all made by themselves, and the cloth manufactured by the Indians of Los Altos is extremely good and very like our Scotch tweed.

The cut and colour of the dress of an Indian is said to tell to an experienced eye the village or district from whence the wearer comes; for myself I could never distinguish much difference between any of them. In some places all the women wear red cord plaited in their hair, and about the colour and quality of this cord they are particular even to superstition. Thus in Central America red has its devotees the same as in China, where a red bracelet is regarded as a safeguard against evil spirits; or in Scotland, where the Highland women tie red cotton round the cows' tails before turning them out to grass in the Spring, and red silk round their own fingers to keep off the witches.

To return to the market; as noon approaches a crowd of hungry customers gather round great jars out of which the proprietor deals little calabashes full of a whitish soup, which from the demand must possess pleasanter properties than its appearance would suggest. Such laughter and pushing as each one tries to hand in his porringer before his neighbour! An exquisite joke is when the arm of a too eager but successful aspirant has received a judicious—but of course unintentional—shove, and the contents of his calabash are deposited on the black head of some little urchin who has been vainly striving for some time against superior weight.

But not a smile is once seen to light up the tall sad-eyed figure of one of many, who wrapped in his poncho looks mournfully at the merry groups. Probably he is thinking that his last cuartillo is spent, and to-morrow he will have to do a day's work; at all events he is the ideal of the Spanish song:

"Soy un cuadro de tristeza
Arrimado a la pared!"[*]

Outside the market in the sunny street are chattering

[*] "I am a picture of sadness
Leaning against the wall!"

muleteers, carelessly dressed soldiers, pedlars with their goods spread out on the pavement, Indians and beggars; the latter chanting in a monotonous voice a regular litany, which they change to profuse thanks or a torrent of abuse according as their supplications are attended to or disregarded.

A few steps leads us back into the great Plaza, a vast paved rectangle, with a covered colonnade on three sides; here are situated the Government buildings, such as the Palace, the City Hall, and the Court of Justice, all without the slightest pretension to architectural beauty. On the fourth side stands the Cathedral, an imposing edifice of simple but elegant design, devoid of the image-decked façade so common to Spanish American churches, which gives them their vulgar plaster-of-Paris appearance. The building is ornamented with a handsome clock, whose utility by the way is somewhat impaired by its not having any hands, a fact of which an old resident, who pointed out the dial to me with some pride, was previously totally unaware.

The centre of the square is taken up by another thoroughly Spanish American object, in the shape of a great heavy stone fountain. This structure has more attempt at artistic workmanship than the generality of such erections, but still it is bad enough to make one remember with pride those much abused basins in Trafalgar Square.

The general idea conveyed by the ornamentation is apparently that of horses playing at bowls, the game being superintended by another steed which looks proudly down from a central elevation. This latter is said to have once had a rider, Charles IV., but at the time when the project of throwing off the Spanish rule was first mooted over fifty-five years ago, the royal equestrian was dismounted and broken up. This seems to have been rather an unnecessary proceeding as the stone extinguisher that covers the statue almost enshrouds the animal, and must have sufficiently concealed its royal rider.

Two sides of the surrounding colonnades are occupied by small shops whose principal wares are cheap foreign jewelry, stationery, cakes of priest-blessed medicines and lottery tickets. The pavement on the side where native goods, such as baskets, bird-cages, pottery, &c., are sold, is worth noticing, being composed of the back bones of cattle and horses arranged in a sort of mosaic; this is also a favourite method of ornamenting the entrances to court-yards and other places.

On and about the steps of the corridors may be seen indolent ladinos and lazzaroni of the place, idly watching the soldiers at drill or enjoying a sun bath. A sun bath, alas! is about the only bath in favour in Central America, where it is amusing but rather painful to notice the universal aversion to water. No true Guatemaltecan would think of washing even his face when travelling, were his journey to last a few hours or some weeks. If he committed such an absurdity, cold and fever would be the result in his estimation. A dry towel, or better still a hot tortilla, does duty for water.

It may be some comfort, however, to be able to use the illustrious name of Michael Angelo as an example of the non-ablution principle, that is if he followed the advice of his father given in a recently published letter. "Take care of yourself," says the anxious parent, "considering your profession you are a ruined man if you lose your health (which God forbid!). Above all take care of your head; keep it moderately warm, and never wash yourself; have yourself rubbed down, but do not wash."

A friend of mine was seriously warned against the danger of pairing his finger nails after a short journey he had just made from the coast.

Fresh air is also a source of discomfort to many, and in the cool mornings and evenings you are continually meeting people with their faces muffled up and with all the signs of severe tooth-ache.

Tying up the head in a sling is a favourite remedy in Guatemala for most complaints, from a bronchial affection to a pain in the big toe. Fortunately the delightful climate of Guatemala keeps disease away; indeed, they say that were it not for the doctors there would be no sickness at all.

The air is deliciously healthy and invigorating, and above all the sun; though warm, is sufficiently tempered to render a long walk most enjoyable. How true is the old Italian proverb: "Dove non va il sole, va il medico," and its converse!

I left Guatemala before the rainy season—which begins about April—set in, but from what I heard it cannot be very bad, sunshine and showers alternating. At certain seasons tremendous thunderstorms occur and the lightning on these occasions is very fatal.

Let us now take a glance at the general aspect of the city. It is certainly gloomy and dull; owing to the uniformity of the houses, whose walls rise straight from the narrow side-walk, the regularity of the streets, which run parallel and at right angles to each other, and the absence of traffic; and the few signs of life are depressing. One of the sights that most strike a traveller—and a pitiful sight it is—is the enormous loads which the Indians carry on their backs; a weight of one hundred pounds they will carry for long distances over almost impassable roads, but in the towns twice that burden is easily disposed of. The loads are supported between the shoulders by a broad band, which passes over the forehead in such a way that the weight rests there and on the spine.

It is rather comical to see sometimes an enormous box, about the size of a small wooden house but probably containing only millinery or some such light article, trotting away down the street on what looks like its own little pair of brown legs.

It must not be inferred from outward signs that there is little trade, for business affairs are mostly in the hands of foreigners or their sons, and I am inclined to think they find their trades very lucrative. It has been the custom with those interested to run down the chances of commercial gain in this country, but the fact is that those who are embarked in trade do not desire to court competition by informing the world of the fortunes they are making in Central America.

As a precaution against earthquakes, the houses as a rule consist of a single ground floor; large gates or doors open into the court-yard—patio—which is surrounded by a broad verandah on to which the rooms open. The windows facing the street are heavily barred with upright iron rods, forming a balcony almost overhanging the side walk, and in whose cushioned depths sit the ladies of the house like birds in a cage. Generally towards sunset flocks of male birds may be seen hovering around, and cooing soft nothings through the prison bars. I once saw, quite unintentionally, a gentle pair playing at the innocent game of bob cherry between the cruel irons.

In Guatemala it is the custom to drive at the very early hour of two or three, consequently there was but little time for a walk after that meal, so I generally contented myself with a stroll to the Cerro del Carmen from whence is the most beautiful view of the city, especially at sunset. I must ask you to accompany me there.

The steep hill on which stands the church of the Carmen, one of the most ancient of the country, is grass-covered and of no great elevation, but made picturesque by the outcroppings of quartz, and by the oriental appearance of the old edifice, with its cupola surrounded by a grey stone wall which crowns the summit. One grand palm, with graceful drooping

Cerro del Carmen.

leaves, stands within the walls which are moss grown and covered with grasses.

The interior of the building which is seldom used, is dark and gloomy; the walls are hung with examples of art in its earliest infancy, the subjects being strictly restricted to views of purgatory, and tortures of the most revolting description. It is a relief to get out of the mouldy old place into the open air. Behind the church, the plain stretches away to ranges of purple hills already changing to a rose pink by the light of the setting sun. On either side are the outskirts of the city, with cultivated patches of garden produce, laid out in squares and parallelograms, and fringed with plantains. Turning to the south-west the volcano of Pacaya is exactly in front of us; at our feet lies the city, a mass of reddish-brown roofs interpersed here and there with great white churches and convents whose domes and turrets stand out in giant relief, contrasting with the low and flat tops of the surrounding houses.

When in the streets but few trees and flowers are beheld; up here, however, we wonder where all the vegetation now seen can have hidden itself, until we remember that we are looking down upon the shrubs and plants that fill the numberless patios.

The hills which bound the plain on our left are indescribably soft and beautiful, the deep shadowed ravines showing to advantage the bright green of the sugar-cane, and the darker smoothness of the coffee plantations. But the grandeur of the scene is centered in the three towering volcanoes that rise sharp and distinct against the amber sky far beyond the city. So sharp and distinct is the symmetrical outline of the Volcan de Agua on the right, the serrated ridge of Fuego, and the isolated cone of Pacaya on the left, that it seems impossible that the two former can be nearly thirty miles away, and the latter only half that distance. The sky flecked with tiny dark clouds looks like the breast of an oriole; gradually the sun sinks behind the peaks, the rose-light which has flushed them changes to a golden haze that in its turn gives place to a soft purple veil which covers the wide expanse around us. From the neighbouring church of Candelaria the Angelus rings out, warning us to return through the now dark and already half deserted streets.

No mountains that I have ever seen have left such an impression on my mind as these volcanoes; their majestic loneliness and grand repose strike one with a solemn awe, and when viewed, whether in the clear purple brightness of day, or in the changing tints of evening, they are emblems of eternal silence and motionless calm.

CHAPTER IV.

FEAST DAYS—LE JOUR DES MORTS—ENTRANCE TO CEMETERY—
THE INTERIOR—A CONTRAST—PICKPOCKETS—EARLY HOURS—
HOSPITALITY — SOCIETY — PRESIDENT BARRIOS—PRIESTS AND
NUNS—EXAMINATION—PRESIDENTIAL CAPACITY—GOVERNMENT
—IMPROVEMENTS—A NEW ROAD—PUBLIC INSTITUTIONS—THE
THEATRE—A COINCIDENCE—PROGRESS—AMUSEMENTS—PICNICS
—START FOR THE COAST.

THERE are so many feast days in the Roman Catholic calendar, that in Guatemala you are never sure of finding the shops open, especially if you are in immediate need of something. The old saying that Spanish holidays were three hundred and sixty-five, not including Sundays, used formerly to be applicable to Central America, and though they are not now of such frequent occurrence, still they come round more quickly even than the revolutions.

The people, too, are honourable in their division of the holidays, and instead of the rich keeping the feast and the poor the fast days, as is the case in some places, they share and share alike. I was not therefore much surprised one day shortly after my arrival to find the stores closed; but I was astonished at seeing the street crowded with people in black all hurrying in one direction. On inquiry, I was informed that it was "the day of all the dead," and that the population was strict in its observance of it.

In the early part of the eleventh century All Saints' Day was a time of rejoicing; but it has become gloomy in having been superseded by the "fête of the dead," a ceremony said to be peculiarly in harmony with French and Spanish instincts. The ancients had the custom of depositing food in the graves of the departed, now the moderns deposit bon-bons and presents on drawing room tables and garlands on the tombs.

On this occasion, the sombre crowd was wending its way to the cemetery adjacent to the fine hospital of the city. The entrance to the principal burying ground was through a shady lane, flanked by ill kept enclosures—dead men's fields—intended for the resting places of Protestants, or heretics, as they here term them.

Here congregated sellers of refreshments, whose small tables were covered with glasses of "tiste" and other liquids, whose various colours would have been suitable for filling the large bottles in a chemist's window. Traffic was also going on in grave-wreaths, beaded wire crowns, immortelles, and images.

A gateway on the right led into a large area, filled with tombstones and monuments. The high and thick surrounding walls also served for graves, the coffins being placed lengthways in a deep recess, which is afterwards closed up, whitewashed, and in some cases inscribed with the name of the occupant. After seven years these "columbaria" are cleared out and made ready for the reception of others.

To a foreigner, the bad taste of the monuments and their tawdry ornaments is most painful, for just as it requires a cultivated taste to appreciate a cemetery, so does it require a cultivated taste to arrange one. On all sides are tall cenotaphs and temple-like erections that would be hideous enough in marble, but which in whitewashed mud, painted in bright colours, add vulgarity to ugliness. Plaster figures of curious shapes watch over marble urns, which are inscribed with gilt letters forming ill-spelt words.

No natural flowers, trees, shrubs, or even grass are to be seen ; nowhere are there the signs, so common in our own burial grounds, that some loving hand still keeps green the memory of the dead, and with tender care trains simple blossoms over the quiet grave. The very mourners themselves, as they drape their crosses and funereal urns with tissue and fancy leaves, have an air of doing it for fashion's sake, and are of opinion that he mourns most who decorates most largely. On few faces will you read a longing

"For the touch of a vanished hand,
And the sound of a voice that is still !"

Human grief, according to Baron Haussman, dies out after the lapse of thirty-five years, that is to say graves commence then to be neglected. He could never have travelled in Guatemala.

Another painful feature is the fact that these gewgaws, these artificial flowers, these mock pearls and cheap decorations have to be watched all day for fear of theft. All the pickpockets from the city choose this occasion for meandering through the crowds, and when they have secured all the available pocket-handkerchiefs and other trifles, for no one thinks of attending the fête with anything of value about him, they turn their attention to the offerings to the dead. These gentry must have taken a hint from Baron Hügel's advice to botanists, " Put everything into your pocket." At sunset everything is removed, and carefully packed away to do duty the following year.

Sunset in Guatemala is the signal for closing business, and one might almost think for going to bed, so quiet and empty do the steets become; there is little inducement indeed to remain out of doors after dark, as the city is only lighted by a few oil lamps, and with the exception of a band which plays occasionally in the street in front of the President's house, there are but few amusements to attract either strangers or residents. Fortunately for me I had the entrée to the hospitable houses of our Minister Resident, and of our Consul, and thus evenings which would otherwise have been dreadfully dull and tiresome, were delightfully pleasant and amusing.

Here were to be met the members of the Government, eleven entertaining men, willing and glad to do any kindness for a stranger, and without any of that narrow-mindedness and reserve so characteristic of the old Jesuitical régime. In all cities society resolves itself into groups, cliques, and coteries, but here among the native residents the two chief antagonistic elements were the Jesuits and anti-Jesuits, *i.e.*, the enemies of the present Government and its friends.

On most subjects, the views of the two parties were so diametrically opposite, that it was a difficult matter to find out the true merits of any question that might be discussed. I remember once questioning two gentlemen at different times about the talents and qualities of Carrera; each had known him personally, and each gave me a totally different account, and I came away knowing little more of that extraordinary man than I did before.

That the present President—Barrios—should be detested by the Jesuit party is not surprising, for a more determined and successful enemy it never had. On the death of Carrera he succeeded to the reins of government, and as Juarez had done in Mexico, set himself to the task of the disestablishment and disendowment of the Church. But with greater wisdom than that displayed by Juarez, instead of pulling down the churches and convents, he turned the latter into the more useful institutions of schools, post-offices, and buildings of a similar character. This could not be accomplished without stirring up the strong opposition of the clergy; but he was equal to the emergency. All Jesuit priests were ordered to leave the country, and the nuns were brought in from all parts of the land, and domiciled under one roof in the city of Guatemala. Passing one day by this nunnery, the President observed that great precautions had been taken by the priests to prevent access to this sanctum by the outside world. He immediately ordered a notice to be attached to the convent gates, declaring that the public had a right to entrance, and must be admitted within the walls; also granting the nuns the privilege of going and coming at will. Archbishop Pinol promptly placed a placard beneath that of the President, excommunicating anyone who should dare to enter the building.

Two hours afterwards the representative of the Pope was *en route* for the borders of the State, guarded by soldiers. Then an anathema of excommunication was fulminated against Barrios by Urruela, Bishop of Teya of which a following is a translation, and will give some idea of the intolerant attitude of the priesthood.

"We, Doctor Mariano Ortez Urruela, by the grace of God and the Holy Apostolic See, Bishop of Teya, and with accessory jurisdiction in the district of Guatemala, and other dioceses of Central America, to our very beloved sons and brothers in our Lord Jesus Christ, we make known—

"That by virtue of the sacred bull, 'Quambis fratres,' extended in favour of the faithful in Central America who have not forgotten their duty as Christians, at page one hundred and seventy-seven of our ecclesiastical protocol, will be found the capitular and diocesan resolution, the tenor of which says:—

"1. Forasmuch as the Canons of Holy Mother Church lay down that all those who, like obedient sheep, are added to our Christian fold, will be taken and held as faithful sons of the holy religion of the crucified, who died on the cross for all good people asking recompense for all His true proselytes.

"2. That if there should be one who, by act or word, according to the sacred Canons, should offend or scoff at the ecclesiastical ceremonies, or against its august Ministers, or should raise himself against the Scriptures, or who should mock the Ministers of Christianity, he should be chastised once, twice, and as many times as might be necessary for the vindication of offended religeon.

3. "Seeing that our Brother José Rufino Barrios has become an apostate from our sacred maxims, outraging our communities even to appropriating their rents and capitals, refusing to hear the clamour of Christian humanity, giving the lie to Catholicism, usurping the immunities of the Holy Apostolic and Roman Church, under whose protection we ought to live and die to meet eternal happiness, and

"4. That according to the canon, 'Si quis violantes manus injecerit in clericum vel monacum anathema sit,' our Brother José Rufino Barrios has placed himself outside of the communion of our flock, by buffeting some of the Ministers of the religion which we profess. United together in our Holy Communion under the text 'Ubi sunt duo vel tres congregati in nomine meo, ibi sum in medio eorum,' and having lighted the candles as prescribed by the Holy Council of Trent, in accordance with legitimate Lateranism and consulted the traditions of St. John Chrysostom, transmitted to our legimate pastors, the only descendants of St. Peter, we order and command,

"1. That the man who is called José Rufino Barrios is held to be excommunicated from our blessed congregation, and to-day I prohibit from taking the name of one of the saints of our Roman martyrology.

"2. We caution the faithful not to communicate with him who is called José Rufino Barrios, who has been placed outside of the mercy of God.

"3. If our accused Brother (Rufino Barrios) wishes to continue in the government of the dioceses of Guatemala let him be accursed by all generations, and let him be held once and a thousand times as a Pharisee and a Publican of modern times, and

"4. Let the fate of the accursed excommunicated follow all those who will lend to him their support to throw to the ground the altars of our religion, &c., &c.

"MARIANO, *Bishop of Teya.*"

President Barrios, who personally commands the army, is a general of experience, undoubted bravery, and has much natural capacity for military affairs. It was feared that his former career as a soldier would prejudice his successful administration of the Presidency, and although undoubtedly a free use of the lash has been employed, and arbitrary punishments inflicted on political opponents, yet at the same time it is certain that revolutions and disorders have been put down more rapidly and with less bloodshed than ever before.

It may be alleged that the government of the State is despotic rather than republican; people are afraid to talk politics, newspapers fear to question any presidential act, and the people are without even the shadow of representation, the sole law-making power being vested in the President. The answer to this might be made that at all events the ruler is a good despot, and in a country of such a revolting character as Central America it is better to have a good despot than a weak President at the head of affairs. A powerful and inflexible will, backed by a hand of iron, is necessary for the maintenance of order in these States, the revolutionary nature of whose members seems to be a satire on the great republican dogma—the capability of all men to govern themselves.

President Barrios has also given a great impetus to public improvement and private enterprise. He has established a system of public education, and made the attendance of children between certain ages compulsory; the excellent "Kindergarten" systsm too has been introduced with success. He has established well conducted postal arrangements, and has opened lines of telegraph in various directions. At present there is in course of construction a fine road which is intended to be the highway between the city of Guatemala and the port of Izabal, on the Caribbean Sea.

It is asserted that this road when completed—if

ever—will in a measure take the place of the Panama route, but this I receive with a good deal of doubt, at all events as regards passengers. For the transport of coffee and the rich products of Guatemala, and also for mail business, the new road will be of immense service, and therefore a great boon to the country itself; but it is a question whether the amount of traffic will be able even in a small degree to compensate for the outlay and attendant expenses. It is not improbable that a railroad from the coast to Escuintla would be a more profitable undertaking, but at present there seems but little chance even of its commencement.

Besides the buildings already mentioned, there is a University, a Normal school, an Orphan asylum, a college for girls, a handsome theatre, and a small but valuable Museum belonging to the "Sociedad Economica."

This Museum receives unfortunately but a small grant from Government and is dependent on private liberality, and this again is restricted to the zeal and generosity of the few rather than of the many.

The theatre reflects the greatest credit on the city; instead of being pushed away and crowded out of sight as so many theatres, it stands in the centre of a large plaza surrounded by orange and other trees. The interior is as chaste and elegant as the exterior, and when filled, as it always is on a Sunday night, with the rank and beauty of Guatemala, it presents a very beautiful appearance.

The opera company, of which I have before spoken,

arrived during my visit and gave some very excellent performances. It was a curious coincidence that the carriages which conveyed the last of the nuns to San José for embarkation, brought back the members of the ballet troupe connected with the opera.

Although Guatemala has not yet joined the "breathless march of a civilization driven by steam" (as Charles Blanc puts it) yet one cannot help feeling astonished at its present social progress in comparison with the days of Carrera.

A stranger is surprised at the brilliant coup-d'œil on a theatre night. Beauty, diamonds and Parisian toilettes are enhanced by the strict evening dress of the male part of the audience in the boxes, and when the curtain rises on a well painted scene with appropriate accessories one is apt to forget that he is in out-of-the-way Guatemala. Nor are the occupants of the gallery less exacting, a false note or an awkward gesture calling forth as many cat-calls and as much whistling as they would among the gods of the Theatre Royal, Dublin; it might almost be supposed that talent of high order had been with them since their birth, instead of its being a newly imported luxury.

There is only one public promenade in the city, and that is a small shady garden where a band plays twice a week, which attracts almost as much attention as a large round-about in which children and even adults ride the wooden horses, and which is situated at one end of the grounds.

Two clubs add to the conviviality of the city which is certainly wanting in social festivities, dinner parties, except among a few of the foreigners, being of rare occurrence, and a ball or dance still rarer. Picnics are in favour, in spite of the natural disadvantages of the environs which have not been adapted by nature to the enjoyment of such entertainments. I must except one spot though, near the picturesque village of Chinantla on the banks of whose river a pleasant party of us once passed a most delightful day and which lost none of its charm because all the adjuncts to a very recherché luncheon had been remembered instead of forgotten.

There is little or nothing in the way of sight seeing in Guatemala, and after a short sojourn I was very glad to accept an invitation from an Englishman, who owned a coffee and sugar plantation on the coast, to accompany him on his journey home.

He, of course, had his own servants and mules, and as I had no difficulty in hiring my three animals, a pack mule and two riding ones for the muleteer (arriero) and myself, we started early one morning on our trip to Los Altos—the Highlands of Guatemala—from whence we were to descend to the coffee district by way of Quezaltenango.

CHAPTER V.

INDIAN MOUNDS—AQUEDUCT—INDIANS GOING TO MARKET—
MIXCO—COMPOSITION OF AN AVERAGE VILLAGE—BARRANCAS—
SANTA MARIA EARTHQUAKE—CATTLE FAIR—CHIMALTENANGO—
LOOKING BACK—TEMPERATE ZONE—A FLOUR MILL—TECPAN—
CHURCH—INDIANS—GOITRE—INTERIOR OF CHURCH—MIRACLE
STONE—IXINCHE—ASCENT TO LOS ALTOS—ATITLAN—A WEIRD
SCENE—A MARIMBA—RAINSTORM — ENCUENTROS — MOUNTAIN
VIEWS—SANTO TOMAS—RELIGIOUS FESTIVAL—A FRUGAL MEAL
—SANTA CRUZ DEL QUICHE—THE CONVENT—HOSPITALITY—A
NIGHT'S REST.

FOR a short distance our road was the same by which we had reached the city from San José; then branching off to the right it led over a plain towards the mountains.

On this plain were numerous Indian mounds, most of which were intact, as the few that had been opened had revealed no greater treasures than fragments of pottery and some old bones.

We passed one of the aqueducts which supplies the city with water, and which is a work of considerable magnitude, as the sources of the rivers are some miles off.

The road was quite animated with groups of Indians hurrying towards the city with their goods for the market; the men mostly with great loads of freshly cut maize, the women and children carrying vegetables, tortillas in neat white napkins, and poultry. Indian women generally move along at a brisk jog-trot, at the same time emitting a peculiar sound, something between a whistle and a grunt, which is supposed to help them on their way.

One woman amused us very much; she carried an open-work basket of fowls and ducks on her back, on which was also slung a baby, in her arms she bore a fine young sucking pig, and on her head was a tray of tortillas; as she jogged along the baby cried, the porker squealed, and the poultry made noise enough almost to drown her own grunting.

The village of Mixco, from whence these country people come, is three leagues from the city; but morning after morning they hasten in, sell their produce, spend the proceeds in liquor, get drunk—at least the men do—and stumble home late at night, to repeat the programme next day.

We found Mixco a clean little mountain village with a large church, fountain and plaza. These three things are inseparable to the average village of the country, which, before you have seen it, you may safely describe as consisting of an enormous white plaster church, in a most dilapidated condition, an

Origin of Barrancas.

ill-kept plaza with a heavy stone fountain, from which issues a meagre stream of water, and a collection of mud huts.

The inhabitants of Mixco are said to be descendants of some people who were settled there by Alvarado, one of the generals of Cortez; they certainly differ somewhat in appearance, and are much more cleanly in their houses and habits than the usual run of Indian villagers.

The next village we reached was Santiago, with a very picturesque plaza; the houses were so embedded in trees that we did not appreciate the size of the place, until on looking back from our continually ascending road we saw it to be of considerable extent.

Soon after we crossed a deep barranca, at the bottom of which was a stream spanned by a stone bridge erected in 1852. Barrancas, as the thickly wooded ravines which intersect the country are called, form the principal feature in the scenery of the great plateau of Guatemala. Their presence is notified by long lines of dark green, which, on approaching them, open out into terrible abysses of almost perpendicular depth.

There are various theories concerning the origin of these barrancas. Some say that the streams, acting on the volcanic material that has filled up the natural valleys, have worn their beds to the original level of the earth; others that the ground underneath has been burnt by fire, and has gradually given way, aided probably by the strong draught caused by volcanic eruption. To whatever cause they may owe their origin they are at any rate a source of continual annoyance to a traveller, who thinking he is near the end of his day's journey, suddenly finds himself on the brink of a precipice, the descent and ascent of which will probably take some hours. Barrancas have their utility in spite of their inconvenience; they are said to be a safeguard against earthquakes. The present city of Guatemala is surrounded by them, and hitherto has been free from shocks.

On this occasion we experienced no difficulty in crossing the barrancas that lay in our path, as the road between the capital and Quezaltenango is good and traversed by stage-coaches of rather primitive aspect.

At Santa Maria, which we reached after a long and steep ascent, we stopped for breakfast at a small hut by the wayside, and I mournfully renewed my acquaintance with tortillas and black beans. Followers of the Pythagorean maxim "Beware of beans," had better not venture into Central America.

The surrounding country was well cultivated, maize being the principal product, and the undulating hills and deep ravines had an abundance of wild flowers.

Zumpango was the next place we passed, then Tejar, lying in a grassy plain, on one side of which were the ruins of the village of San Luis Pastores, which was utterly destroyed by the earthquake of 1874. A great cattle fair is held here towards the end of November in each year, and is attended by people from all parts; thirty thousand head of cattle are frequently collected there.

Plain of Tecpan.

We slept at Chimaltenango, the chief town of the department of that name, and found the small inn clean and comfortable, and sufficiently advanced in civilization to possess knives and forks, luxuries which betokened more substantial victuals than frijoles and tortillas.

By five o'clock next morning we were galloping over the fertile plain in which Chimaltenango is situated, and after a sharp ascent of a pine-clad hill turned to look back over the road we had been travelling on. The view embraced a wide extent of country; in the far distance lay the city of Guatemala, on our right were the volcanoes, the white mists of early morning rolling up their shapely sides, and below was the sleeping town in the centre of the plain, which glistened like silver as the rays of the sun struck across the rising vapours. Through the branches, whose foliage quivered in the light air, appeared the sky, like a bright blue mantle without speck or cloud. It was so simple and tranquil a scene that even a small caracara eagle that was perched on a neighbouring fir tree, refrained from disturbing its repose with his usual harsh cry.

Soon afterwards we passed more Indian mounds, and presently arrived at a picturesque hill forming a natural fortification, and which had been used as such during Carrera's war. In front lay the plain of Tecpan, fertile and cultivated with maize and wheat. The temperature was delightful, as the plain is at an elevation of 6,000 feet above the sea, and it was pleasant to see the cereals and fruit trees of the temperate zone. Flocks of small green parroquets that screamed and wheeled about in the cool air looked like inhabitants of another clime. Eagerly watching these noisy birds were numerous little hawks of a species that is very common in Guatemala.

At Patzitzia—another village that was destroyed by the earthquake of 1874—we were able to appreciate the intensity of the shock that had shaken to pieces most of the houses, by the appearance of a large church whose entire front had slipped down, and lay almost unbroken on the ground ; when the occurrence happened the priest was alone in the church, standing near the altar, and he escaped unhurt.

After leaving the plain an immense barranca crossed our path, but it was impossible to regret its depth, so beautiful was the winding road, mountain on one side and ravine on the other, here starred with the exquisite blossoms of some wild flower, there decked with rocky beds of deep green moss and graceful ferns.

When we had crossed the river that flows through this valley and had ridden a short distance along its banks, we came upon a scene of animation quite foreign to native industry. A large flour mill—the only one I believe in Guatemala—appeared in view; over its dam the water flashed like a sheet of silver, people hurried to and fro, buildings were being erected, a saw mill was at work and the busy air was not that of Central America. I was told it belonged to a Swiss who had thus established a very lucrative business in the centre of a wheat growing country and with no competition.

Following the Tecpan river, we afterwards passed an old Indian flour mill which in utility contrasted very absurdly with its modern neighbour, but which for picturesqueness quite carried the day. Near this point the old road to the city joined ours and we soon reached the Indian town of Tecpan Guatemala.

We dismounted at the posada and were informed that the mistress of the house was ill, and consequently there was nothing to eat; we suggested that, as probably the hens continued laying in spite of their owner's indisposition, we would be quite satisfied with a few eggs. Eventually a slight repast was served to us in the farm-yard of the inn, an old mattress acting for a table cloth, and two high-backed church chairs for seats.

After our meal we visited the church, which is said to be one of the finest in the country. In size it may deserve its reputation, but as usual, on near approach, the tawdry plaster figures that ornamented its façade deprived it of any effect that distance might have given. In the large courtyard of the edifice were groups of strange-looking Indians, in large woollen cloaks and tall black straw hats in shape and size like our own.

On the steps we were accosted by beggars, most of whom in addition to a variety of complaints were afflicted with goitre. This disease is very common in some villages of the high lands of Guatemala, where, as in some parts of South America, to be without one is regarded as a deformity.

The interior of the church was filled with tarnished gilt altars, picture frames and trumpery of all sorts; an old Indian woman was making a pilgrimage on her knees, kissing all the bricks that composed the walls within her reach, and uttering doleful sighs.

We were disappointed in not finding the miracle stone described by Fuentes; we consulted the padre and some of the oldest inhabitants, but they all assured us they had never heard of such a thing, and certainly there was nothing like it in the church. This stone was said to be composed of some black transparent substance, on whose face appeared the answers to questions when it was consulted on matters of war or judicature; its resting place was on the top of the grand altar.

About a league to the south of Tecpan Guatemala, is the site of the ancient city of Ixinché, but as nothing now remains of the ruins of this once powerful place, the very stones themselves having been removed in the building of the present town of Tecpan, we decided not to visit it, as my companion was anxious to reach home by a certain date.

The ascent into Los Altos commenced shortly after leaving Tecpan by a steep hill (cuesta), up which the road wound for a distance of three leagues. It was a very delightful ride, so varied, such a blending of grandeur and loveliness that one could not determine which part was the most beautiful. The mountain sides were covered with wild flowers, fuschias, geraniums, salvias, red and purple asters, and the deep blue convolvulus, whilst the deep gorges were filled with drooping foliage and trailing plants with here and there a glimpse of flowing water. Of all the flowers so bountifully spread over the mountains, none were so welcome as a few violets that we found nestling under a large uprooted trunk on a sunny bank. Although mere dog-violets they then seemed just as fragrant, yes, more fragrant, I think, than their garden cultured brethren, and we gathered these sweet home-links with a care and reverence that would hardly have been bestowed on the rarest hot-house blossom.

Before we had accomplished the ascent the golden sunshine, that had been streaming on the grand vistas and rocky caves with almost too great a power, vanished, and was succeeded by banks of fog and mist that rolled up the ravines in dull white masses. Thus the views of the Lake of Atitlan which lay far below us, which I had heard described as being of wondrous beauty were lost to us. Whenever we arrived at a point from whence we ought to have descried the lake and its volcanic shores, nothing was to be seen except the creeping storm-mist, bringing with it the sound of thunder, betokening a storm which subsequently overtook us, and which we afterwards heard had raged with considerable fury around the lake.

I was however in some degree compensated for the loss of the views by the knowledge that the road on my return journey would pass along the shores of the lake.

Gradually darkness settled down, and had not the road been broad and good it would have been a difficult matter to have continued our journey. Suddenly from out of the distant gloom appeared flashes of light, and at the same time there came a sound of the strangest music I had ever heard. My companion at once recognised it as proceeding from a marimba,* and we presently came upon a party of Indians indulging in a dance by torch-light on the roadside. They stopped at our approach and made preparations for departure, but at our request they continued their festivities.

The scene was intensely picturesque; all around were the great mountains looming up in the black night, out of whose darkness flashed thousands of fireflies; a few pine torches showed the slow, monotonous movements of the dancers, keeping time to the clear wild music of the marimba whose notes sounded high above the growling of the distant thunder, and altogether the

---

* A marimba consists of a series of vertical tubes arranged and graduated like those of a pan's pipe. Their bases have a little side opening covered with thin parchment. Over each tube, and supported on cords at their extremities, is a bar (also graduated) of hard resonant wood. No nail is used in making the instrument, all the parts being held together by cord. Sometimes the tubes consist of natural gourds carefully selected. The music is produced by rapidly striking the bars with sticks of cane, or whale-bone tipped with India-rubber balls. It is played with both hands and usually by three performers; the marimba most commonly used has twenty-two tubes, and its clear and sonorous sound can be heard a great distance.

picture was as weird as could be found amongst the witch legends of the Brocken. Long after the waving pine torches were hidden from our view we heard the dull chant of the singers, and longer still the notes of the marimba pursued us, as if the dusky musicians intended to play on in spite of night and the rapidly approaching storm.

It is said that few travellers cross these mountains without encountering heavy rains, and we proved no exception to the rule. Wet through and chilled to the bone, we did not reach our resting place for the night until eleven o'clock. This cheerless halting spot is known by the name of Encuentros, and the Government has here erected a wooden shelter for the benighted. The man in charge showed us into a large room in which were several bedsteads and a table, but as unfortunately our pack-mules had not yet arrived there were no blankets to put on the former, and the lady of the house being absent, there was very little to put on the latter. It is astonishing what a little it takes to upset the arrangements of a family in this country!

The night was very cold, and I could not help thinking that as Government had taken the trouble to build a house, they might have added to their kindness by putting a fire-place in it, there being no scarcity of fuel, and the region a very cold one.

Very early next morning we mounted our shivering animals, and instead of pursuing the direct road to Quezaltenango turned off over a long mountain ridge on our way to Quiché. The little path we followed kept carefully for some distance along the dividing wall of two deep valleys, but at last was compelled to give in, and then commenced a series of ascents and descents strongly suggestive of a game of see-saw on a gigantic scale. Beautiful views, varied and widespreading from the tops of the hills, narrow and vista-like from their bases, came in rapid succession. Native huts, surrounded by maize and other signs of cultivation were not unfrequent in the valleys and on the hill sides, and their sturdy owners passed us now and then with the invariable greeting "Dias, patron"—good day, Sir. Some of these Indians carried a little shuttle from which they were spinning a fine thread. So rapid are the changes from valley to mountain top in this land, that a few hours' walk will take you from the warm temperature, where a little cotton is cultivated, to the cold regions of the fir and pine.

From the summits we could see ridge after ridge of mountain trending off to a plain, on which stood a few white villages, with here and there an expanse of water, glittering as though it had drained the adjacent mountains of all their mineral veins; the background was formed by the rugged outlines of the Sierra Madre, whose rocky sides contain a wealth of lead and silver as yet hardly touched. About noon we reached the Indian village of Santo Tomas, and being very hungry hoped to enjoy a good breakfast. But here again our ill-luck in the matter of food attended us. All the houses were closed as a religious festival was in progress, and the inhabitants were witnessing the procession. As part of a religious ceremony, this procession was certainly as strange a one as I had ever seen. It was headed by ragged Indians playing drums and whistles; these were followed by Devils in grotesque dresses and masks, and after them came some spangled saints and a few historical characters.

It has often struck me that the Indians of this country must be of a most forgiving spirit, as in all their festivals and ceremonies they introduce with most honour figures representing Cortes and the Spanish generals who assisted in the overthrow of Montezuma, and became the conquerors of their race. But probably they know nothing of their own history, and have been content with the saints that the priests have given them instead of their ancient idols. The sight of these stagily dressed saints always reminded me of the answer made by an old Indian to his priest, who urged upon him the necessity of putting away his ugly idols, and the easy change it would be to substitute the blessed saints. " Padre mio," was the reply, " if the difference is so slight it is hardly worth while to make the change."

After a diligent search we succeeded in buying a few eggs and oranges, and with as little delay as possible bade adieu to the inhospitable village.

Just outside we rode through a very pretty ravine with fern clad sides and overhung with orange trees; then came more barrancas, an undulating plain, a lake, and the village of Lemoa. From this point our destination looked quite close, but the intervening ravines delayed us so much that the sun had set before we entered Santa Cruz, Quiché, which we did in the midst of a violent rain-storm.

As no one ever goes to Quiché for pleasure, accommodation for man and beast is limited; muleteers and others whose business takes them there, pass the night in the open corridor which runs round the plaza. As we preferred a more comfortable lodging, if possible, we made inquiries and were directed to the convent adjoining the church and fronted by a paved quadrangle.

Clattering over the stones we pealed at the bell, and on the gates being opened were informed that the padre had gone away and that there was no accommodation for us. Finally we persuaded the domestic to give us shelter, and ourselves and mules were soon ensconced in the cold stone cloisters. After leaving us for a short time, the aged housekeeper returned with a solitary candle and an enormous key, with which she unlocked a door and introduced us with much ceremony to a large cell without a vestige of furniture of any sort. With many apologies she assured us that there was no bedstead, chair, or table in the place, and worst of all she had not a particle of food left. Sticking the wretched candle in a crevice of the wall, she bowed herself out and we never saw her again.

The only thing for us to do was to send the servants in search of eatables and a table, or something to sleep on, but our chances of obtaining anything were small, as after dark it is difficult to get provisions even in more civilized places than Quiché.

In the meantime my companion sat down on the floor and proceeded to inflate an air-mattress he had brought in case of emergency, and I commenced the same process with an india-rubber bath. This occupation we prolonged as much as possible, as it suggested the perhaps vulgar but natural idea that it would probably be the only "blow out" we should get that evening. However, our servants proved themselves equal to the occasion, and returned with eggs, tortillas, coffee, a table and a broken bedstead.

The owner of the two latter pieces accompanied them, and after asking a considerable sum for their use, at last consented to take about the entire value of the articles in question.

With a promise to send a guide early next morning to conduct us to the ruins, our kind but expensive friend left us, so our arrieros stretched themselves in their ponchos on the altars in the cloisters, the mules munched their sacate where the nuns had once tended their flowers, and we were soon fast asleep, wearied by our long day's ride in barranca-land.

CHAPTER VI.

RUINS OF QUICHE—IDOLS—THOUGHTS—ALPINE SCENERY—TOTO-
NICAPAN—INDIANS OF LOS ALTOS—CAPTURE OF TOTONICAPAN
—AN "ON DIT"—STRANGE ASPECT OF COUNTRY—WEALTHY
INDIANS—QUEZALTENANGO—ITS VOLCANOES—PLAZA—ANCIENT
DIET—CATHEDRAL—DEATH OF FLORES—A CENTRAL AMERICAN
DRAWING-ROOM—A NEW ROAD—ALMOLONGA—HOT SPRINGS—
POTTERY MANUFACTORY—INDIAN SUPERSTITIONS—AN INDIAN
GOVERNOR—ASCENT OF VOLCANO OF QUEZALTENANGO.

THE ruins of Quiché are about a mile and a quarter from the town; our path to them was bordered with aloes, most of which were in full blossom, their lofty stalks, fourteen or fifteen feet high, bearing hundreds of blossoms.

After crossing a small ravine, our guide pointed out to us a hill range once the exterior fortifications of the ruined city, now, almost entirely ploughed up and cultivated. The entrance to the ruins was through a deep and narrow gorge, the winding passage only permitting one mule to pass at a time.

Palace at Quiché.

Entering a small gateway we found ourselves on a plateau, entirely surrounded—except where we had come in—by an immense barranca with almost perpendicular sides, forming what must have been in the old days an impregnable position. This plateau was the stronghold of the royal house of Quiché, and on it stood the palace, place of sacrifice, and a few other buildings whose ruins are all that is left of the once regal city. Fragments of walls, two or three massive piles of stone and cement, a tower and a well-preserved floor, also of cement, constitute the ruins, but every part so destroyed and overgrown with brushwood that it is impossible to imagine the original structures with any certainty.

According to the old historians of Guatemala who derived their information from manuscripts, the palace was a magnificent edifice of hewn stones of various colours, and would compare favourably with that of Montezuma in Mexico. It was divided into six divisions; the first was occupied by the body guard, the second by the male relations of the king, the third by the king himself who had different apartments for morning, noon and night. Here also were the court-houses, aviaries, the grand saloons, armouries &c. The queen and ladies of the Court occupied the fourth and fifth divisions; the sixth being the residence of the daughters of the king and other females of the royal line. Gardens, baths, and fish-ponds were freely distributed about the grounds, which gave the idea of the most princely magnificence.

If the writers were correct in their accounts—and they have even given the dimensions of the different buildings—it seems marvellous how all that they have described, or even half could have been contained in the comparatively small area of the plateau. It looks, rather, as if it were an inner fortress, the last place of refuge in case of an advance by a victorious enemy.

Of the city itself, which must have stood outside the great ravine, nothing remains, and in a few years it is probable no vestige will be left even of the palace and its surroundings. The little that time has left is fast disappearing, and the very Indians themselves who rose *en masse* and threatened to kill the violators of their capital when they were searching for treasure, unless they immediately left the country, now employ their spare moments in dragging the squared stones and other useful building materials to the new city.

It is not unlikely that there never was a city the people of which were not scattered over the fields, or herded together in open hamlets, like the inhabitants of ancient Greece, whose royal family and its immediate followers alone lived in the stone edifices. Small images and idols are continually being found amongst the stones and rubbish that have accumulated on the side of the ravine where the ruins stand, and some of the natives have quite a collection of them.

One little stone idol I purchased from a man, who was at first very unwilling to part with it, as he declared it would bring him bad luck, but the sight of a réal (a shilling) overcame his scruples and he said he would risk the ill-fortune. Our guide was very voluble, and imparted a good deal of what he thought was valuable information, but after he had informed us that Quiché was celebrated as the meeting place of the three kings—Montezuma, the King of Quiché, and the King of Spain—we felt we could not place much reliance on his statements.

The remains of a great people cannot be looked on without feelings of pity and sorrow, and although we did not find the extensive ruins that we expected, still there was much to exercise the imagination. As we stood on the top of the pyramidal structure where human sacrifioes had been offered up, the eye wandered over the lands of what was once a rich and populous kingdom. There were the situations of the fort Resguardo (defence) and of Atalaya (the look-out tower), which guarded the entrance to the royal residence, and beyond them a line of fortifications indicating a military genius that the mind can hardly conceive when thinking of the present Indian race.

For ages the kings of Quiché prospered; victorious in war, wise in administration, and surrounded with wealth and luxury. Then the Spaniards appeared, and for an act of treachery towards them the last king was hanged. Again and again did the fierce Quichés battle against their invaders, but Spanish discipline overcame them, and the whole kingdom fell into the hands of Alvarado.

We rode away from the ruins pondering over the fate of the brave old race, and glad that we had seen one of the great military sites of ancient Indian civilization. Crossing the plain of Quiché, on which were several ponds, where long-legged white cranes were wading, and numerous wild-fowl swimming, we entered an Alpine region of mountain, stream, and forest. Range behind range rose the pine-clad hills, until we thought we must be moving in a circle, such a family likeness ran through them. Up and down these endless mountain banks we followed the bridle-path, now deep in some green and quiet valley, and now toiling up some slope gay with the bright yellow masses of wild marigold; then higher up still, amongst the solemn pines through which we caught glimpses of the lofty range under whose crest ran the white high road between Guatemala and Quezaltenango, some ten thousand feet above the level of the sea.

At last, far down below us, we saw in a beautiful and picturesque valley the town of Totonicapan, behind which, and far over-topping the intervening high table-land, rose the magnificent cone of the volcano of Santa Maria. It was a grand landscape, and a fitting finale to the romantic scenery through which we had passed. A steep and stony path down the mountain brought us out into a narrow street of the town, and we were soon comfortably lodged in a clean, well-furnished posada.

Totonicapan, although the chief town of the department of that name, and containing about twenty-five thousand inhabitants, most of whom are Indians, requires but little description. Like most other towns in Guatemala, it is merely an extended edition of a village without any points of interest.

The following morning we left for Quezaltenango. The road seemed very lively, especially after the silence of the forest we had traversed the preceding day, and Indian market-women, pack mules, droves of pigs, and country people were met and passed continually. The country is an agricultural valley, and produces fruit, wheat, barley, and other cereals in abundance; we saw flocks of sheep in the pastures and plenty of cattle were spread over the plains.

The Indians of Los Altos are the most industrious of the Central American tribes, and their manufactures of wool and cotton meet with a ready sale; these and articles of pottery and wood form their chief exports to the other departments. They are said to be a superior-looking race, and certainly are hardier and more intelligent than the Indians of the low-lands. The cool and healthy climate naturally accounts for their industrial habits and bodily vigour, and perhaps their greater mental acquirements may be assigned to the fact that a large number of them are descendants of the ancient noble families of Quiché. One thing I noticed though, and that was that the love of strong drink was as prevalent amongst them as with less favoured tribes.

Shortly after leaving Totonicapan, we ascended a steep hill by a winding road, edged on one side by a deep gorge.

After the death of Carrera, his temporary successor

Cerna was encamped with his troops at Totonicapan; hearing one day that his opponent Barrios was at hand and about to attack the town, it is related that he gave orders for part of his army to retire at night behind the afore-mentioned hill, and at a given signal to attack the enemy, who would then be assailed from front and rear. The story says that in the morning Cerna had not recovered from his night's potations, and consequently no signal was given. Whether such was the case or not, it is at all events true that Barrios triumphantly entered the town, and Cerna quitted the country.

From the top of the hill, our road ran through a cultivated district forming a wide plain, intersected by ravines and bounded by volcanic mountains. The appearance of the country we had left and of Quezaltenango was very peculiar, and gave the idea that in times past the entire valley from the foot of the surrounding mountains was an immense lake; you could see everywhere the form of promontories, and their steep declivities were strongly suggestive of a shoreline.

As we progressed on our journey, we passed some well-to-do villages, one in particular that was half-hidden in a barranca on our right, contained, I heard, many wealthy—that is for Indians—inhabitants. But an Indian will not change his mode of life or add to its convenience, no matter how many dollars he may have lying idle. So long as he has his corn patch, and perhaps a cow, a bed to lie on, and plenty of tortillas, he is content, the rest is vanity and vexation. He still goes on accumulating coin, but either buries it in the ground or spends it in gifts on saints and altars to his church, and in paying taxes to his priest.

After descending a lime-stone cliff, we crossed a broad but shallow river by a bridge, passed through a village standing on its banks, and, after a few more miles entered the town of Quezaltenango.

Quezaltenango—the abode of Quezal—is the second city of Guatemala as regards commerce, population, and wealth. The road from the capital stops here, the distance between the two cities being about forty leagues. The town is situated near the extremity of a plain, and is shadowed by the two volcanoes of Santa Maria and of Quezaltenango. The latter is a rugged volcanic ridge of huge lava piles, with crater from whence still issue smoke and steam. The former, which rises to a height of over twelve thousand feet, is a perfect cone of great beauty ; it is thickly wooded from base to summit, and standing quite alone presents an appearance of quiet grandeur that one never tires of looking at.

The inhabitants of this country say that the vegetation at the top is dying away, in which case no one can foretell what calamnity the peaceful giant may be about to inflict. Should a violent eruption take place the lava flow must either be in the direction of the town or towards the coast ; in the former case, a repetition of the destruction of Herculaneum would probably ensue—in the latter, a laying waste of the rich coffee and sugar plantations. Still, to produce such dire effects the eruption would have to be on a very grand scale, as though the distances to travel over are but small, yet fortunately they are intersected by ravines whose depths would swallow up rivers of lava.

The large plaza formed always a picturesque scene; the market was held there, and the vendors displayed their goods under huge plaited leaf umbrellas, among which a motly crowd in various costumes was constantly moving.

Bernard Diaz says that the people of Quezaltenango used to rear a certain species of dog that never barked, was very good eating, and whose flesh was always for sale in the market. In the present day, that sort of food has given place to beef and mutton, and the peculiar canine race is extinct.

The cathedral stood on one side of the square and contained nothing worthy of note, but it was an object of some interest, as it was here that in 1826 Cirilo Flores, the Vice-President of the Republic, was murdered by a fanatical mob. Being a Liberal, he was denounced by the priests as an enemy to religion, and when on a visit to the town, his house was surrounded by the enraged populace who demanded his death. He fled to the church, but was dragged by the hair of his head from the pulpit in which he had taken refuge, thrown into the hands of a furious crowd of men and women, and in the name of religion beaten to death.

Besides the municipal buildings, Quezaltenango

Hot Springs of Almolonga.

contains several schools, a hospital, and an Orphan Asylum of which the inhabitants are justly proud. Although the population amounts to about thirty thousand, yet the number of foreigners may almost be counted on one's fingers; most of them own coffee estates, the journeys to and fro passing away the time, which would otherwise hang heavily in a place where there are but few amusements.

The houses are the usual heavy one story adobe buildings, square, and with a garden in the centre. They are cool and airy—too cold I thought—but owing to their solid walls and grated windows, present the appearance of so many prisons when viewed from the outside. I had always been amused at the formal arrangement of the furniture in a true Central American drawing-room, which consists in placing eight high-backed chairs or four sofas vis à vis, and in two scrupulously straight lines, at either end of the room; but at the house of a rich ladino in Quezaltenango the same uniformity was observed with two entirely different sets of furniture; where you expected to see one clock there were two, and instead of four vases you found eight, in fact everything was doubled except the pianos, and of those instruments there were three. The apartment was long and narrow, but not of sufficient size to deaden the harmonious effect if the ladies of the house ever practised their scales at the same time.

The prettiest ride outside the town is to the hot springs of Almolonga, and one morning we set out before our breakfast to pay them a visit. At some distance we passed large gangs of prisoners hard at work on a new carriage road, which is to form the fashionable drive to the Springs; they seemed a merry lot, proud of their position and glad to see strangers from whom they requested cigars and tobacco as a toll. Continuing along the old road, we dipped down into the valley in which stood the village and the Springs. It was a great change from the cold morning air of the plain—which is over eight thousand feet above the level of the sea—to the warmth of the valley; from a country of wheat and oats, we had descended into maize fields and orange groves, where humming birds poised themselves over some fragrant shrub, or hid themselves for a second in the deep heart of a trumpet-flower.

In Europe, such a valley as that of Almolonga would be considered one of the most charming resorts, and the picturesque hill-sides would be enlivened by many a white villa and cosy dwelling, but here it is still in its primitive state, and Indian huts and Indian customs reign supreme.

The water from the spring is very hot, and whilst some of it passes into small bathing houses where a slight charge is made for their occupation, the greater part finds its way into a circular pool in the ravine. In this pool congregate the natives; men, women and children, all dressed in the garb of nature, sit and lie about in the utmost tranquillity. The waters are a cure for skin diseases to which the natives are very prone,

An Indian Governor. 69

and consequently the number of daily visitors is large. I have before mentioned that the inhabitants of different villages can be distinguished by their costume; the villagers of Almolonga have another distinction, and that is that they are nearly all great drunkards and it is a curious circumstance that within a league of that place there is a total abstinence village.

On our return home we visited a pottery manufactory, of which there are several in Quezaltenango. The owner was a ladino, the workmen were Indians and ladinos; they did not appear to possess much invention, but the cups and other utensils that they turned out were simple and well shaped.

I was anxious to ascend the graceful volcano of Santa Maria, but we found it so difficult to obtain a guide that we gave it up, as my companion wished to reach his estate on the coast with as little delay as possible. The Indians are very superstitious, regarding the volcano of Santa Maria, and have many stories of fairies and spirits that have been met near the summit.

We found time, however, to make a trip to the volcano of Quezaltenango, to obtain a guide for which we called upon the old Indian Governor. We found the old gentleman ill in bed, but he was delighted to see us and at once gave the necessary orders. He was very intelligent and courteous, and gave a good idea of the ancient Indian noble; his people regard him with great reverence, his will being law. Like the interior of the huts of the rich Indians, it was destitute of any convenience except a wooden bedstead, all available space being occupied by a great altar on which were crowded innumerable saints, crosses, and other paraphernalia of his religion.

The ascent of the volcano was easy, until we left the wood and emerged on the lava beds, leaving our animals in charge of a native. Then commenced a rough, but by no means difficult climb over the huge boulders and piles of rock that intercepted our course, until we reached the ridge on the northern side of the crater, from which issued small jets of steam. These jets puffed up at intervals among the loose rocks more strongly, and the smoke would collect in a cloud until blown aside by the wind. We had noticed these clouds from the plain, and their appearance suggested a greater eruption in the crater than we found to be the case; in fact the ascent was hardly worth the trouble, the coast view we had expected being entirely shut out by the more lofty Santa Maria.

On our return, I found among other plants some beautiful specimens of a lovely little fern,* whose bead-like fronds sprang from the interstices of some moss-covered rocks. With these and other treasures of a like sort I felt recompensed for our scramble, and all the more anxious to inspect the wonders of the tropical world for whose regions we started the following morning.

* Cheilanthes Lendegeria elegans.

CHAPTER VII.

A MUD ROAD—MULES—BAD LANGUAGE—CHANGE OF VEGETATION
—TREE FERNS—VIEW OF COAST—BIRDS—ARISTOLOCHIA—A
FINCA—COFFEE ESTATES IN GUATEMALA—ADVANTAGES AND
DISADVANTAGES—IDEAS ON SELLING AND BUYING PLANTATIONS
—DESCRIPTION OF COFFEE RAISING—AVERAGE PRODUCTION—
PROCESS OF PREPARING THE BERRY—LABOUR SYSTEM—COFFEE
CULTURE OF SERVICE TO THE COUNTRY—ESTIMATE OF COST
AND PRODUCTION OF A NEW COFFEE PLANTATION.

"IS the road always as good as this?" I could not help asking, as my mule, after wading through a sea of mud up to its girths, stumbled over a ridge on to its nose, and would probably have deposited me in a quagmire had it not been for the high pommel of my Mexican saddle.

"Always," was the reply, "you see it now in its best, in the wet season the road disappears altogether."

We had been for some time slowly wending our way down the road leading from Quezaltenango to the coast; at intervals, the otherwise very fair track was broken by long stretches of mud, a perfect ocean over whose billows our animals could hardly lift their legs so deep were the furrows into which they were plunged. Sometimes they remained astride these ridges, then all you could do was to dismount, and wait until a supreme effort had extricated them from their unpleasant position.

Still it was wonderful how knowingly they picked out the best places, and with what care they dragged out their embedded limbs, sniffed about as if their powers of scent could tell them what deep holes to avoid, and after feeling for a sure foundation, slowly drew themselves from valley to valley over the intervening hill. The pack mules seemed to enjoy it most, and never missed an opportunity of wedging themselves in between the furrows; they would rush frantically over four or five ridges, and then settle down on the next, their legs momentarily sinking deeper and deeper on either side. Then was the opportunity for the arrieros to show off their powers of persuasion; such swearing, whistling and entreating, now coaxing each animal by its pet name, and now invoking the anger of all the saints on the unlucky brutes.

The speech of the lower class in Central America is invariably enlivened by oaths and religious phrases, but muleteers exceed all in the force and variety of their expressions. Most of these have long lost all power and significance, and the popular use of them reduces their effect to a mere "God bless me!"

but to a foreigner the invariable "Jesus," "Buen Dios," "Maria," "Cristo," "Caramba," &c., &c., that fill up the pauses of a conversation, fall unpleasantly on the ear.

So rapid is the descent from the Highlands of Guatemala to the coast that after a few hours' travel we had left the cold region, entered the temperate and were quickly approaching the hot. Vegetation had changed; the cold-loving wild flowers had given place to plants of a more luxurious foliage, the helianthus appeared instead of the fucshia and palms with their crowns of foliage contrasted strangely with the artichoke-like aloes we had so lately been admiring.

The mountain-side on our left hand was covered with ferns and creeping-vines, which grew in profusion under the lofty trees, and on our right the deep ravine was almost hidden in a thicket of greenery. Here and there in some shady nook, and generally in one moist from a trickling stream, stood beautiful tree-ferns, most of them with their waving leaves fully spread, but a few whose undeveloped fronds assumed the exact shape of a bishop's crozier.

Fot the first half of our journey the views had been confined to our immediate surroundings, the winding path through the gorges and the intervening hills having shut out anything beyond, but at last we came to a point from whence we overlooked the coast-land to the sea. On both sides of us the mountains extended far away, here showing an abrupt, precipitous knoll of rock, there divided by valleys and ravines.

In the foreground the tree-clad hills we were crossing sloped gently away, broken here and there by green glades, until they seemed to stop suddenly, and beyond was a bay of verdure, a velvet carpet of waving tree tops, extending to the white sea-shore. The intense green of this expanse was varied by the paler tints of the sugar plantations and the dark shade of the coffee trees; a silver line streaming through the woven woods marked the course of a river, whose banks, occupied by a few small huts, showed the only signs of life in the silent depths of that forest ocean.

We had seen but few birds on our way down the mountain—some large hawks, with a few bright crimson cardinals and red birds, being all that had deigned to show themselves; once or twice we heard the low warble of the blue-bird—called here elazulejo—otherwise no song had enlivened our day's ride. Now, as we drew near to the *tierra caliente*, parroquets appeared, and towards sundown, large green parrots flew overhead in pairs, uttering screams of defiance. Giant ceibas—venerated by the Indians—threw their huge buttressed roots across our path, their magnificent domes affording a safe shelter for gay-plumaged birds.

We passed strange trees and plants at every step, and from one creeper-covered shrub were suspended the curious flowers of the *aristolochia grandiflora*. The natives call it "the devil's bonnet," and when in full bloom it does resemble a Phrygian cap, lined with chocolate colour, but before it is developed, it is like the figure of a bird suspended by its beak. Some of these flowers must have been nine or ten inches in diameter.

It was dark when we passed through some rough gates, which showed that we had entered the plantation district, and it was nearly ten o'clock before we arrived at my companion's estate, passed through an avenue of young india-rubber trees, and pulled up before the verandah of his welcome cottage.

Next morning we made a tour of inspection of his sugar and coffee plantations, and after the wild and primitive cultivation we had so lately seen, I was struck with the excessively neat and carefully tended appearance of the property. But this is characteristic of most fincas—as the plantations are called—in Guatemala. It is a very pretty sight to look at, and a very pleasant walk to take through a well-managed coffee estate. Broad, well-kept roads run through acres of evenly-pruned trees, amidst whose shining dark leaves the fragrant white blossoms and red and green berries are seen at the same time. The ground underneath is perfectly clear of weeds, and whether on undulating hills or level plain, the smooth and trained aspect of the trees reminds one of a prosperous evergreen nursery garden.

I had heard in the city of Guatemala such different accounts of the value of coffee plantations as a profitable investment, that I was glad to have the opportunity of finding out for myself, by personal inspection and inquiries on the spot, their true merits. I had no ambition to own a coffee estate myself, but as one sometimes meets or hears of a man who is either in possession of too much or too little money, and is anxious to increase his store, it is well if asked to be able to give some direct information on the advantages and disadvantages of coffee culture in this country.

The disadvantages, I think, may be summed up in a few words, viz., the want, at present, of good roads, and the liability of losing most of your labourers at a moment's notice, in the event of their being required for military service. The latter event had taken place previous to my visit, but in spite of it, there was no want of activity visible, old men, women, and children all taking part in the different processes.

On some plantations, too, water has to be conveyed in flumes from a distance. These drawbacks, together with the trouble of searching for workmen, who usually are imported together with their entire families from distant places, are the chief disadvantages against which a planter has to contend. The introduction of Chinese labour would, I think, be attended with marked success, and it is a matter of surprise that in a country where it is most wanted, it should be unknown.

The advantages are that the climate is pleasant, as the plantations are situated between two thousand and four thousand five hundred feet above the level of the sea, heights at which coffee grows best; and that hitherto there has been no disease, all the conditions for good crops being extremely favourable. From what I can judge, coffee buyers and sellers are quite contented to leave matters as they are, and by a little judicious misrepresentation to too inquisitive strangers, keep the trade in their own hands and with as little competition as possible.

It has been urged that the number of plantations in the market is a proof of the barrenness of the enterprise; but it must be remembered that many of them have merely been bought for a speculation, some have been badly managed, or are in badly chosen situations, whilst others have amply repaid their owners who are glad to retire from business. The prevailing want of ready money is another great inducement for parting with a finca. It is no longer an easy matter to purchase a well-located plantation, planted, and with machinery, &c., ready for use; such a one may now and then be obtained for a reasonable figure, but prices here, as everywhere else, are rapidly increasing. But, as I said before, on account of the scarcity of ready money, it is easier to buy an average finca than to sell one. The one great imperative necessity for the success of a plantation is the continual presence of the master, and this is an item frequently overlooked by men who have failed in coffee-raising.

At the end of this Chapter I have given an estimate of the cost and production of an average coffee plantation. It was made out for me by the friend at whose estate I was staying, and though I have been told it gives too sanguine a view, yet I would prefer taking his knowledge and experience to that of others. It is merely added to give some idea of the requirements for a coffee plantation. It may prove of interest to give a rough description of this great industry of the country. Coffee is not indigenous, but was introduced into Guatemala about eighty years ago by French colonists, from seed obtained of the Paris Botanical Society. After proving its adaptability in the island of San Domingo, it rapidly spread over the extensive regions where it is now grown. The variety thus propagated was the Arabic.

To start a plantation, the first thing to do is to choose a suitable situation, having a vegetable soil and perfectly level, that will form a nursery for the young plants. Long and narrow beds are then made with spaces between, of sufficient size to allow the man in charge of them free access. The seed—which is the berry deprived of its outward fleshy covering, and the two kernels separated, but each retaining its outer skin—is planted in rows about nine inches apart; the holes are then covered with fine earth to facilitate as much as possible the germination of the seed. It is indispensable that the kernel should have the inner skin, or it will not bear, and it is also best to remove the outer covering, as this facilitates germination and prevents two plants from coming up together.

Having planted the seeds, the next step is to cover the earth with a light layer of plantain leaves, taking care to keep the soil always moist. After thirty or forty days the seed begins to sprout, then it is necessary to remove the leaves and substitute another covering. As the young trees require to be protected from the rays of the sun, low forks are placed at regular intervals through the nursery, upon which transverse poles are laid, and upon these is spread a covering of palm or plantain leaves, forming a shade at about three feet from the ground. This operation is indispensable if the seeds are uncovered in the dry season, but not so necessary if it is the rainy. Thus shaded, the young tree grows quietly on until it is time for transplanting it. The transplanting is managed with implements made expressly for this work.

During the third year the tree matures a few berries, and in the fourth a small crop is produced; in the succeeding years much larger crops are raised, but the average is subject to much variation. Some fincas will not produce more than two or three pounds to the tree, while others, older and more favourably situated, yield two or three times that amount. The tree is kept pruned down to eight or nine feet, and has a very symmetrical appearance. The berries grow in clusters, and as soon as they begin to ripen the process of picking begins and is continued, as successive portions become ready, until the setting in of the rainy season.

After the berries have been picked, they are passed through a machine which removes the outer covering and pulp, a stream of water being kept running constantly over them. They are then thrown into large vats of water and allowed to soak a day or two, when they are taken out and spread upon a pavement of tiles or cement to dry in the sun; in late improvements machinery is used for drying. When thoroughly dried, they are subjected to the action of another machine, consisting of large heavy wheels revolving around a circular box path. This removes the inner skin and dry pulp. They are then passed through a series of sieves which separate the berries from the pulverised skins and pulp, after which they are placed upon large tables and carefully sorted over by hand; the large and small berries are separated and the useless ones thrown away. They are then sacked and are ready for market.

It will be seen that considerable patience is required to await the fifth year before a planter begins to receive a return for his outlay, but it is a question whether the low price he originally pays for his uncultivated land will not eventually more than compensate him for the quicker return of a ready-made plantation and its consequently heavier outlay. Of the existing labour system there is a good deal to be said on both sides, I shall merely remark that in course of time, probably, a better one than the present will be adopted. There is no doubt that the culture of coffee has greatly improved the condition of the country, not only in making the people richer, but also by the introduction of new necessaries and luxuries which they can only obtain by bodily exertion and industrial habits.

Estimate of Cost and Production of a Coffee Plantation of one thousand trees, planted at 3 yards by 2, during five years.

Cost of two caballerias of land (225 acres) suitable for coffee		$4,000
Clearing one caballeria, or 1000 cuerdas, 4 reals.	500	
Staking and holing for 100,000 plants at 3 p. mil.	300	
Planting and holing for 100,000 plants at 2·4 p. mil.	250	
Cost of plants, 100,000 at $25 p. mil.	2,500	
	3,550	
Rancheria for mozos (labourer), tools, &c.		500
		$8,050
Maintenance of finca (plantation) for five years, say, five cleanings per annum, each 1000 cuerdas, at 2 reals, or $1,250 per annum.	6,250	
Mayordomo, $40 per month, or $480 per annum	2,400	
Cost of planting 500 cuerdas of grass.	500	
Cost of necessary machines and buildings for crop of 2000 quintals* to be erected—5th year.	5,000	
Incidental expenses.	500	
Cost of picking and preparing 2,500 quintals at $2.	5,000	
		19,650
Total cost up to end of fifth year.		$27,700
Corn to be raised in year of planting 2000 redes at 4 reals		1,000
Probable yield in 4th year, at ½ lb. per plant, 500 quintals at $10.		5,000
Probable yield in 5th year, at 2 lb. per plant, 2000 quintals at $10.		20,000
Total product		$26,000

---

* A quintal is 100 lbs.

Result at termination of fifth year.

Value of 100,000 trees at 3 reals.	$37,500
Value of 500 cuerdas potrero (pasture)	500
Value of Machinery, &c.	5,000
Value of Product as above	26,000
	$ 69,000
Cost as above.	27,700
Net profit.	$ 41,300

CHAPTER VIII.

A FINCA—COFFEE TREE—ANTS—HAMMOCK BRIDGE—GRAVE INDIANS—COSTA CUCA AND COSTA GRANDE—RETALULEN—AN INN—A FOREST KING—SAPOTE TREE—BIRDS—BUTTERFLIES— INDIAN WOMEN—A SPORTSMAN—PARROTS—CHITALON—VOL- CANOES—WASHERWOMEN—A KNOWING MULE—WIFE BEATING —PACING—COCOA PLANTATION—VAMPYRES - GOITRES—AN ANI- MATED FLOWER-BED—CUESTA D'ATITLAN—ASCENT—VIEW—A CURIOUS TREE—INDIAN SUPERSTITION—CABILDS—LIGHTNING EFFECTS.

HE early sunshine was lying warm and bright over the far reaching greenness, and the mountains stood half hidden in soft blue haze, when after a few pleasant days passed at my friend's house, I bade fare- well to the pastoral scene and continued my journey. I still had the same agreeable companion, as business, he said—but I think it was in reality kindness to me— called him to the town of Retalulen where we were to pass the night.

After a short ride ride along the outskirts of several plantations we entered the Mercedes estate, with one of whose proprietors we were to breakfast. This large plantation seemed to me to be the beau ideal of a well regulated finca. Beautifully situated on undulating ground, it presented the appearance of a well trained wood of laurels, with broad green rides, some crossing at right angles, others diverging from a common centre.

The machinery was in admirable order, and superintended by a young Scotchman who had lately brought it from Scotland with him, set it up with his own hands, and was now instructing others in its management. A broad carriage drive bordered with coffee trees, growing on high banks on either side, brought us to a large open space lined with the cottages of the labourers, forming a small village. Farther on stood the house of the proprietors, with a charming view of ravine and mountain. The property had lately come into the possession of our hosts, who informed us of many alterations and improvements that were in prospect, but everything was so neat and orderly that it was difficult to understand where the changes were needed.

After breakfast we mounted again, and for some distance passed through groves of coffee, where a busy scene of life and animation was presented. Indian women and children flitted among the dark bushes, filling their baskets with the ripe berries; others were carefully weeding the spaces between the trees, or spreading about the pulpy refuse of the berries to enrich the exhausted soil. A few ox-carts stood waiting for their load of berries, and near them were the overseers ready to give a check for each basket load deposited. The pickers keep these checks until Saturday night, when they present them and receive payment according to the number. A good picker can earn about two reals—two shillings—a day, though this of course, is subject to much variation.

The plantations are often bounded by coffee trees, which have been allowed to grow to their natural size, and they often attain a height of twenty feet. I know of no other tree, except the orange and cocoa, which is in bloom and fruit at the same time, which at once shows the different stages from bud to decay in such various colours. The berry changes from green to a greenish yellow, then from rose ripens into a purplish red, and if not picked fades into a dull brown and turns black. The flowers are white, like jessamine, and deliciously fragrant, and in Java a lover compares his lady to the pure and scented blossom of the coffee tree.

After leaving Mercedes, our road took a southerly direction, and we gradually descended from the coffee region to the hotter climate of the coast. Here signs of foreign occupation grew fewer, and the weed-covered land of the unpruned coffee trees, which betokens the plantation of a native, was now replaced by similar ill-tended patches of sugar-cane and cocoa. With the exception of these occasional wild gardens our path lay through a forest of giant trees, whose tops, tied together with various creepers, formed an agreeable shade from the hot sun.

We waded through a mountain stream at almost every quarter of a mile, and the number of these gave a refreshing coolness to the air, and gladdened the views by the rich green of the ravines through which they ran, past the grey shadows of rocks and slopes and into the flowery depths of an impenetrable jungle. Very remarkable and interesting were the numerous columns of ants we were constantly meeting. One of them extended for nearly half a mile in a compact red line. The colour was due to a bright red leaf, which each individual carried in an upright position. Parallel with this line was another going in the opposite direction, but each one with empty mandibles, having already deposited his burden, and now returning for another. Perfect order existed, except when an unfortunate leaf-bearer got mixed up with the wrong line, and was hustled about and finally overthrown and trampled on by the advancing column. Two or three times I have seen an ant thus treated, and on no occasion did it drop its load, but bravely held on to it to the last.

Sometimes the moving armies were carrying yellow leaves, and their appreciation of colour was very remarkable, as I have watched them loading themselves from shrubs whose leaves were both yellow and red, and when one colour was the order of the day, none of them ever took the other. The wonderful sagacity of ants has as yet hardly received the attention due to it, but that it is of a high order cannot be doubted, when we remember that they can excavate passages under rivers, build the floors of their houses so firmly with pebbles that sections can be lifted without breaking, and some species even form guards out of their communities, for the protection of those among them known as workers. Their vices are better known than their virtues, and it is a common saying in Central America that if an army of large ants enters your house you must leave, as they will not, and nothing will stop them.

One broad, swift river which we crossed, was made highly picturesque by a swinging hammock-bridge, composed of twisted vines and fastened to a tree on each shore. It looked very fragile and uncertain, but a pile of Indians stick in hand, each carryiug as usual a high crate, containing his household gods, passed over steadily and easily without a glance at the pretty scene, and with the customary "Dios patron" continued their march. The natives here are apt to look shyly on strangers, as they cannot account for their presence for any other purpose than that of seeking coffee lands, and they imagine that every new-comer is an injury to themselves.

Hitherto we had been travelling in that part of the country known as the Costa Cuca, which is separated from the Costa Grande—-one the finest coffee districts— by the river Tilapa. This we presently crossed, and at night-fall entered the small town of Retalulen. This place has the reputation of being one of the hottest in the country, and probably it is in the summer, but we did not find it too warm, and fortunately, as the inn was very dirty, and the guest chambers devoid of ventilation, except through the door and a tiny barred window high up in the discoloured wall. I have been told that these inns are vast improvements on the old ones, especially in the matter of cleanliness. They are only found in towns of some importance, and are almost entirely confined to places west of the city of Guatemala, and are all built and furnished in the same style.

On asking for a room, you are shown into a place with four adobe walls, containing a few boards placed on a frame, which is the bed. There may be a table, perhaps, but anything else is considered superfluous. In a few of the better class you may find a chair and a jug, but these are luxuries. As the rooms always open out into the patio, you can perform your toilet, and at the same time watch your mules, and see that they consume their proper allowance of sacate.

The next morning, after a very early cup of coffee, I said good-bye to my late companion and set forth alone with my arrierro, Leon, who was three-fourths an Indian, a heavy-visaged, taciturn fellow, but quick and obliging. That day's ride was the most beautiful I had experienced. Almost as soon as we had left the village, and before the sun had risen above the hills, we entered a broad green glade running through a dense tropical forest. On both sides there was a bewildering density of rare shrubs and plants, whose leaves and branches were united in tangled confusion by innumerable lianes to the gnarled trunks and spreading limbs of a race of forest giants. Some of these trees, particularly the ceibas, were of enormous proportions, and covered as they always were with an infinite variety of other plants, formed such hanging-gardens of Nature's own handiwork that it was difficult to tear oneself away from their contemplation! Leon, whom I had sent on ahead with the mules, was constantly returning to see what had become of me, and could not imagine what I was gazing at in a common tree. Probably he would have been just as unconcerned at the sight of a Hamadryad, who certainly ought to have had her home in the thick foliage of these leafy solitudes.

From the roots to the topmost branches these grand old trees form a playground for the most fantastic parasites, and a nursery for the most delicate ferns and orchids. Mosses and coloured lichens like those of our own woods, but more luxuriant, make a ground-work for the ferns and begonias which cover the trunks; on the branches huge bird-nest ferns, quaint orchids, and arrow-shaped caladiums perch themselves, whilst clinging "with Nessian venom," and climbing over their humbler brethren, may be seen the thick-veined leaves of the arum, dracontium, and pothos, whose deep verdure and elegant forms contrast with the pale grey of the deep tillandsea and the stiff regularity of the bromelias.

The gradation of colour, too, in this green mass is very beautiful, growing with an increasing brilliancy from the emerald mosses and pearly fungi to the bright orchids, until up in the thick crown the eye is bewildered by the confusion of the purple passion-flower and the gay blossoms of the ipomea, and other creepers, which mingle with the large yellow flowers of the heavily-burdened tree. Nor are the snake-like vines and creeping banhincas, in their upward struggle to the light, content to interlace the trunk and branches, but they throw out long tendrils, which, deriving sustenance alone from the tree and air, swing from the overhanging limbs until they reach the ground, when they take root, and again commence to climb.

Such was the appearance of numbers of these woodland monarchs that stood out in solitary grandeur, each a welcome oasis in a living sea of green. Another of the most striking objects in this forest scenery was the sapote tree, whose massive dome forms a canopy of bright orange-red flowers, very conspicuous amongst the darker shades. Lofty erythrinas, too, are frequently seen, their leafless branches adorned with red blossoms of a peculiar shape and of a rare intensity of colour.

The harmonies of these sunlit vaults are not confined to vegetation alone, there is a chime in the morning air, as birds fly from tree to tree; one beautiful little fellow with blue head and crimson breast pipes forth a tiny strain, which is soon eclipsed by the brilliant notes of an oriole; insects and feathered beauties vie with each other in saluting the rising sun, and even the nasal strains of the parrots are subdued and not out of accordance with the forest sounds of the awakening day. Silver-blue butterflies, whose outstretched wings would cover the hand, flit about heavily and lazily, studying botany with a coolness and deliberation very different from the brief investigations paid by the restless humming-birds in their electric flights from flower to flower.

Unfortunately this pleasant dawn lasts but too short a time, soon the hot sun has dispersed the vapours of the night, the birds cease their music, and the drone of the insects alone wakes the stillness:

" An atmosphere without a breath,
A silence sleeping there."

As the day advanced we met many groups of Indian women, some with fruits, others carrying oval pitchers of water, gracefully balanced on their heads, and all giving a colour to the scene by their crimson kerchiefs or light blue mantles coquettishly adjusted around the head or skirt.

Another and less picturesque figure that crossed our path was a ladino of poaching appearance, whose game-bag was pretty well filled with small birds, chiefly parrots and orioles. On asking him what he intended to do with them, he replied that he should sell them in the town (Retalulen) for food. I suggested that he might find some larger game for the exercise of his skill, but he said that small birds were more plentiful, and a man must live. I felt inclined to quote the words of the old French aristocrat, " Je n'en vois pas la nécessité," but refrained, and, instead, bought for some small coins a few of his specimens for preserving.

It is related that an Indian was once resting near here under one of the great trees, when suddenly a voice up in the branches exclaimed "Ave Maria." Falling on his knees, he began to mutter his prayers, when from another tree he distinctly heard the words "Ora pro nobis." Rushing into the village, he reported the miracle, and in after-days many of the inhabitants, when passing through the same part of the forest, heard "Ave Maria" uttered from the clouds. At last somebody noticed that it was a parrot which spoke the words, and for some time these birds were held in great respect, and even now an extra-superstitious native will cross himself when he sees one. Some people declare that a ladino who was moving with his family to another residence, lost a tame parrot when travelling along this road, and that this one had taught the others to say their prayers.

The number of streams and rivers we had to cross equalled that of the preceding day; one of them being so deep that we got thoroughly wet, and as the jocose pack-mule chose the opportunity for a swim, my bundle of rugs and the rest of the luggage were well soaked. This was of very little importance though, as we had to pass the night at the house of a planter to whom I had a letter of introduction.

Late in the afternoon we reached our destination, Chitalon, passing through part of the owner's large sugar plantation. I had hoped to have seen here the whole process of sugar-making, but as the cane would not be ripe for some days, my wish was not gratified.

Chitalon is situated about two thousand eight hundred feet above the level of the sea, and commands a beautiful coast view, but the most striking part of the scenery is the volcanic chain which runs east and west almost parallel with the Pacific. Volcanic action is an unmistakable feature in the mountains of Central America, and the volcanoes have the peculiarity of forming part of the Cordilleras and Sierras themselves, instead of standing isolated, as they do in other countries.

From the top of the house at Chitalon the peaks of eleven of these volcanoes can be counted; the graceful forms of Santa Maria, Zunil and Santo Tomas standing out clearly, and in apparently close proximity. Away to the right rise the bare summits of Santa Clara, San Pedro and Atitlan, and still farther on are visible the rugged heads of Fuego and Acatenango.

The outlines of the mountains are shown with wonderful transparency against the blue sky, and over all the panorama the shifting shadows of evening fall with a variety of tints, which brighten and darken the wooded hills and broken gorges. Then a grey mist steals up and hides the grim volcanoes, and one gladly turns to the soft champaign land which slopes towards the sea.

My host was a Swiss emigrant, and had not attained his present comfortable position and extensive property without misfortunes. Amongst others, he had lost by fire all his valuable machinery for the preparation of coffee and sugar. Nothing daunted, he set to work and in time replaced his loss and with newer improvements. Then came a heavier blow, for in one year his wife and child died. He led me to the little chapel where they lay, which he had built near his house, and the much worn path showed that in that foreign land, far from home and friends, they were still his best companions. Hearts grow hard as stone for a less cause, with such grief it is a wonder they do not break!

When I parted with my hospitable friend the next morning, he gave me a letter to his brother-in-law, who was forming a new coffee plantation a few leagues off, and with whom I was to spend the night previous to the ascent to the table-land.

At the village of Mazatenango a good bridge carried us over a broad river, whose shallower parts were—as is always the case in these village streams—occupied by crowds of Indian washer-women. It is a curious circumstance that the garments of the natives seldom look clean, although life with them is one perpetual washing-day. Before we reached this place my mule had cast a shoe; as these provoking animals generally choose some out-of-the-way spot for any accident of a like nature, it was surprising that this should have occurred near a large village; but it turned out that the sagacity of the creature was not astray. We passed two or three forges, but none with their fires lit, and on asking, were told that it was a feast-day and the men were all busy getting drunk. It is only due to the mule to say that it suffered no inconvenience, and seemed rather to rejoice at having got rid of what it considered an unnecessary appendage.

Varied Duties of a Proprietor. 95

From Chitalon to our destination was only a few leagues, and at an early hour we turned into the plantation, and found the master busily engaged in superintending the erection of shades over the young coffee trees. He proved to be very agreeable, and was delighted to meet a stranger, as with the exception of his native labourers, he seldom had anybody to talk to. Young, active, and well educated, he, nevertheless, appeared to enjoy his lonely life, and when not engaged out-of-doors, employed his spare moments in playing on a " mouth harmonicon," out of which, by constant practice, he managed to extract some very fair music, considering the capabilities of the instrument. His love for such a retired life was partly due, I suspect, to the fact of his being a member of an old Spanish family, whose political opinions were strongly antagonistic to the present government of the State.

After a refreshing bowl of rice-water, he showed me round the estate, and it was amusing to see the enthusiasm with which he used his inseparable machete, cutting down a small tree here, marking a large one there for future destruction, now pruning an overgrown coffee shrub, then dashing in amongst the thick bushes after a snake, or with a few smart blows repairing a damaged fence.

In these localities a man must be able to turn his hand to anything, and that evening I had a proof of some of the requirements of the situation. An old Indian couple, two of his labourers, were brought to him; the unfortunate woman had been so injured by blows from a heavy glass bottle, inflicted by her husband in a fit of drunkenness, that one of her eyes was actually hanging out. The proprietor, with whom such affairs were not uncommon, took his medicine chest, replaced the eye, bound up the wounds, and treated all so skilfully that the moans of the poor creature soon died away, and she was carried off quite relieved and muttering her thanks. He next turned his attention to the culprit, whom fear had sobered; he first administered to him a sound flogging, and then chained him by the leg to the door of an outhouse, where he was to undergo some hours of confinement. Having thus performed his medical and judicial duties, my friend washed his hands and resumed his variations on the harmonicon.

The natives are a hardy race, and have not the same physical sense of pain that white people have, and wounds and blows that would be of serious consequence to others are treated with great indifference by them. That their mental feelings are not so hardened, was proved by the fact that a few hours after the above mentioned affair the old woman was discovered stretched beside her repentant spouse, preferring to undergo punishment with him rather than nurse her wounds in her own solitary hut. At her earnest entreaty the man was released, and the aged couple hobbled away with many promises of good behaviour in the future.

As I wished to ascend the great *cuesta* (hill) before the sun had attained its full power, we had agreed to start very early in the morning, but at the last moment it was discovered that my host—who intended to accompany me for a short distance—had forgotten to fasten up his horse the previous day, consequently it was five o'clock before we set out. The morning was fresh and fair, and as the green path was broad enough in places for a canter, we made the most of our opportunities.

In Central America every well-educated horse or mule can "pace," which is something between a trot and a canter; it is an agreeable and easy motion, and as the animals can keep it up a long time, a journey is soon got over. The accomplishment, however, is generally confined to private property, hired mules seldom exceeding a trot, and even then requiring a liberal use of the spur. A few plantations of cacao adjoined the road, but besides these there was not much cultivation. A cacao tree is something like an orange tree in shape, and has long glossy leaves; the pear-like fruit and yellow blossoms growing close to the branches. Its cultivation is not carried on here to the same extent that it is in other Central American republics.

As we rode through the village of San Antonio, I remarked a large number of empty houses and a ruined church. There is a legend that the whole of the population was once killed off by a race of vampyres. The most remarkable thing now, with the present inhabitants, is that they all appear to have goitres. Here my companion left me and returned home, and the road once more turned towards the mountains.

H

After crossing a ravine and passing through a small Indian village we entered a valley, in which stood a few farms and groups of mango and other fruit trees. In the middle of one of the freshly cultivated patches, we saw what appeared to be a bed of variegated tulips. At our approach the bed took wing and proved to be a flock of macaws (*ara aracanga*), who must have been enjoying some peculiarly attractive food. It is unusual to see so many of these birds together, and the few that I had seen hitherto had always been flying high overhead in pairs, and utteriog harsh caws like rooks. Many of those whose meal we had disturbed, flew up into a neighbouring tree, and looked at us very unconcernedly as we passed under.

The sun was high when we reached the fort of the mountains, where, after crossing a pretty stream, we came upon what might have been a very comfortable camping ground. It is probable that the Indians use it for a sleeping place in making their trips up and down the mountain, as there were four posts supporting a rough roof of palm leaves, under which were the remains of fire. The Cuesta d'Atitlan is the oldest Indian highway in the country, and is certainly better adapted for the pack-bearing natives than for mules. The narrow and, in some places, almost perpendicular track is one continuous ascent for no less than four leagues—twelve miles. Here and there high steps have been cut out of the rock, but in many places the ascent is facilitated by a rough staircase of wooden poles.

We dismounted at the stream, filled our gourds with

water, as no more is met with during the climb, and after relieving the animals of their head-gear, gave them a flick with the whip, and away they went like mountain-goats up the earth-bound ladder. The path was very slippery, steep, and rock-encumbered, but the varied scenes were so delightful that its eccentricities were forgiven. If the sun did pour down too hotly, it only gave greater coolness to the picturesque gorges, whose fern-covered sides almost met overhead. Sometimes the turns in the road were so abrupt that the forward mule appeared to be going in an opposite direction, and over the heads of those in the rear.

As each successive terrace was reached the outlook expanded, and when after about three hours' toil we had gained half the ascent, we paused to enjoy the view. All around were great sweeps of wooded mountains, whose soft outlines were broken by rocky palisades, moss-stained and wild. There was an endless variety of light and shade, and the sun's rays streaming into the great depths cast a golden shimmer over the bright tree-ferns, and dappled with shadows the dense foliage of the jungle. On the coast side, two cliffs draped with vines rose up, and through the vista, formed by their approaching heights, was a lovely glimpse of the lowlands stretching away to the distant ocean.

After leaving this point, the road was less stony and not so steep; an occasional narrow ridge did good service by crossing deep valleys and following windings and curves which seem endless, but which eventually lead to the summit. In one of the deepest ravines, about two-thirds of the way up the ascent, is a curious relic of Indian superstition. An almost hidden trail, leading off the road, runs nearly perpendicular down into the dark recesses of a gloomy gorge. On the other side of this is an open space in which grows a tree bearing very peculiar foliage; from the branches hang numberless strips of rags of different colours and lengths. The explanation of this decoration is that when a male child is born to an Indian, the father hastens to this secluded spot, and fastens up the strange offering to the woodland deity. This is supposed to ensure strength to the child, and enable him in future years to ascend the cuesta.

We were five hours in making the ascent, having in that time passed from the zone of heliconias, palms, and sugar-cane, though the regions of ferns and ericas, into the precincts of oaks and lichens. Very different was the aspect of the scenery on the other side of the mountain from that through which we had been passing. Instead of the fresh green verdure of the coast, nothing was to be seen but bare volcanic hills. Soon we saw, stretched out at our feet, the much-praised lake of Atitlan, enclosed by rocky walls, barren in some parts, green and wooded in others. A picturesque volcano rose sheer from the water's edge at the near end of the lake, and under its shadow stood the village of Atitlan, to which we were bound.

An hour's descent over rocks and lava boulders, and

along the dry bed of a once broad river, brought us to the town, where we took up our quarters in the cabildo. In towns and villages where there are no inns, the cabildo, or town-hall, is the invariable stopping-place of travellers. It seldom consists of more than a lock-up and one room where the alcalde performs his magisterial duties, but as this is generally furnished with a table and chair, it suffices well for a night's lodging. The alcalde, an old Indian, welcomed us kindly, and after ordering fresh sacate for the mules, sent me a bountiful supply of eggs and tortillas. Afterwards I strolled out, and from the large plaza of a fast-decaying church witnessed a very fine display of lightning over the surrounding mountains. As the only inhabitants were Indians, and the streets were nothing but lava boulders, I soon returned to my room, and before long fell fast asleep in spite of the hard table-bed and the want of a pillow.

CHAPTER IX.

LAKE OF ATITLAN—INDIAN LEGENDS—CERRO DE ORO—GEM OF ATITLAN — CUESTA — NORVAL — VIEW OF LAKE — GODINES — NAMES IN GUATEMALA—STEEP PRECIPICE—EXCHANGE OF CIVILITIES—ASCENT TO TABLE LAND—PATZUN—FEAST DAY—TO ANTIGUA—ACCOUNT OF THE DESTRUCTION OF THE TWO OLD CAPITALS—ENTRANCE TO CITY.

THE lake of Atitlan is situated at a height above the sea of more than five thousand feet, and though it receives rivers and mountain streams, it has no visible outlet. Its length from east to west is about eighteen miles, and its breadth ten. The depth is unknown, so the Indians are pretty safe in their statement that its waters cover an ancient city. Indians delight in mystery, and according to them there are but few of their lakes, forests, and caverns that do not hide strange ruins and remains of lost races, or in whose depths are not buried vast quantities of treasure. But there is no doubt that this lake has many peculiarities; it contains no large fish, but an infinity of small ones; it is subject to very violent hurricanes;

and on its banks stand eleven villages, whose situations are so varied, that their climates and productions are those of the cold, temperate, and tropical regions, and whose inhabitants speak different dialects.

The southern shore along which our path ran on leaving the village of Atitlan, is not so abrupt and precipitous as that of the north and west, but it is barer and more rocky. The volcano of Atitlan rises behind, and has strown with lava the surrounding country down to the lake. There was formerly an old Indian custom of appeasing the wrath of the deity of the volcano by throwing a young girl into its crater, and so great was the honour of this yearly sacrifice considered that the maidens of suitable age used to fight for the privilege.

The soil is everywhere very fertile, and between the boulders and creeping over the huge slabs are many grasses and flowering plants; one of the latter, having mauve blossoms like our lilac, was very plentiful, and its graceful festoons softened the rough character of the rocks. The vegetation was varied; high up on the rocky places grew cactuses and agaves; lower down were salvias and species of solanum, and still lower we saw fuschias, helicanthus, and other kindred forms. Wherever space allowed, down in the ravines or along the mountain side, there were fields of beans, maize, and other cereals.

A very prominent hill that we passed is called Cerro de Oro, but I did not hear that the natives had ever attempted to extract the gold, of which they declare it is composed. Shapely and wooded, it rises like an islet from the débris of rock and lava. At the southeastern extremity of the lake we came to a lovely little village, San Lucas, which must be the gem of Atitlan. Embowered in fruit-trees, it stood on a green slope, backed by an amphitheatre of pasture land surrounded by a semi-circle of wooded hills, in the centre of which was the volcano. The opposite shore of the narrow bight rose perpendicular from the water, a green wall of shrubs and creepers.

On ascending the cuesta leading to the table-land above the lake, we were overtaken by a young ladino, who reminded me strongly of "Norval on the Grampian hills." He was very communicative, and said that, being tired of farming, he had determined to leave his home at Solola, and go to some college in England or Germany; he said he had plenty of money, five hundred dollars was the sum he named, I think, and wanted to know which was the best of the English colleges. As I did not give him much encouragement in his search for knowledge, he offered to sell me a coffee plantation, as of course I was looking for one, and was quite disappointed that I did not jump at his offer. He was very amusing, and I was quite sorry to part with him at the small farm to which he was bound, near the top of the hill.

Before reaching San Antonio we got a magnificent view over the lake which lay far below us. Almost opposite rose the picturesque volcano of San Pedro, a small bay alone separating it from the village of Atitlan.

To the right of San Pedro, a succession of cliff-like escarpments was broken by a green valley running up from the lake, and in this plain were situated the white villages of San Jorgé and Panajachel. To the left were the brown lava hills sloping up to the black crater of Atitlan, their points and ridges feathered with waving grass and luxuriant creepers. Nearer still, and at our feet, were the green precipices, and ravines filled with tropic plants, which faced the pastoral village of San Lucas, while the higher table-land on which we stood was terraced with wheat and maize fields stretching up to the distant pines.

Turning from the bold scenery of the lake, the eye caught a pleasing contrast in a vignette of the coast region. Two parallel mountain ranges trended off towards the sea, and through the overarching spray of the green trees that covered their steep sides one saw the soft hazy blue that enveloped the fertile lands of the Costa Grande. It was a scene to be enjoyed the more, the longer one looked at it, there was so much that at the first glance seemed barren and rugged, but that gradually won the feelings by their beautiful lights and colours; numberless little nooks and corners that might escape a casual view, but which would well repay a close investigation. Then there was the great charm of the silver water, varying in shade from the dark tones of the overhanging cliffs to the bright gleam of the open expanse; and above all there was that inexpressible feeling of utter rest, where no voice of water or note of bird breaks the stillness.

I had been disappointed with the view of the lake from its shores, as the peaks and precipices which surround it did not seem of sufficient magnitude to compensate for the absence of verdure; but from an elevated point the scene had that air of quiet grandeur that leaves a deep impression on the mind of the spectator. The road still kept winding up after we had passed San Antonio, and was so unshaded that the heat and reflection of the sun became rather oppressive. It was a relief to reach the aromatic pine glades where some flocks of sheep were wandering, and in a short time we arrived at Godines.

It must not be imagined that because a place in Guatemala has a name that it is of the slightest importance. Some places, with high-sounding names, merely consist of two or three houses, or even of only one hut, but they are conscientiously recorded in the Government books. A stranger too is apt to be puzzled by the frequent recurrence of the same name. Each of the twenty departments into which Guatemala is divided, is sure to contain four or five villages, or haciendas, with the same appellation, and even among the larger places (pueblos) there will probably be one or two alike. Godines consisted of a few uninhabited huts, and three houses that gave some signs of habitation. As it is a halting place for muleteers, we were able to get food for ourselves and our animals before continuing our journey.

When we again set out we joined a good road which wound down the sides of a steep precipice into the valley below. For the rest of the day we were perpetually ascending and descending mountain sides, the views everywhere very picturesque, but at length very monotonous.

As we were crossing a fine river at the bottom of a ravine we met a large party of equestrians on their way to Godines, where they were to sleep that night previous to continuing their journey to some pretty village on the shores of the lake of Atitlan. Most of the ladies rode singly, and, as usual, on what we consider the wrong side; but two of them—and they seemed by far the most contented of the party—had double saddles, the hinder part of which was occupied by a gentleman who supported his fair companion with one arm and with the other held the bridle. They cheerfully told us we should never reach Patzün that night with our tired mules, to which I replied that, had we known of their approach, we would never have eaten up all the food at Godines, and then with mutual congratulations we continued on our different roads.

After riding for some time through a beautiful ravine we ascended our last hill and emerged on the broad table-land. Soon we passed one of those stupendous barrancas that intersect the country; its perpendicular sides nearly touched the road which was already crumbling away at the edge. In one of the wheat-fields we witnessed a very primitive mode of threshing, consisting in the wheat being placed in a small circular corral, round which a number of oxen were driven.

The sun had long gone down behind the volcanoes

of San Pedro and Atitlan before we came in sight of Patzün, which we entered amidst the ringing of bells, gun firing and the explosion of numerous rockets. The houses which lined the narrow street were illuminated with coloured lanterns; arches of leaves and flowers crossed the road and everything betokened general rejoicing. It proved to be the feast of the village saint, and one of the most important in the year. Open house was kept, and cakes, confectionery, and aguardiente freely distributed. In the plaza of the church two large bonfires were blazing, and rendered distinct the groups of swarthy Indians, soldiers and ladinos assembled on the stone steps. The interior of the church was decorated with green branches and coloured calico ; pine leaves were thickly strewed over the floor, and an abundance of candles threw a brilliant light over the trophies of saints and angels that were arranged down the centre. At last the procession was formed, the trophies were raised on men's shoulders, and following in the wake of the chief saint, with attendants dressed in gauze and with silver wings, all moved out of the church to the music of a march played on a piano. After visiting the stations at each corner of the plaza, the procession, headed by the priest and a discordant Indian band, passed out of the gates, and made the tour of the town, finally returning to the church from whence it had started. Then amidst fireworks, ringing of bells and much din, the saints were returned to the boxes where they are kept until required for another fête. Although as a rule the inhabitants of a town or village have great respect for their patron saint, yet if occasion demands they will not hesitate to depose him and adopt a new one. Only very lately a certain town was afflicted with some disease that its patron saint—San Martin—ought to have kept away; another grievance against him was that he did not give rain when it was wanted, neither did he stop it when they had too much. They therefore displaced San Martin, and are trying Ignatius Loyola.

The following day we resumed our journey, and as our road soon joined the highway to the city of Guatemala, we retraced our original route as far as Chimaltenango where we turned off to the right in order to visit Antigua, the former capital and the most interesting city in the State. After crossing a wide plain, we rode through a narrow and beautiful valley full of rich coffee and nopal plantations, and watered by two rivers. Then by a long straight road we entered the ruined city, which stands in an expansion of the fertile valley surrounded by green mountains and hills, high above which tower the grand volcanoes of Agua, Fuego and Acatenango. Antigua, as the city is now called, was the second capital of Guatemala, and was one of the richest and most populous in all Spanish America. It was founded in 1542 after the destruction of the original capital—now Ciudad Vieja—which was situated farther up the valley at the foot of the Volcan de Agua.

The following details, gathered from various authors,

may be interesting and will account for the impression of a terrible disaster that now hangs like a memory over the ruins of the unhappy cities. The catastrophe which destroyed the Ciudad Vieja occurred during the celebration of the obsequies of Don Pedro Alvarado, the conqueror and governor of the country. The ceremonies were conducted by his widow—Doña Beatrice de la Cueva—and were of the most pompous description. Whilst in progress, a terrible tropical rain storm commenced and lasted three days and nights. On the night of the third day, 11th September, 1541, a dreadful earthquake took place, broke down the sides of the crater of the volcano, letting loose a vast torrent of water which swept down on the city, carrying earth, rocks, trees, and buried six hundred inhabitants. At the first shock Doña Beatrice fled to her oratory, ascended the altar and clasped the figure of Christ, uttering words of supplication. Here she met the same fate as the rest of the unfortunate citizens.

The sun next morning revealed an unparalleled scene of devastation. The volcano had changed its form, the summit had broken away and the sides were seamed and strown with rocks. The site of the city was a mass of uprooted primeval forest, the tangled trunks mingled with stones in wild confusion. The fertile fields were buried in mud. The survivors then established themselves in the second capital—Antigua. The history of this city is one of uninterrupted disasters. In 1558 an epidemic swept off great numbers of the inhabitants. Then followed a series of earthquakes,

Disasters of Antigua. 111

more or less alarming, and in 1581 the Volcan de Fuego began to emit fire, and so great was the quantity of ashes thrown out that the sun was entirely obscured, and artificial light was necessary in the city at mid-day. The years 1585 and 1586 were dreadful in the extreme; earthquakes followed each other in such rapid succession that not an interval of eight days elapsed during the whole period without a shock. The greatest damage took place in December, 1586, when the greater part of the city became a heap of ruins, burying under them many of the inhabitants; the earth shook with such violence that the tops of the high ridges were torn off and deep chasms formed in various parts of the level ground. In 1601 another pestilence carried off great numbers, and raged with so much malignity that three days generally terminated the existence of those affected by it.

On the 10th February, 1651, in the afternoon, a most extraordinary subterranean noise was heard, immediately followed by three violent shocks, at very short intervals from each other, which threw down many buildings and damaged others; the tiles from the roofs of the houses were dispersed in all directions; the bells of the churches were rung by the vibrations; masses of rock were detached from the mountains; and even the wild animals were so terrified that they quitted their retreats and sought shelter in the habitations of men. In 1686 there was another epidemic which decimated the inhabitants. In 1717 the volcano again began to emit flames, attended by a continual rumbling noise. The eruption increased to great violence, and the terrified inhabitants carried the images of saints in procession through the streets. The year 1773 was the most melancholy epoch in the annals of the city ; it was then destroyed, and, as a capital, rose no more from its ruins. On July 29th of that year a tremendous vibration was felt, and shortly after began the dreadful couvulsion that decided the fate of the city. In September a severe shock threw down most of the buildings that were damaged in July, and on the 13th December one still more violent terminated the work of destruction.

Before the last shocks, the governor and public authorities had removed to the little village of La Hermita, and at a Congress there held in January, 1774, it was resolved to make a formal translation of the capital to the valley of Las Vacas. This was gradually effected, until in 1777 the population had totally abandoned the old city and occupied the site whereon the present city of Guatemala now stands. No wonder that after such disasters the Spaniards described the ancient city as standing with "Paradise on one hand and Hell on the other." It was past such scenes of ruin and decay that we rode on our entrance to Antigua. Crumbling walls, roofless churches and desolate houses stood side by side with inhabited buildings; the plaza was alive with chattering groups; and along the roughly paved streets moved a gay and laughing crowd strangely at variance with the mournful aspect of the shattered city.

CHAPTER X.

A SANATORIUM—A RUINED TEMPLE—THE PLAZA—SANTA MARIA
—CONVENT QUARTERS—A CONCERT—MIDNIGHT—START FOR
VOLCANO—A SHORT CUT—HEIGHTS OF VOLCANOES—A NAP IN
THE CRATER—INSCRIPTIONS—VIEW FROM SUMMIT—MANO DEL
MICO—FLOR DE MADERA—RARE PHEASANT—DRUNKEN INDIANS
—AZTEC LAW—RETURN TO GUATEMALA.

S soon as Dame Nature had proved her power in conquering man and in driving him forth from his chosen home, her malignity seemed to be satisfied, and now Antigua is not only the most beautiful spot in Guatemala but in also its sanatorium. Its climate is delightful, and its waters are remarkably pure and health-restoring. However hot the sun may be, there is yet a freshness in the air that makes a long ramble in the shaded country just as agreeable as a lazy basking in the garden of some ruined temple; in fact a lotus-eating land, " a land where it was always afternoon."

Some idea of the extent of the old city may be formed from the fact that the remains of more than fifty churches may be traced ; in some cases merely an arch or pillar is standing, but in others the edifice, shaken and cracked certainly, but almost entire, looms out of a wilderness of trees and thick underbrush. Here stood four richly ornamented walls, with lofty trees showing high above the fallen roof, there a superb basilica, grass-grown and yawning, denotes a style of architecture massive and grand. A distinctive feature in these ruined churches and convents was the amount of rich and graceful decoration bestowed on their façades, and the beautifully carved friezes over their doors and windows. Very different from the heavy stuccoed front, with no ornamentation save three or four ungainly niches in which stood still more ungainly and generally broken figures, which are the distinguishing character-istics of Spanish American churches of the present day.

One half-ruined temple that stood outside the town under the eastern slopes was very attractive to me ; not that it differed much from many another, but its site was so retired and peaceful, and the ruin itself so enhanced the beauty of its surroundings that my steps strayed towards it again and again. It stood in a large garden utterly neglected, but running wild with roses, orange and coffee trees, and almost hidden by lofty fruit trees such as the mango and avocate. The building had no roof, but the front had an exquisite tracery of arabesques above which was the framework of a beautiful arched window. The stone work that probably had embellished it was lost, but was replaced by living creepers and vines that mullioned the empty space with a hundred twisting stems, and coloured the white walls with the luxuriant festoons of their brilliant tinted flowers. Passing up the moss-grown steps into the interior one saw nothing but a wilderness; the blue sky looked down on a rank growth of shrubs and flowers that buried the pillars and stones in a living tomb; the perfume of the orange-tree filled the air once laden with incense, and through the open spaces that had borne stained windows, now darted the humming-bird and rare painted butterflies. Such is the character of many of the ruins that lie in and around Antigua. From the plaza of the city there is a magnificent view of the volcanoes which seem to rise from the very streets, and in their quiet grandeur strike the beholder with as great an awe as they would when emitting fire and smoke.

The Plaza of Antigua resembles others in Central America, in presenting an epitome of church, state, and commerce. The municipal buildings occupy one side and the cathedral another, but neither requires description, although the latter was once exceedingly rich both in treasure and works of art.

Native art is still, as formerly, cherished in Antigua, and small figures made of rags form no small item in its commerce. They are admirably made, and show singly and in groups the dress, customs, and different occupations and pursuits amongst the Indians. They are also skilful in their execution of Lilliputian vases and bowls in different coloured clays, and of imitation birds, all of which find a good market in Guatemala, especially at Christmas time. Another speciality is the carving of coffee sticks, on some of which I have seen beautifully cut heads and figures; but probably this industry has been introduced lately by foreigners.

After a few days spent in wandering about the city and suburbs, I started off to make the customary ascent of the Volcano of Agua. Never having ascended a water volcano, I thought it would be more interesting than Fuego, but I subsequently heard that very few have ascended the latter mountain, and no one had ever quite reached the top; that is, the highest of its numerous ridges.

Following the advice of two German gentlemen, who had made the ascent a few days before my arrival, I left one afternoon, accompanied by Leon, for the Indian village of Santa Maria, which is situated on a spur of the volcano, about two thousand feet above Antigua. There we intended to spend the night, and next day ascend to the summit.

It was pleasant to leave the rough cobble stones of the city, and ride along the good road which extends up to Santa Maria. Just outside the town we passed a very pretty alameda, shaded with fine trees of the amate and sycamore species. Then leaving the Ciudad Vieja on our right, we followed a shady lane as far as the foot of the mountain, up which the road wound, until we reached our resting-place, a little over two leagues from the city.

We were assigned quarters in the convent, in a room

used as a children's school, and without a particle of furniture except a wooden form. The next room was occupied by the schoolmaster and his brother—two good-natured young ladinos, who did what they could to make me comfortable, but as their own chamber only contained a table and a mattress, I could not complain of my narrow bench. We had fortunately brought some provisions, and as the mules had plenty of fodder, we got on well enough.

Leon and the teacher made arrangements with the alcalde for guides to be ready at two a.m. the next morning, and I stretched myself on the form, with the hope of falling asleep; however, I found that it was out of the question to sleep on a very narrow bench fastened to the wall, and as I heard sounds of music I went in search of them. They proceeded from two guitars that the brothers were playing with some skill, and as they were not a bit shy of a stranger, the concert was kept up until midnight. I then retired again, but not to sleep, as there presently began such a shouting and calling in the street outside the convent garden, that I thought something had happened—perhaps an earthquake. I roused Leon, who, wrapped up in his serapé, was sleeping soundly on the floor of the verandah, and he discovered that the noise was nothing unusual, and was merely the every day preparations by the Indians for going to market at Antigua. As it was useless to attempt to go to sleep, and it was very cold, I prepared for our trip up the volcano, and waited patiently for the guides.

Leon having made a fire on the floor we boiled some coffee, and shortly after two o'clock the guides appeared. One was a sturdy young fellow, who at once proceeded to place our provisions and water-gourds into a basket which he carried on his back in the usual manner; *i. e.*, supported by the broad forehead strap. His companion was an elderly gentleman, bare-legged of course, but wearing a high black hat, which, however much it added to his dignity, was rather unsuitable to the occasion. I afterwards found that he only intended to accompany us to the spot where we had to dismount, and there await our return.

Before we left the village, we were delayed for a short time by taking what our guides called a short cut. This led us through a private garden, whose proprietor had carefully fenced up the only exit; with some difficulty we aroused him, and for a small consideration he consented to remove the obstruction. Tolls of a similar nature are not unknown in other countries, but it was unexpected to meet such a high phase of civilization in a remote corner of Guatemala, where the trouble entailed could hardly have been compensated by the amount demanded, or by the large number of travellers.

For the first part of the ascent the slopes were cultivated, then we entered the forest belt, where the path gradually became steeper, and we at last had to dismount, and leave our mules in charge of the old Indian.

After a tedious climb up a path overhung with dense

foliage, and surrounded with old trees, whose branches were matted with vines, and whose trunks were almost hidden by mosses and rank fungus, we at length caught a few glimpses of the sky, and ere long emerged from the gloom into the open region above.

The path hitherto had presented no difficulties, but was so excessively steep that we had found it necessary to stop every few minutes to regain our breath. The same steepness still continued, but instead of the rocky steps which interspersed the forest, we now traversed a narrow, deep path, with high grass on each side. The few trees that dotted the sides were stunted and blackened as if by fire, but as an offset to their dreariness, the grassy nooks and rock-hung hollows were bright with fuschias, begonias, and other wild flowers. Soon these ceased, and after a brisk climb we arrived at the summit of the crater.

This volcano has an altitude of between fourteen thousand and fifteen thousand feet above the level of the sea, but as the plain from which it rises is five thousand feet above the sea level, and the village of Santa Maria nearly two thousand feet above that, our ascent that morning had been hardly eight thousand feet.

The Volcan de Fuego is higher, I should judge, than this mountain, but I have seen such totally different estimations of their heights that I am inclined to doubt whether they have been really ascertained by scientific observations.

To obtain a perfect view from the top of Agua, it is necessary to arrive there before sunrise, as usually after that clouds hover around the peak. We had been so delayed at the start that we were too late to witness the sunrise, and already clouds were sweeping past underneath us. Hoping that these would clear away, we descended into the grassy oval bosom of the crater, and whilst a fire was being made to prepare our breakfast, I crept into a soft cozy nest between two boulders, and tired with the want of rest during the preceding night, soon fell fast asleep.

I much regretted having followed the advice of my well-meaning friends in Antigua by stopping at Santa Maria. The crater would have been far more comfortable, as it was quite sheltered from the wind, and with plenty of wraps and a fire would have afforded a much more desirable night's lodging than the convent. The certainty too of being in time for the clear view at sunrise is another and important inducement in favour of the crater.

After breakfast we ascended the sloping sides, passing on our way several rocks and slabs whose faces were inscribed, needless to say, with the names of former visitors, some being deeply carved into the imperishable stone, others rudely painted with the less romantic blacking brush. The walk round the crater's rim is rough, but affords magnificent panoramic views whenever the drifting clouds are for a moment dispersed. On the land side the eye wanders away over the old ruined cities, across low ranges of hills, to the new capital of Guatemala; white villages stand out clearly on the level plains, and nestle in shadow at the bases of dark wood-covered heights, and beyond up to the horizon, mountains rise behind mountains, their trending lines growing faint and far in the dim distance. Looking toward the sea the great height of the volcano is more evident, as its side slopes down to the low coast region where the ports of Champerico, San José, and the town of Escuintla seem mere specks. A little to the left, near the town of Amatitlan, the hill chain is broken by quaint rocks and pinnacles, bare or wooded, which fling deep shadows across the narrow valleys which intersect them. Sparkling lakes here strike in between the mountains and diversify the scene with light and colour, and when the sun's rays in full glory are reflected on the waters, its silver gleam amidst the red rocks and dark woods form a wonderful contrast with the blue haze of the coast, and the clear transparent atmosphere of the inland country.

The view we obtained was not, I suppose, what would be considered a successful one, but I think I enjoyed it more than if there had been no clouds; for they themselves were well worth looking at, now rolling past far below in fleecy masses, then opening into a filmy veil through which were the most lovely glimpses of the sun-lit plains; sometimes driven down by the wind they clung to the spectre limbs of the blackened pine trees, then expanding like an india-rubber ball they would creep upwards, shroud us in vapour and in an instant leave the landscape as clear as if clouds were only dreams. It was so quiet too up there; the very wind as it chased the phantom clouds in cold eddies around the crater was noiseless; no sound arose from the dark forest or sunny valley, the silent voices of nature alone were heard, and spoke with more appeal than human tones :—

> " Two voices were there ; one is of the sea,
> One of the mountains; each a mighty voice."

Our descent was rapid, and as uneventful as our ascent; two or three Indians who had come to cut grass were the only human beings we met, and we soon reached the spot where our mules were picketed.

Amongst the numerous rare trees and plants we passed in the wooded region, the most peculiar was a tall tree which bore blossoms like a glove. The ground underneath these trees was strown with hundreds of these Lilliputian hands, which are well-named "*mano del mico*"—monkey's hand. The palm and back of the hand is light vermilion, and the tapering fingers have narrow yellow stripes of a powdery description. Another curious object on some of the trees was an excrescence like a stem opening into a sort of blossom, called "*flor de madera*" —flower of wood. A beautiful species of tillandsia was also very abundant, and hung in curly festoons from most of the old moss-covered trees.

We did not see many birds. A small black and white wood-pecker was the chief representative of his kind ; but these volcanic regions possess several beautiful species. In the wooded recesses of the Volcan de Fuego is found a large pheasant—

"*oreophasis derbianus*"—having a horny protuberance on its head; this species has also been met with near Coban in Vera Paz.

After leaving Santa Maria on our return to Antigua, we met the natives who had so disturbed our night's rest, on their way back from market. But they were in a very different condition from that in which they started; now they were nearly all drunk, some staggered from side to side, supported by friends in the same state as themselves, others had fallen down in stupor, and lay there surrounded by their families, patiently awaiting the recovery of their husbands and fathers. Nor were the female members of some of the groups less intoxicated than their lords and masters. The love for strong liquors is so great with this race of people that their earnings, however hardly gained, are nearly always spent at once in aguardiente.

They lose no opportunity for a festival, and turn the most solemn ceremonies into occasions for a debauch. A very ludicrous incident occurred shortly before my arrival in a small Indian community on the coast. A baby was to be baptized, but the only church was some leagues distant from the child's home. Arrangements were made for the ceremony to take place at a certain time, and all the friends and relations, together with those most concerned, set out to keep the appointment. When they had gone about half way, they sat down by the road-side and soon forgot their business in a general jollification. Night passed, and before daylight one less muddled than the rest suddenly remembered what he had come for, and arousing his companions they all stumbled off to their destination. They arrived in time at the church, found the priest ready, and just as he was commencing the service it was discovered there was no baby. Then there was great commotion, messengers were despatched, and the infant was found quite safe in the spot where it had been deposited during the festivities of the previous night.

I have often thought that the old Aztec law—or some modification of it—as regards drunkenness, might be revived with profit. This law ordered that all young drunkards should be stoned to death. Older men lost their rights, and if noble, their nobility; if plebeians, they shaved their heads and burnt their houses. But drunkenness was allowed at certain times and feasts, and after sixty years of age they were allowed to drink as much as they liked. A rapid change, certainly, from the death penalty to the permission of free indulgence! It was pleasant to turn from these besotted examples of human nature to the beautiful valley which had by this time exchanged the bright joyousness of morning for the pathos of evening light. From our position we could trace the large extent of ground occupied by the old cities. Amid the various shades of vegetation the ruined churches and dismantled walls appeared in strong relief, and every field of nopal or coffee indicated the former presence of some large convent or lofty portico. Away to the north rose the white walls of San Geronimo, almost perfect and unharmed, whilst nearer to us, all that remained of the great church of San Domingo was visible in the grand arch of its choir. And all about Antigua, side by side with the fallen temples, and clustered around the ruined palaces, were seen the modern dwellings and restored churches of the re-peopled city—a strange mingling of ruin and recovery, therein resembling her native aloe · whose dead and withered parent stem surrounds itself with a living progeny of fresh and fertile plants. Surely there there is something inspiring in witnessing this proof of man's courage and determination in fighting against destiny. Before we re-entered the city the sun had purpled the frame work of hills, and like a great opal had disappeared behind the Volcano of Agua.

The next morning I returned to Guatemala—nine leagues distant—after a picturesque ride over an excellent coach road—thoroughly pleased with my expedition to the coast.

CHAPTER XI.

POT-POURRI—VOLCANIC FIRE—A STRANGE THEORY—SUN'S RAYS—NACIMIENTO—FEAST OF GUADALUPE—ITS ORIGIN—JOCOTENANGO—SAN DOMINGO — ZOPILOTE — STARLING — TOUCANS — A MESON—EL CARABAN—WHO GOES THERE?—WAR—PASSPORTS—START FOR COPAN AND ESQUIPULAS.

TO escape for a time from the tediousness of recounting the exact routine of each successive day, which it is difficult to avoid during the progress of a journey, I shall make this chapter a sort of "olla podrida"—a medley of things heard and seen which may perhaps give a pretty accurate idea of the character and customs of the country, and indicate that distinctive colour which every city is said to possess.

A traveller in Central America naturally takes much interest in all matters appertaining to earthquakes and volcanoes. Shortly after my return from Antigua I read a little book about the causes of volcanic eruption entitled, "Memoria sobre el Fuego de Los Volcanos." The author, a learned professor of Guatemala, starts with the admitted fact that most volcanoes are situated on or near the sea-board of continents or on islands, and from that he deduces a necessary relation between the sea and volcanic phenomena. The nature of this relation is explained by the following—to me— novel hypothesis, viz. : "that under certain conditions of sun and sea the latter acts as a great lens of hundreds or thousands of miles area which concentrates the sun's, rays at the bottom of the ocean, or on the shelving shores of continents, with such force as to fuse them instantaneously and cause eruptions from the very foundations of the earth in the form of volcanic islands in the sea and volcanic mountains on land." He then explains the nature of the common lens—one of which, the diameter of a dollar, concentrates the sun's rays sufficiently to ignite powder or burn holes in cloth. "When of a larger size," he adds, "it burns green wood or wood soaked in water in a moment; water in a vase exposed to the focal effect boils in an instant ; the most obstinate metals melt under its ardour; the hardest stones, bricks and earth dissolve or vitrify ; and the diamond itself is burnt and dissipated." When we reflect that such results may be obtained from a small bit of glass of a certain figure, we can form some notion of the consequences from one of grander size— say five yards in diameter. With this we might melt the base of the Hill of Carmen and dissipate it as if it were of straw. And if one could be made of the size of the grand plaza, one hundred and fifty yards in diameter, who could calculate its power? And then if it were five hundred yards in diameter, &c.

Regarding the convex surface of the ocean as that of a great lens, we can comprehend how under certain angles of exposure, and under peculiar relative positions, the sea might act as a true lens, with a focal column of great length, and of a power far surpassing anything which the human mind is capable of conceiving. Let the focus of the oceanic lens be formed for ever so brief a space at the bottom of the sea, and the earth to its very depths, for the whole length of the focal column, must be reduced to its elements, dissolve in gases, or rise in the form of pumice or lava to the surface. A remarkable theory certainly, but apparently not more far-fetched than that which makes the whole interior of the globe a molten mass of which volcanoes are the safety valves. As an example of the strength of the sun's rays through a lens, it is related somewhere that at Tours, in France, a man has invented an apparatus for driving a steam engine by the sun. A silver-plated concave reflector, five feet in diameter, collects the rays on to a boiler, the water in which in about twenty minutes becomes so heated that the power has to be lessened to prevent the boiler from bursting, by all the water turning into steam.

In Guatemala the devout character of the people is very marked as far as appearances go. Every house has its shrine, and as the period of which I am speaking was approaching Christmas, most of them had also a "Nacimiento," or set scene representing the birth of Christ, and incidental events supposed to have taken place in Bethlehem. The season is one of visiting and rejoicing; houses are thrown open and the general public are admitted to witness the spectacle.

Shortly after Christmas Day I went with a party of friends to see what was said to be the best "nacimiento" in the city, which was very interesting on account of its mechanical movements, and all being the work of its proprietor—a wealthy architect. After paying our respects to the ladies of the house, we were shown into a room, one side of which was fitted up as a stage. At a glance it was evident that all devout character had been made subservient to tricks of mechanism, and the most incongruous elements had been introduced to give variety. It must have been Bethlehem from a Spanish American point of view. I will try to describe it. The figures were about two inches high, and of course the various parts of the scenery were in proportion. The curtain rose on a country scene with a large village, trees, woods, hill and dale, outlying farms, plantations, pastures and river flowing into the sea, of which the background was a well-painted scene of the Bay of Naples. A few small natural flowers and plants were arranged about the rocks and river banks. In the foreground to the right was the house of Joseph, with Mary seated in the verandah. At the touch of a spring everything was set in motion. Joseph began to carpenter, Mary to spin at a spinning wheel, and an angel swept an outhouse with a broom. At a blacksmith's horses were being shod and near at hand a woman was seen making tortillas. Cows ate, horses moved their tails, and goats butted at one another; some men were drinking, or fighting with sticks, others cutting wood and drawing water from the well. A priest entered with an animated conversation with his parishioners who bowed and scraped profusely. Labourers worked in a coffee plantation, and others cut sugar-cane. A band on a platform struck up with modern instruments, and an acrobat walked along a tight rope, receiving great applause at the hands of a group of Indians, who in the garb of nature contrasted strangely with a party of Orientals in long flowing robes. Finally, a storm commenced at sea and the vessels rolled most suggestively, a little thunder aiding the illusion. Such was the latest improvement on what was originally a purely scriptural subject.

The fondness for external religious observances may be noticed continually, and that the feeling seldom goes deep is very evident; what is fanaticism with the Indian might be termed hypocrisy with the Ladino, *i.e.*, speaking of the lower class of the latter. The man who wore the most sanctimonious aspect during a long cathedral service would not hesitate to appropriate your purse or handkerchief outside the church, and he who remained longest on his knees during the passing of the Host along a street, would probably be the first to cry out against a Protestant who did not conform to his prejudices.

To a stranger, the ceremony just mentioned is very disagreeable, as he may not be able to escape by a side street, and though in Guatemala the taking off the hat is generally considered sufficient recognition of the Host by a foreigner, yet scowling faces are not rare, and it is unpleasant to be the only one standing when all around are on their knees. The people themselves kneel even if they are not in the same street as the actual procession, but as long as the warning bell can be heard they fall on their knees, at window, shop-door, or balcony, in the mud or on the stones, and remain there until the sound has ceased. It certainly has a magic effect, the profound silence following the noisy clamour, and the motionless attitudes succeeding the busy movement of the streets.

Nowhere is the shallow religious pretence of the people, their rapid change from grave to gay, and the strange mingling of reverence and contempt, more evident that in the processions of their saints. From out of their number let me take one—that of the Virgin of Guadalupe, which on account of the beautiful display of fruits and flowers, leaves a more pleasing impression than others do. The streets through which the procession was to pass were decorated with arches of palm-leaves and evergreens, among which flowers, garlands, and strings of gourds and grenadillas were interspersed. The houses were hung with flags and lanterns, and the balconied windows were draped with coloured silks and gay curtains.

In the afternoon, the procession commenced its march. First of all came ragged Indians playing drums and carrying whips, with which they endeavoured to keep in order the crowd of unruly boys and dirty leperos who pressed too close. Then came a series of saints and angels carried on litters by eight or ten men, the former dressed in silks of the most modern fashion, and with wings to match, the latter like opera-dancers all gauze and spangles. Military music and a company of soldiers followed, and after them in double rank marched black-robed penitents carrying candles and chanting. Priests, sheltered by red umbrellas, came next, heralding the principal Saint —Our Lady of Guadalupe—which was carried on a large platform, literally a bed of roses and lilies. The figure, with hands clasped and eyes looking upwards, was dressed in white, and from the shoulders fell a rich purple mantle studded with silver stars, the heavy train being borne by six children in the costume of monks. More saints and altars of flowers succeeded, and another row of Indians closed the procession.

A motley crowd kept pace with it during its monotonous march, and rivalled the choristers and acolytes in their jokes and cracker-throwing. But the majority of the spectators collected at the street-corners, where they awaited the arrival of the chief personage, before whom they fell on their knees, then rising, would scamper off with much merriment to the next suitable position and repeat the salutation. Flights of rockets and other fireworks were introduced during the whole route, and gunpowder and crackers were most lavishly expended.

It was dark before the procession returned to the Church of Guadalupe, and the large green outside was thronged with people, most of whom were from the country and intended to pass the night there. Large fires had been lighted, and the blaze of pine-torches fell upon a picturesque scene; here were families grouped round an improvised table, evidently having their supper; there a vendor of sweetmeats was trying to satisfy the demands of a crowd of hungry urchins; some preached sermons, others sang songs, and at the moment when an angry dispute was at its height a sudden falling on the knees and complete silence announced that "Our Lady" was about to re-enter her church. For a minute the figure on the steps faced the kneeling crowd, and then passing through the door was lost to view.

The Spaniards originated this feast about the year 1500 in Mexico, as they did not think that the Indians were converted fast enough. They managed it in this way:—A poor native was on his way to the city over the mountains when he suddenly saw a female descending from the clouds. The figure told him not to be alarmed, that she was the Virgin Mary, and had determined to become the patron saint of the Mexican Indians; that he must go to the city and tell the bishop that she wished to have a church built at the foot of the mountain and dedicated to her. The Indian hastened to the city and delivered the message to the bishop, who was incredulous and sent him away. The next day the Indian met the Virgin at the same place and told her that the bishop would not believe him. "Then," said she, "I will give you a proof that the bishop will not doubt. Go to the top of the mountain, fill your apron with the roses you will find there, and carry them to the bishop." The Indian found the roses, and as none had ever grown there before, they must have been placed there by a miracle. When he opened his apron to exhibit the roses to the bishop, he found to his amazement that another miracle had been performed, and that a portrait of the Virgin, dressed in blue velvet spangled with stars, had been painted on it. The bishop could not, of course, resist such evidence as that, and the church was built, the Indians contributing all they possessed and joining the true faith by thousands.

In Guatemala the religious processions and fête days are no longer countenanced by the presence of the President and civil authorities, and in general in Spanish America the white race is with unmistakable advances asserting its independence of the Church. Though the Jesuits control Ecuador and have not as yet been expelled from San Salvador, yet they are becoming more and more objects of distrust throughout the Republics.

The churches of Guatemala possess on the whole but little merit. Their interiors are overloaded with gilt ornamentation and carved wood, painted or gilded in the rococo style. Large and indifferent paintings fill the chapels and overhang the altars, and figures of martyrs, sculptured with various degrees of skill, are very numerous, but there are very few real works of art. Among the few, the Church of La Merced possesses a most exquisite piece of sculpture—Christ bearing the Cross. The patient suffering face is carved with a delicacy of expression most touching. Various stories are related about this masterpiece; one is that the sculptor—a native of Antigua—had received orders in a dream to complete the work he had begun and laid aside, and directly he finished it he died. Another is that, when on Good Friday it is carried through the streets, great drops of perspiration appear on its forehead.

The good padre who had shown me the church and had taken some trouble in explaining the different objects of interest, was very reticent regarding this figure, and I did not press my inquiries too closely. I could not help thinking of the story of the man who, after many sneers at the religion of the priest who was accompanying him round a celebrated cathedral finally said, " You talk of your Church and your priesthood as being in the line of St. Peter, but you seem to have lost the power to work miracles." " Oh, no," was the answer, as the intruder was summarily forced out of the building, " we still retain the power to cast out devils."

The church of Jocotenango, which stands in a pretty suburb of the same name, has peculiar sanctity attached to it. Among the virtues which it is supposed to possess, are certain miraculous powers in regard to those whose matrimonial expectations have been disappointed, and it is for this reason frequented by numbers of native women on certain days.

For heaviness of ornamentation, both inside and on the outside, the church of San Domingo is pre-eminent. It contains two enormous pictures by an old artist of the country, which are fair examples of the mixture of ardent devotion and the love of depicting horrors which is so conspicuous in most of the church decorations. The old convent attached to this church is now a college of music, and as if in contrast to the harmony which proceeds from thence, the ear is deafened by the crowing of hundreds of game-cocks, who live in their noisy abode on the opposite side of the street.

This cockpit, or "Teatro de los gallos," as it is proudly named, is a great resort for a certain class of men, especially on feast days and Sundays. After paying a small entrance fee, the visitor crosses a half-cultivated enclosure, at the end of which is a covered building with open sides, round which are arranged tiers of seats. Each of the numerous pens outside has its bird occupant. Some of these game-cocks are most beautiful specimens of their class, and ought to be winning prizes at poultry shows, instead of fluttering out a brief existence in the ring.

At the proper hour for commencing, the two cocks who are to open the proceedings are brought in and exhibited in the arena, the spectators selecting the one on which they choose to risk their money. Then the birds are removed, and their owners proceed to arm them. Out of a leather case containing several pointed knives, slightly curved and sharp as razors, one is at last chosen, and carefully fastened on to the left leg of the combatant. The firm attachment of these murderous gaffs is a matter of no small importance, and requires considerable skill; among others, the President is celebrated for his ability in that line. The birds then re-enter the ring, and the wretched sport commences.

Any one who sees a cock-fight for the first time, must be astonished at the scientific way in which the combatants spar, and the wily feints they employ to invite attack, and the cleverness with which they avoid it. It sometimes happens that at the first spring one of them falls dead, pierced by the gaff; but the most cruel sight is when, after several attacks and failing to inflict a mortal wound, they seize each other by the comb (which is not cut) or neck, and fight at close quarters until they fall exhausted. Occasionally a veteran will, after first facing his antagonist, pretend utter indifference, and will scratch the ground or pick up a stray seed, but all the time keeping an eye on the enemy, and working round for a good opening. Sometimes, too, after closely examining one another, with heads down and neck feathers bristling with anger, one springs at the other with feet outstretched, ready to give the death-blow, but instead of responding to the attack, his antagonist lies close to the ground, and his enemy passes harmlessly over his head, receiving a considerable shock on his descent from the unexpected non-resistance.

It happens not unfrequently, that in their fury and excitement they are not aware when they have received their death-blow, and at the only fight I ever attended, two magnificent birds, after several rounds, retreated a little, and looked as if each considered himself the victor, then after a flap of the wings and a loud crow they both fell dead. The gladiators of old could never have exclaimed more opportunely :—" Morituri salutamus."

The ladies of Guatemala do not attend these exhibitions, but the same compunctions do not deter them from witnessing the bull-fights, which also take place on Sundays.

The Plaza de Toros is situated in the suburbs of the city, near the old church of El Calvario, which, by the way, contains some interesting pictures. Due notice of an intended bull-fight was always given by a procession through the town of the "company," attended by some grotesque figures. The large amphitheatre was always well filled, and the entertainment invariably commenced with some curious evolutions by the military. They could not be called military evolutions, but resembled rather the intricate diversions of a ballet. Those engaged would open out like a fan from a common centre, then gradually forming out into two circles, would lay their rifles on the ground and extend to the limits of the arena. One circle would then move to the right and the other to the left, and after an in and out movement like the last figure of the Lancers, would retire in order and pick up their arms; then a few more figures of a similar character would follow, and the review ended.

It is unnecessary to describe the bull-fight which followed, as probably in no city could a tamer exhibition be presented. The bulls were the most harmless animals, and were only too glad to follow the old steer that came to coax them out whenever they had been sufficiently teased. I do not remember ever seeing one of them even angry, and perhaps fortunately, as the "picadores" were so badly mounted that their horses sometimes fell of their own accord. The sympathies of the public were with the bull, and though the dart-headed rosette with which he was sometimes adorned —and skilfully too—did not appear to inconvenience him much, yet it would have been a satisfaction if he had lifted his tormentor over the barricade.

What the bull thinks of the sport is doubtful, but there is no question about the pleasure it affords the people, who look "as happy as if it were the middle of the week," as some keen Sabbatarian in a Scotch village angrily remarked. Looking at them, one is reminded of the Puritan sentiment that forbade bull-baiting on a Sunday, not because of the pain to the bull, but on account of the pleasure it gave to the spectators.

Sunday's routine with this people is certainly an odd one, when regarded from our point of view: matins in the early morn, cock-fighting at noon, a bull-fight in the afternoon, then probably vespers, and assuredly the theatre in the evening. It used to be said that Mexican ladies began the day in black, on their knees in chapel, and ended their waking hours amid the blaze of dress and jewels in the family box at the opera. The matin prayers may be a little out of fashion, but an opera box is still an indispensable necessary of life even in Guatemala.

Among the enactments of the so-called Blue laws,

ordained by our forefathers a couple of centuries ago for our American colonies, is the following:—"No one shall run on the Sabbath Day, or walk in his garden, or elsewhere, except reverently to and from meeting." What would they have thought of a Sunday in Central America?

The zopilote—black vulture*—of Guatemala, is such a conspicuous object everywhere, that it deserves a few more words than I have given it. Hideous and repulsive as the bare, wrinkled-neck creatures are, yet they are of incalculable use as scavengers, and would put to shame even the dogs of Constantinople in their greed. They swarm on the roofs of all the houses and churches, sitting with outspread wings airing in the sun, but with an eye to everything going on in the street below. If a pail of dirty water is but thrown away within sight, down they pounce at once to see if there is anything that will suit them, and the object must be very hard indeed that they cannot expeditiously make away with. They are the most ungainly birds on the ground, and when they attempt to fly have to take several shuffling leaps before they can rise, but when once in the air they swoop about very gracefully, ascending and descending without giving a flap of the wings, but with head and neck continually moving, and their great black eyes perpetually in search of prey. From frequent observation both in towns and country, I can hardly doubt that, as a rule, they hunt by eye and not by scent, as has been often asserted,

* Catharista atrata.

although, considering the vast extent of ground they cover in their flight, they must frequently come within sight of carrion that otherwise they would not have seen.

Another very common bird in Guatemala is a species of starling—Quiscalus macrurus; like our own, they may be seen in numbers following the steps and perched on the backs of the cattle, but they differ from ours in having a clear, penetrating note, for which reason the natives call them " clarineros."

Most of the birds of this country are named by the inhabitants from some striking point about them, or from some peculiarity in their movements ; for instance, the toucan is called "cucharon"—big spoon—on account of its enormous beak, and in some parts "predicador"—preacher—because of the solemn way in which it wags its head.

Whilst I was in Guatemala I bought two of these birds from an Indian for about two shillings, cage included. They were a delicate species,* and of a bright green colour, the upper mandible being yellow and the lower one black. One of them quickly became so tame that it would fly and perch on my shoulder whenever I entered their room, and in the morning if I did not bring its food in time, it would tap with its great beak against a glass door that opened into my bed-room. One morning it broke one of the panes and never tapped again. They used to drink a good quantity of water, and it was very

* Aulacoramphus prasinus.

amusing to see their preparatory motions. Indians declare that they make the sign of the cross, another reason I suppose for their nickname of "preacher." They are very greedy birds, and certainly do credit to their beaks which they fill to repletion, and then with violent tosses of the head swallow the contents. When they are asleep they resemble a ball of feathers, as they hide their beaks under their wings; they also sleep with their tails turned over, and almost touching their backs. The Indians say that their beak, when reduced to powder is the only certain cure for epilepsy, and this is certainly the strangest use I have ever heard alleged for their extraordinary snout-like appendages. Their long feathered tongue is suggestive of a honey-sucking or bee-eating bird, and the great beak looks capable of cracking nuts; but they live chiefly on soft fruits, and the light porous bill has not even power to hurt your finger. Can any student of the theory of evolution offer a reasonable answer to the questions,—what has led to the production of the wonderful bill of the toucan and what is its use? If the smallest as well as the most conspicuous peculiarities of birds and animals are, or have been, of use to them, or have been developed under the influence of general laws, then I think the toucan's bill has yet to be explained. I have seen it stated that the use of the large bill is to enable the bird to re-masticate its food, but I have never been able to detect it in the act.

The people of Guatemala are very fond of singing birds, and in the market and "mesones" there are generally many cages full, chiefly consisting of rioles, mocking birds and of a charming songster called here "guarda barranca"* from the peculiarity of its notes.

To bird lovers, memory has few stranger associations than the familiar songs of the feathered race; in great sorrow or joy the note of a bird will sink into the mind, and ever after be listened to with the same old feeling of gladness or of pain. So, in recalling some half-forgotten place, the memory of the sweet sounds that haunted it soon re-pictures the scene itself, and thus the clear metallic notes of the little singer of Guatemala which, when once heard, are never forgotten, brings to the recollection the deep ravines and grand pine forests of its sheltered home. The grief and gladness which shadow the voices of the birds have been beautifully depicted in "Deirdrè" by Dr. Joyce:

"Then she replied, 'O King,
Long time the wild bird's song to me would bring
But joy, yet now mixed up in every note
Some tone of sadness to my heart will float.
Long time I laughed; but now, I know not why
Their warbling songs both make me laugh and cry."

The "meson," which I have mentioned as being one of the places where birds may be bought, is quite a feature in Guatemala. It is an inn where muleteers and men of that class congregate. There are several of them, but they differ very little from one another. Round the large "patio" are numerous little shops, where the natives sell their own produce, such as woollen stuffs, hats, cottons, &c., at more moderate prices than elsewhere. Next to the market, a visit

* Myiadestes obscurus.

to the "meson" gives a good idea of the native produce and industry of the country.

A curious bird called "caraban" is often found in the "patios" of private houses; it is extremely useful for keeping watch, as no stranger can enter the yard without being greeted by its shrill cries. It also has the peculiarity of uttering its warning notes at certain hours. I was once asked by a gentleman to accompany him to his house in order that I might hear a bird of this kind give its strange cry, and as he had predicted, it suddenly screamed and immediately a neighbouring clock struck four.

One night, when returning home from a dinner-party, I was surprised at receiving a challenge from a sentry who was posted where there had been no guard previously; however I answered "Amigo," thinking that probably the reply was the same as in most countries; the sentry muttered something and I passed on. The next day I was inquiring about the unaccustomed presence of the guard, and was informed that on account of the expected war some additional posts had been assigned. I was amused at my answer of "Friend," as I found out the challenge, and its reply was as follows. "Quien va?"—"Who goes there?"

"Libertad."—"Liberty."

"De que gente?"—"What sort of people?"

"De paz."—"Of peace."

It was also suggested that it was advisable if possible to avoid these posts, as there was no knowing when the musket of the sentry might go off.

The impending war which I have mentioned was against San Salvador. The causes which produce wars and revolutions in these countries are not always apparent, but on this occasion it was believed that the President of Salvador was obnoxious to the members of the Government of Guatemala, and they intended to give the position to somebody else. Doubtless the Jesuits of Salvador had much to do with it, as the Liberals of that State favoured the proposed measures of President Barrios.

Troops were assembling on the frontier of Salvador, and it was considered a bad time for me to make my visit to the ruins of Copan, but as war had not been declared, and I had no time to lose, I obtained a passport and a letter from Señor Samayoa, the Minister of War, and prepared to start.

A passport is absolutely necessary for anyone leaving Guatemala, but it is easily obtained, and the Government have instituted the very fair measure—which might advantageously be adopted elsewhere—of only making a charge for them on people of those countries where passports are in vogue.

As my road lay to the east of Guatemala, where towns are fewer, and accommodation more primitive than in the west, I bought a camp-bed *(catre)* and having obtained a capital arriero in place of Leon—discharged—was ready to set out. I had postponed my journey as long as I could, for I wished to make it when the great pilgrimage to Esquipulas—the Mecca of Spanish America—was at its height; I therefore left Guatemala early in January.

CHAPTER XII.

A PILGRIMAGE—A BLACK SAINT—CERRO REDONDO—PASCUAL—ARPINO—A TORTILLA—THE ROAD-RUNNER—SWALLOW-TAILED FLY-CATCHER — CUAJINIQUILAPA — ESCLAVOS—AZAGUALPA—JUTIAPA—ORGAN-CACTUS—AGUA BLANCA—SAN ANTONIO—VOLCANO OF SUCHITAN—SANTA CATARINA—EL RIO—AMATILLO—SILVER MINES OF ALOTEPEQUE.

THE town of Esquipulas is situated only a short distance from the frontier of Honduras, and about five days' journey from the city of Guatemala. In January of each year thousands of pilgrims—not only from the neighbouring provinces but also from the confines of Mexico, and from some of the South American States—assemble here to worship "our Lord of Esquipulas" or as the figure is called the "Black Christ."* For days previous, large bands of pilgrims had passed through the city singing as is their

* Benoit de Palermo thus quotes the phenomenon of a black saint in the Calendar: "Nigro quidem corpore, sed candore animi præclarissimus quem et miraculis Deus contestatum esse voluit."—*Grégoire, De la Littérature des Nègres.*

custom, and all along our route we met or passed hundreds of these Indians going to or returning from their sacred shrine.

Our road first of all took a south-easterly direction through a hilly country thinly populated, and with but little cultivation. Looking back from one of the high ridges we see the country we are leaving spread out in the blue distance, and the volcanoes on our left standing out clearer than ever against the cloudless sky.

The heat was very great, and as at this time of year high winds prevail, the dust was almost suffocating. Still up we went, and presently overlooked a valley much broken and divided in the centre of which rose a strange conical hill—Cerro Redondo. It had all the appearance of a miniature volcano, thickly wooded half way up, and then rocky and rugged to the summit, where the signs of a crater were not wanting. I could find out nothing about it, and it was the only object I met in that and subsequent journeys of which my arriero, Pascual, could give me no information.

I must introduce Pascual, as he proved an admirable servant both on this occasion and later when he accompanied me to Peten. He was slightly built, but strong and active, and had the happy faculty of making himself at home wherever he went. He fell into my ways in a very short time, and afterwards I never had any trouble. He had a very comical expression, and I never met anyone who could help laughing when they addressed him. This, I think, had much to do with making him believe that he was a wit, and he seldom spoke without an accompanying laugh. This was rather unfortunate, as his love of talking was intense; from morning to night he never stopped, and even when there was nobody to talk to he chattered to his mules, or the birds, or to himself. He spoke so fast, too, that often I could not understand, and when I informed him that I did not know a word of what he was saying, he would repeat it quicker than before, and with all the gesticulation and emphasis that he could command.

It is the custom in Central America for the arrieros, when speaking of their employers, to use the Christian name with the prefix "Don," and as my shortest name was "John," I had been amused once or twice at hearing Pascual talking of me as "Don Manuel." On asking him the reason, he replied that not knowing my proper name he thought "Manuel" would answer as well. However he was quite satisfied with "Juan," and I think added "Manuel" to his list of jokes.

The incident reminded me of a story I heard in San Francisco. When a German lady asked her new Chinese servant his name, he replied,

"My namee Ah Sin Foo."

"But I cannot remember all that," she said, "I'll call you Jimmy."

"Velley welle; now wachee name I callee you?"

"My name is Mrs. Van Auckenkrast."

"Oh, no, can 'membel Missee Yanneauhengrass; too

big piecee name ; I callee you Tommy—Missee Tommy."

We had intended to sleep at the village of Cerro Redondo, but we found it so dirty and void of accommodation that we determined to push on for another two leagues where we heard there was a house. Crossing a plain with a shallow lake on our left, in the middle of which stood one large white crane looking like a ghost in the evening mist, we soon arrived at Arpino. In one of the three huts that composed the village, there was a vacant room which we took possession of, and the owner speedily provided eggs and frijoles. I then found I had omitted to furnish myself with knife, fork, and spoon, and heard with sorrow that I should not see those articles until I reached Esquipulas. I found that among other uses of a tortilla it does duty for a spoon, and when Pascual was eating his supper I noticed that he used one for a plate on which to put his frijoles, then he used it as a spoon with which to eat his eggs, and finally he demolished the tortilla itself. The luxury in these houses may be imagined from the fact that the only basin I could get in which to wash my hands was a moderate-sized gourd.

Next morning we rode through a country of a different aspect from that of the preceding day. It was undulating grassland, with here and there a little square house perched like a chimney on the top of the hills. There was no shade or tree, except in the villages, and our path was lined with thick brushwood. From out of this thicket we heard at intervals a rich, mellow note like a bell, and occasionally the bird* that uttered

* Geococcyx affinis.

it would run across the road or stand watching us from a short distance. The natives call it "El reloj" —the clock—and declare that it sounds the proper hours. In appearance it is like the Californian roadrunner, but the cere round the eye is of a bright blue. One of these birds was most persistent in its endeavours to make me chase it, running on ahead of my mule and then stopping until nearly overtaken, when off it would start again. There were also numbers of the swallow-tailed flycatchers,* and it was very amusing watching them as they tried to bear up against the high wind, or to balance themselves on some slender stem, their long tails impeding them greatly.

In the villages many of the large trees were adorned with a most beautiful rose-coloured orchid—I think a Lycaste Skinneri—whose large flowers gave a wonderful glow to the grey trunk and green leaves among which they were perched. It appeared to me that they had been transplanted, as they were seldom far from the ground, and generally on trees overhanging a native hut; to an Indian an orchid is a sacred flower, and as none of the trees in that locality, except those near houses, were similarly decorated, it is not improbable that superstition rather than a love of gardening accounted for their appearance.

Guatemala is rich in these lovely plants—the élite of the floral kingdom—and every day I had cause to regret my limited knowledge of botany; and after I had left the country, when showing what I had col-

* Milvulus forficatus.

lected and describing what I had not, I often found I had taken the chaff and left the grain.

In all parts of the country the trees themselves, especially ceibas and that species, give a curious character to the landscape. Where we now were, the roots of these trees were just as conspicuous as the domes, sometimes rising in high buttresses which reached almost to the lower branches, at other times twisting and twining along the ground so as to form a perfect wall for many yards on both sides; it looked, indeed, as if the earth had sunk and left the tree to balance itself as best it might.

When we arrived at the town bearing the euphonious name of Cuajiniquilapa we found the utility of the letter which the Minister of War had given me, as the place was occupied by troops, and no one without permission was allowed to proceed. The soldiers must have eaten up all the provisions, as no breakfast was to be obtained, and we had to ride on to the village of Esclavos, where in a hospitable native hut we found coffee and eggs. Afterwards we crossed the Rio de los Esclavos by a fine bridge, from which there was a very romantic view as the river ran in a succession of steep falls through a narrow and picturesque gorge. The bridge itself is worthy of notice, as it is of ancient date and built entirely of stone ; its length is over 300 feet, and its breadth about 30 feet. Our path then passed through a long and very hot valley, at the end of which we turned off up a steep hill to the left, leaving on our right the road to San Salvador. The cuesta we

ascended was long and quite unshaded ; it seemed that
we were never to find shelter from the sun, as in the
entire distance we had then travelled from Guatemala
not a particle of shade had been granted us, and trees
had been cut down quite unnecessarily.

It was almost dark when we reached Azagualpa, and
as the cabildo was occupied by some drunken Indians,
we quartered ourselves in a tiny convent built of mud
and whitewashed ; the mules we stabled in the cloisters,
to reach which they had to pass through the only room
the building possessed. It is customary when travelling in this country to start soon after daybreak and
to breakfast about eleven, then to continue your journey until evening. A good arriero will know the best
halting-places, and the day's route is arranged accord-
ingly. When we left the convent, and had paid the
alcalde a very exorbitant charge for the accommodation
and for the eggs and frijoles—this was the only occasion
during my journeys in which I met with any imposi-
tion—we rode through quite a large village, near
which were several flocks of sheep, and towards noon
breakfasted at the River del Paz. A broad plain
bounded by hills then opened out before us, and at
the farther extremity we saw the white houses of
Jutiapa, a town situated on the edge of a deep barranca,
and the capital of the department of the same name.

The plain was arid and but little cultivated, the few
patches of maize being surrounded by hedges of the
wild pine, whose long sharp-pointed leaves were of a
brilliant crimson. The hills were bare in parts, but

here and there were groups of trees, hiding a small cottage, whose owner tended the goats that browsed near at hand. Some of the trees had no leaves and were covered with clusters of flowers, like lilac but of a deep pink; these gave variety to the scenery and relieved the stiff formality of the organ-cactus whose chandelier-like branches were tipped with snow-white cotton.

We did not visit Jutiapa, but crossed the plain on its left, and in a few hours entered the valley of Agua Blanca. This valley was full of trees similar to the apple, but on whose trunk and branches grew stemless gourds. Groups of pilgrims sat under these trees and were busily employed in painting the gourds which they had halved and cleaned. The rind is very hard, and consequently the "morros," as they call them, form good cups, and the Indians make money by selling them. Cattle and pigs are very fond of the pulp, but as their owners have to open the gourds themselves, the animals are not as well provided with the delicacy as they could wish. The village of Agua Blanca was evidently a favourite halting-place for the pilgrims, as long rows of sheds had been run up for their accommodation, and each little partition was occupied by numerous travellers. Not finding any of these horse-boxes vacant we rode on to San Antonio, and as there was no cabildo, a kind-hearted native offered us his house, and at once moved his belongings into another.

In this part of the country the chief industry is carried on by the hens, and they are the only inhabitants of the villages who are never idle. It was a great matter to be always sure of finding plenty of eggs, and as the hens never disappointed me, I felt very grateful to them. I often recalled the old joke that to a hungry traveller the sweetest bird's "lay" is that of a hen. As if aware of my friendly feelings, several of them roosted in my room that night, and though I frequently called in Pascual to eject the intruders, yet they always came back through the roof.

Next morning when we quitted the village, crowds of pilgrims were kneeling in front of the church and chanting their prayers, whilst others, staff in hand, were continually arriving and pressing on to their journey's end. After crossing a wide grassy plain dotted with sugar-cane and banana fields, we ascended a ridge and had a fine view of the Volcano of Suchitan, and of a large lake in its vicinity. A very steep and stony descent brought us into a beautiful valley in the centre of which was the tropical looking village of Santa Catarina. Its situation was delightfully picturesque, and the road, which was crossed by a small stream, entered the village between houses which crowned rocky eminences and lay embowered in groves of fruit-trees. As in all the villages orioles were numerous, but here I noticed a very handsome species of bird whose name I have been unable to discover. Its brilliantly spotted back made it very noticeable, but its quick flight among the trees and shrubs rendered it difficult to examine it more closely.

The large church and plaza were crowded with

pilgrims, and the festive aspect of the village contrasted with the dilapidated appearance of its guests. Pascual found out the most likely place for obtaining some breakfast, and oddly enough it was outside the village. A broad river ran through rhe valley, and on its banks were a number of bough huts, leafy arbours that had been speedily erected for the benefit of travellers to Esquipulas during the month of January. Here we found not only tortillas but fresh rolls, and for the first and only time good coffee. Usually in the small towns of Guatemala the "extract" of coffee is alone used, and as it is seldom fresh a moderately good cup of coffee is out of the question; in the distant villages, where the "extract" is unknown, the coffee is always so thick as to be undrinkable. Here it was really fresh and clear, and I look back with much pleasure to that simple breakfast under the palm leaf hut on the banks of El Rio. Matters like these are very trivial, but they go to make up the enjoyment of journeyings like the present and leave an easily recalled picture on the memory. I can see it all now; the green huts under the large trees which shaded the pilgrim groups; the broad river sparkling in the sun and rippling over the rocks with the old sweet song that rivers everywhere love to sing; the banks clothed with shrubs and flower-covered trees, about which fluttered the curve-billed honey suckers; behind us the picturesque village with its large white church, in front the wooded hills which stretched across the path we were to travel; and above all—the infinite sweetness of nature in the varying scene—the bending sky, the hill and vale and flowing water.

That evening, after a rough and tedious ride, we arrived at Amatillo where we intended to sleep. The village consisted of a small collection of huts, some of poles, others of mud; we found a vacant one of the latter description and took possession of it. Like all native houses it consisted of only one room, but this happened to be a very large one, and its sole occupant when we arrived was a splendid game cock, which was tied by its leg to the centre pole, which supported what there was left of the roof. The bird gave a certain air of habitation to the room which it otherwise would certainly not have possessed, as the broken walls had two large holes for windows, the mud floor was so hillocky that I had some difficulty in finding a level place for my bed, and there was not even a table or a bench. The arrival of a stranger in one of these villages is of such rare occurrence that a crowd soon collects at the house where he is lodging, and, as usual, my doorway was quickly occupied by inquisitive natives intensely interested in the unrolling and laying out of my camp-bed, an article they had never seen before, and which in their eyes was the perfection of mechanical skill. Seated on the mud wall of the verandah were the wise men and notabilities of the village who had assembled to see the foreigner. They were very anxious to hear about England, the size of it, its distance from Guatemala, and the direction in which it lay. I answered as well as I could, and pointed to the direction, and on the arrival of fresh visitors my answers were repeated to each, a wave of the hand indicating England's situation; gradually this direction veered round until the position of Australia was the one shown to the eager spectators. Their ideas were limited to Guatemala and they knew of no other country. That there should be lands beyond their own was a surprise to them as great as it was to the chickens, in Hans Christian Andersen's story, that had strayed to the limits of the farm whereon they were born. When they discovered that there was an orchard, and still another farm beyond, their astonishment knew no bounds. "Is it possible," said they, "that the great world extends so far?" The pleasure of these innocents in hearing about England was marred by the fact that there were no tortillas there. "How can people live without tortillas!" they exclaimed. When I changed the subject to their own country and asked about Copan and Esquipulas, the old alcalde replied. "In this village we know nothing of such things, we are too poor." One of them afterwards volunteered the information that at Esquipulas there was a marble church finer than anything in the world, and full of gold ornaments.

I was glad at last to get rid of my visitors, and soon read myself to sleep by the light of the moon which streamed in through the broken roof. Long before dawn the game cock announced that it was time to get up, and we were shortly in the saddle again.

In the country around Amatillo are many abandoned mines that were once considered among the richest possessions of Spain. The chief mining district is known by the name of "Alotepeque," and in the time of the Spaniards it produced over forty millions of dollars. Spain lost her supremacy on the seas, her dependencies were neglected, the silver fleets sailed no more, and Alotepeque fell into decay. But the mines are as rich in silver, lead, zinc and copper as ever, and it is probable that before long the eyes of the mining world will be turned to Guatemala as enthusiastically as they were to California and Australia. There are twenty-three distinct mines at Alotepeque, and they still bear their old Spanish names such as San Juan, Plomosa, El Socorre, San Joaquin, &c. None have been worked to any great depth, as mining skill in the olden times was unable to compete with water. The owner of the district, a merchant of the city of Guatemala, is now working on a small scale two of the twenty-three mines which furnish about five thousand dollars in silver per month, whereas they might be made to yield fifty times that amount. The entrances to his other mines are barricaded and kept under lock and key to prevent trespass and damage. He is endeavouring to perfect arrangements for carrying on operations on a scale of some magnitude.

A few years ago a number of Engliah capitalists purchased an interest in the whole of these mines, but worked only the "San Pantaleon," from which they extracted 1,200,000 dollars. But the company shortly fell into a hopeless dispute and general discord marred the executions of all their plans. When the troubles were at their height, the present owner, who then held a half-interest in the mines, determined to make himself master of the whole. To this end he commissioned a London banking firm to buy out all the shareholders in one day, and this was successfully accomplished. The English left some valuable improvements behind them. Two rivers traverse the district, each carrying during the entire year enough water to drive twenty mill wheels. The value of this unfailing water-power can hardly be over-rated. On one of these rivers the company erected fine reduction works, well supplied with all machinery, ovens, assay office, and a complete outfit of all kinds of requisite tools and implements. They also put in place two steam-engines for pumping out water, and built a number of dwelling-houses for the superintendent, doctor, engineers and other attachés. The entire improvements involved an expense of about 200,000 dollars.

Most of these details I gathered from an account given by a mining expert who lately visited this district, and he was sure, from his inspection of the different strata of the rock, that the heaviest deposits of gold, silver, and many other valuable metals, are neither in California nor in Mexico, but will eventually be laid open in the mountains of Central America.

The altitude of these mines is from four thousand to eight thousand feet above the level of the sea, and so isolated is the adjacent country that at present it has hardly been explored and its treasures investigated by scientific men. But the same want of enterprise is shown in the other parts of Guatemala, which abound in dormant wealth.

The hills around Alotepeque are covered with heavy timber, and untouched forests of pine, oak, rosewood, and innumerable other species are standing. The foot hills are of the richest alluvial soil, where sugar-cane, coffee, oranges, and lemons grow luxuriantly, but the natives are quite content with their tortillas, frijoles, and dried meat for edibles, and as long as they get plenty of aguardiente to drink, have no other aspiration.

For several centuries, a Spanish edict was in force prohibiting strangers from visiting these mines, on penalty of deeth. Only a permit, with the Sovereign's own signature and seal, could procure that privilege. Now, the permission is willingly granted by the present owner, and every facility is afforded for their inspection by visitors, who will see in the workmen and inhabitants of these regions descendants of the Indians who worked in the mines when they belonged to the Spanish Crown. As their forefathers were, so are they to this day, hopelessly deficient in education and enlightenment, and keeping their religious holidays more strictly than the people of Rome itself used to do, but still at all other times willing to work for thirty cents a day in their beloved mountains of Alotepeque.

CHAPTER XIII.

MOUNTAIN SCENERY—PILGRIMS' GRAVES—PIEDRAS GORDAS—
MERINO SHEEP—A RESTAURANT—A DELIGHTFUL VALLEY—A
MUD HUT—THE CROSS—A NIGHT WITH THE PILGRIMS—TIL-
LANDSIA—FIRST VIEW OF ESQUIPULAS—A DOUANE—THE CALLE
REAL—BRIDGE AND STONE FIGURES—A FAIR—CHURCH OF
ESQUIPULAS—THE BLACK CHRIST—STRANGE OFFERINGS—LAST
VIEW OF ESQUIPULAS.

HE shade of the pine and oak forests was very delightful, after the unsheltered road we had travelled previous to Amatillo. Our path lay across a chain of mountains, situated between the Andes on the south and the Sierra de Merendon on the east; the latter separating the district of Chiquimula— where we then were—from Honduras. The scenery was bold and romantic, but the ascents and descents dreadfully steep and rocky. Between the ridges were meadows and glades covered with mimosa, where we saw many beautiful gros-beaks of a dark blue colour and with brown wings.

Near a splendid stream that flowed through a narrow

ravine, was another specimen of a root wall; this time the tree was an amate, and the gnarled and twisted roots, like petrified snakes, formed a fence nearly five feet high for a distance of fifteen yards. Near it was a native house, with fruit trees and a plot of maize; this was the only habitation we had seen since we left Amatillo, and it looked very forlorn and desolate.

A little further on we passed the graves of ten or twelve pilgrims who had died on their way to Esquipulas; none looked new, and the crosses over them were decayed and broken. The valley in which they were, presented a curious mingling of torpical and temperate vegetation. The hill sides were covered with pine-trees and oaks, and at their base grew aloes and papayas. In the vale were palms, mango-trees, and oranges, among which screamed parrots and parroquets.

One of the most picturesque of the numerous valleys we crossed was named "Piedras Gordas," from the enormous boulders with which it is strown. Creepers and long grasses festooned the grey masses, which took all sorts of fantastic shapes, and the stream which watered the meadow gave a rich green to the herbage, on which was grazing a flock of Merino sheep. Overhanging the valley, and nestling under the shade of the high rocks, was another group of bough huts, on the top of which were perched four tame macaws of the most gorgeous plumage. Here there was a choice of luxuries from the different establishments: coffee, chocolate, pine-apples, oranges, bananas, dried meat, eggs, and bread. Rows of black bottles in one of the booths suggested something stronger than coffee, and the number of exhausted(?) pilgrims gathered near was proof positive of their contents. The owners of these restaurants are mostly ladinos from the neighbouring towns, and they reap a good harvest in the pilgrims' month.

After Piedras Gordas we again toiled up and down hill till we reached a small oval-shaped valley, in whose centre was a pretty village buried in trees. Leaving this on our left we ascended a rocky pass, and again entered the forest. Here I sent on Pascual with the pack-mule, in order that he might find some lodging in Esquipulas by the time I arrived. Soon after he left me, I arrived at a spot where two paths met, and as there were no pilgrims to direct me I naturally took the wrong road. After an hour's ride I met a native, who informed me I was out of the track, and consequently had to retrace my steps. Presently the level forest path ended on the brink of a precipitous ravine, down which a very fair road wound in a hundred twists and curves.

At the bottom, a shallow mountain stream ran merrily over the rocks, and into it rushed my mule, which I had driven on in front of me down the mountain side. To my disgust, when I approached him he began to move on down the stream, and when I imagined that he would stop to allow me to take off his head-gear, as I had always done previously, in order that he might drink, he put down his head and sucked up the water, as easily as if he had had no bit in his mouth. For about ten minutes I followed this ungrateful animal down the water-course, and only caught him at last when some high boulders impeded his progress.

These delays convinced me that I could not reach Esquipulas that night, and I began to feel anxious about Pascual; fortunately I met some muleteers when ascending the opposite hill, and they told me he was waiting for me at the end of the next valley.

This valley was the most charming we had seen in the journey. The road ran above and parallel with the river, which flowed through it, and on either side rose rugged cliffs wooded on their crests, and divided into thick-foliaged ravines. The far end of the valley was crossed by a splendid range of mountains, between whose rounded and tree-clad contours were undulating slopes of green meadow-land. In the middle distance, rising out of the plain, were cone-shaped hills, at whose feet flowed the river, amid groves of plantains, orange trees, and fields of maize. The valley narrowed at these hills, and then opened out into a wide basin, in the centre of which was the village of Apantes, surrounded with sugar-cane and fruit trees. There were beautiful pictures on all sides, and the returning pilgrims lingered and seemed loth to leave the pleasant-sounding river and the cool shady rocks.

It was quite dark when I arrived at the place where Pascual awaited me, and as it was a long two leagues to Esquipulas and the mules were very tired, we decided to remain in the pilgrim camp where we then were. We were not badly off, as coffee and eggs were forthcoming, and for shelter we took possession of an old mud hut, which fortunately was unoccupied.

Opposite this building, and on the other side of a small stream was a large cross which the pilgrims had decorated with garlands of grey tillandsia; around this they knelt in a circle, and sang and prayed the whole night. Whenever a new comer arrived, he deposited his wreath and joined the kneeling group. A great bonfire threw a glare over the scene, and lit up in fitful gleams the kneeling figures at the cross and the many sleeping forms which were stretched in and about the fragile leafy shelters. All around, the dark mountains loomed up through the gathering mists stern and grand, adding to the wild picturesqueness of the pilgrim bands, who, in spite of cold and falling rain, continued their prayers and chants until the dawn.

It was raining steadily when we left our lodging-place, and commenced the ascent of the intervening range between us and Esquipulas. The mountains were wreathed with a thick white mist, which added to the weirdness of the moss-clothed trees. These hills were thickly wooded, and every tree was draped with the grey tillandsia; any green which might have enriched them was totally concealed in the drooping festoons of the pale moss which waved from every branch. The road on which we were travelling, climbed with many a tortuous curve the mountain ridge, on the other side of which was the happy valley. High up above us, the descending travellers on thei homeward journey looked like huge spiders in the glittering webs of the strange foliage, and as they passed silent and grave, seemed to envy those who had not yet looked upon the shrine.

Our first view of Esquipulas was, as it should have been, sudden and unexpected. We had arrived at the summit of the mountain, and turning a corner beheld a great number of pilgrims collected around a cross. Some were singing and praying, and some were weeping, as they took a last look at the church of their devotion, whilst others were laughing hysterically at the first glimpse of their long-expected goal. Far down below, in the corner of a green and fertile plain, rose an enormous snow-white church, with four towers and a cupola. This was the famed temple of Esquipulas. At some distance to its left was the town, but so hidden in trees that its red roofs alone were visible. Between the town and the church was a moving multitude, which passed to and fro among the buildings that lined the intervening space. On three sides the church was quite shut in by green hills, but on the fourth, away beyond the town, stretched the flat plain to the foot of the encircling distant mountain range.

When we had descended the hill, we found a guard of soldiers waiting to examine the contents of everything brought to the town. After inspecting my baggage and finding out that my passport was correct by reading it upside down, the officer of the guard offered to accompany us to his house where we could breakfast and remain as long as we wished. This offer we readily accepted, and found that we had fallen into good hands, as our host kept a small grocery, and everything was very clean and comfortable. Whilst we were at breakfast a large band of pilgrims passed along the street singing, and though they strongly reminded one of May-day, yet they formed a very picturesque procession. They were all decked with garlands of the tillandsia, and in their hands they carried brilliant orchids. Some of the different companies carried spikes of the beautiful rose-coloured orchid I have before mentioned ; others carried a species of Epidendrum whose rich orange flowers contrasted with the creamy blossoms of an Odontoglot which seemed a great favourite. Panicles of one of the commonest orchids in Guatemala—an Oncidium—were used in great profusion, and their long drooping stalks covered with small yellow flowers looked very graceful. It was a strange contrast to glance from the rare blossoms to their ragged bearers, whose tattered costumes bespoke the tedious march that their fanaticism had prescribed.

The town of Esquipulas is said to be unhealthy at certain seasons on account of its low and enclosed position, and we certainly found it oppressively hot and damp as we traversed the long street—the Calle Real— leading to El Templo, as they call their church. The street in the town itself was lined with large open shops filled with all sorts of merchandize, cotton goods, glass and hardware, saddlery, tawdry jewellery, and all the items that make up a fair. There were drinking-booths without number, and these, with their adjoining refreshment tents, were thronged with an ever increasing crowd.

On a bridge that spanned a malarious swamp were three ancient stone carvings that were said to have been brought from Copan. One of them—a dragon's head—was well executed, but the others—figures of men—were very indifferent and unshapely. Here we were outside the town, and the shops were replaced by booths and awnings, under which were sold prints and copies of the church and its contents. The street and the surrounding plain swarmed with Indians, Ladinos, soldiers and itinerant merchants of various nations, all of whom seemed bent on enjoying themselves to the utmost. A variety of curious sights here present themselves; in one corner a juggler is performing some very modern tricks to a crowd of admirers; in another a family of acrobats is going through the usual balancing and somersault performance on the regular square piece of carpet and to the sound of the inevitable pipe and drum. Here a fortune-teller distributes his magic cards among a gaping throng for the small consideration of one "real" a-piece, and there a wretched pilgrim puts his last cent in a "turning-wheel" and wins a glass brooch instead of the ten-dollar note he had expected. But the sharpers—three-card monte men and thimble-riggers—prove the greatest attraction, and it almost looks as if the pilgrimage had been ordained for their special benefit. Thus modern civilization steps in and makes a satisfactory profit out of superstition!

Ascending a flight of steps we crossed the large square of the church and entered the building. The interior consisted simply of a nave, which was separated from the aisles by massive pillars. Under the lofty dome at the upper end was the heavily gilded high altar, and in front of it swung a large silver lamp—all that was left of the costly treasures that once ornamented the building.

"Public necessity," as they term it in Guatemala, has necessitated the conversion into coin of as much church property as can be conveniently appropriated. Some gilt cases, containing wax and wooden saints and a carved pulpit, were the only decorations that relieved the white walls of the sombre edifice. On the right of the entrance stood the Black Christ—a carved representation of the crucifixion in dark wood, and about three feet in height. This crucifix was sculptured in the year 1595 by Quirio Castaño, in Guatemala, and the church itself was finished in 1758. Underneath the Cross were hung numbers of small gold and silver figures, rough shaped in solid metal by the pilgrims, and each indicating some malady of which the donor prayed to be relieved; for instance, the hand pressed to the head showed a tendency to head-ache, an enlarged foot was a sign of gout, and so on; horses and mules were also introduced, showing that their owners were anxious for their recovery from disease. These little images were about an inch in height, and often of such rude workmanship that it required a good deal of imagination to discover their intention. Some that I afterwards obtained in Guatemala were most ludicrous, but a few were wrought with much skill. As these offerings are not now permitted by law, the priests get rid of them when the pilgrimage is over, and, indeed, I think that, even when they were permitted, they seldom remained long at Esquipulas. Near by was a table on which there was a plate well filled with money, the produce of the sale of ribbons and pieces of linen bearing an inscription and a print of the sacred figure. One woman that I saw touched the knees of "the Christ" and then rubbed her fingers over her baby's face; afterwards she took a piece of flannel that was shaped like a cross, and when it had been blessed by the priest, touched the figure with it and wrapped it around her neck. This, she informed Pascual, was a certain remedy for a sore throat.

Not wishing to stay long in Esquipulas, we soon returned to the house of our entertainer—Antonio Martinez—and from thence proceeded on our journey to Copan. At a short distance out on the plain we found another "douane," and the inspector, who was in a half-drunken state, intimated that he wished to examine the baggage. We had therefore to unload the mule and submit to a strict investigation. The officer proved to be of a very inquiring turn of mind, and not only studied my letters—upside down as usual —but also criticized the texture and quality of various garments. Finally he opened a little box containing some silver-coated pills; these roused his curiosity to

A Cure for Inquisitiveness. 171

the utmost, and I explained that they were a sort of bon-bon and very good for the health. Asking for some water, I pretended to swallow one, and at his earnest request dropped six or seven into the palm of his hand; these he immediately swallowed, stating that he was often troubled with a bad tooth-ache. As we returned to Guatemala by quite a different road, I am unable to say whether his tooth-ache was cured, but, at any rate, it is probable that his inquisitiveness was.

Before we had half crossed the plain the town was hidden from our view, and the great isolated church rising in that wild solitude of mountain and valley looked stranger and more unreal than when we had first beheld it from the lofty hills of Esquipulas.

CHAPTER XIV.

PIEDRA DE AMOLAR—JUPILINGO—SAN JOSÉ—ORIOLES—OSTINOPS
MONTEZUMA—TETERIA VIRIDIS—SWAN ORCHID—COPAN RIVER
—DON PEDRO ARELLANOS—THE MYSTERY OF COPAN—THE
IDOLS—HIEROGLYPHICS — CEIBAS — ANCIENT SEPULCHRE—EL
CERRO DE LAS VENTANAS—CARVED ALTAR—HUMAN SACRIFICE
—STONE HAMMOCK—GARRAPATAS—NIGUAS.

ON the other side of the plain we crossed a river and entered a beautiful country of meadows and glades dotted with clumps of trees; a deep stream crossed and recrossed our path in its descent from the wooded hills that surrounded the grass-land. This was a region of orchids, and each species seemed to have its favourite locality. In one spot a Stanhopea flourished, the flowers of this kind being a bright yellow, barred with chocolate. In another, the trees bore no other species, except one whose flowers were shaped like a China rose and of a delicate pink hue. I gathered twenty of these blossoms off one tree, and I recalled to mind that once or twice in London I had paid five shillings for a single specimen. The other varieties were chiefly those I have already mentioned, and all grew in profusion; such a bouquet of orchids as I gathered during the ride was a treat to be remembered. As we ascended the mountains these plants were less capricious, and two or three varieties grew on the same tree, but before long they disappeared and nothing else adorned the trees except a very common species of Tillandsia which resembled the withered crown of a pine-apple, of which the flower was a spike of insignificant red blossoms.

After a long ride we commenced the steep and rocky descent known as Piedra de Amolar The valley below was hot and misty, and cultivated with tobacco, said to be of very superior quality, which under the name of tobacco of Copan reaches the farthest districts of Honduras. As we rode along hoping to find some resting place for the night, the rain began to fall, but at a cottage we soon reached, we received a kind welcome. The one room that composed the domicile was well occupied, as not only the heads lived there, but also their married daughter and her children. At first there was some discussion as to where I should take up my quarters, but the question was quickly disposed of by my request to be allowed to sleep in the verandah which was gladly acquiesced in. We had a musical evening, as our host played the guitar, and sang some quaint melodies, which the rest of the family joined in efficiently. They insisted on my taking a share in the amusement, and as I could not play the guitar I made it do duty as a banjo, and they were highly delighted with some of tne Christy minstrel songs. The " Old

Folks at Home" particularly pleased them, and though of course they could not learn the words they soon picked up the air, and as we were leaving next morning I heard the children humming it very prettily.

In spite of the rain our morning's ride was not unpleasant, as the path ran by the side of a beautiful stream lined with bamboos and delicate ferns. When we emerged from the forest, the rain ceased and we entered a burning plain covered with dwarf mimosas, and without any shade. After fording the Jupilingo river we ascended the opposite bank, and soon arrived at what I had heard in Guatemala was the large village of Jupilingo where I should find fair accommodation. The village consisted of two huts, one of which was deserted, and at the other there was nothing to eat of any description.

About a league farther on we came to a few more houses, whose collective name was San José; here we obtained some breakfast at a house where all the members of the family—eight or nine persons—had their faces bound up, and were suffering from tooth-ache. I nearly lost our chance of breakfast by an unfortunate mistake. Two of the ladies of the house were so exactly alike that I asked one of them if they were not twins, and the other turned out to be the mother.

In this valley were many beautiful orioles, and among other birds was one[*] of a claret colour with a yellow tail, and large stony bill; in size it resembled a

[*] Ostinops montezuma.

crow. Then there were small birds* with bright yellow breast, black wings and white throat; and larger ones,† about the size of a pigeon, with blackish body and wings, and yellow tail. Yellow seemed to be the favourite colour with the birds of this valley, just as it was the most conspicuous tint among the wild flowers.

Soon after we had resumed our journey, we passed under a tree from one of whose overhanging branches hung a very curious orchid; it was like a bright yellow swan with a reddish bill, and was suspended by a slender stem from its back. There were four or five of these flowers each on a separate stalk, but unfortunately they were out of reach, and the branch was not strong enough to permit of climbing.

Close to this spot was a cross on a slight eminence which marked the boundary between Guatemala and Honduras. In less than two leagues, after crossing this boundary, we arrived at the ford over the Copan river which is here broad swift and deep.

Ascending the hill on the other side we entered the village of Copan which consists of twenty tumble-down houses. In the middle of the small plateau on which the village stands we espied the cabildo, clean looking, and freshly white-washed; Pascual obtained the key, and we at once took possession. A matron from one of the cottages agreed to provide us with food during our stay, and though the few inhabitants soon flocked about us to look at the foreigner, we met with no

* Icteria viridis.   † Ocylus wagleri.

discourtesy, but rather an overwhelming amount of attention.

I had heard that the best guide to the ruins was the alcalde of the village of Cachapa, who lived on the opposite side of the river about two miles off. I therefore sent a messenger asking him to come and see me; whilst I was waiting, the alcalde of Copan—a wretched old Indian—entered the cabildo, followed by half a dozen ill-looking alguazils, and demanded my passport. As none of them could read, and probably had never seen a passport before, they refused to believe it and held a muttered conversation by themselves. Not liking their appearance and wishing to get rid of them, I made a great show of cleaning my revolver, and presently their spokesman came and asked me if I had no other permit. I informed them that I had not, and then wished them a very good evening, upon which they sulkily withdrew. Probably they hoped to make a little money out of me, but were disappointed and never troubled me again.

Pedro Arellanos—the alcalde of Cachapa—proved to be a very intelligent and agreeable young ladino, and promised to come the next day to accompany me to the ruins. The mystery which envelopes the ruins of Copan detracts in some measure from the absorbing interest which a known history would impart, but at the same time gives a charm to these unintelligible monuments of a departed civilization.

As regards the people who built and fashioned the ruined structures there are many surmises. Egypt,

China and even the submerged continent of Polynesia, where pyramidal monuments have been found, have each been suggested as the possible birth-place of the race, but the most general impression is that to the Toltecs may be ascribed the monumental records of Central America. The Toltecs were the most civilized of all the primitive peoples of Mexico, and when in the year 1031 famine, pestilence and war destroyed their monarchy and drove the remnant into Yucatan, what more natural than that they should spread southward, mixing with the Indian tribes of the coast and plain, as at Escuintla, Quirigua, Copan and other places. Against the Toltec origin may be urged the different style of art in these antiquities and those of Mexico, but arguments for and against are so numerous that I do not presume to give more than a passing remark on the subject. One important argument against their Toltec origin is, I think, the fact that all Toltec remains at present discovered, consist of ponderous stone buildings, elaborately sculptured and embellished with hieroglyphics, the stones being heavy blocks and put together with mortar. At Copan there is no vestige of a dwelling of any description. At present the origin of these ruins can only be guessed at, and probably we shall remain in our ignorance until science has deciphered the finely wrought hieroglyphics which are engraven on these monuments. The history of the past can only be revealed by philology—the science of the future.

The small plateau on which stands the present

village of Copan is situated about a hundred feet above the river which flows through a valley entirely surrounded by thickly wooded hills. Looking up the river the eye sees only forest and jungle, but in their dark depths lie the ruins hardly a mile away.

When Don Pedro appeared, according to his promise of the previous night, we at once started, attended by six Indians (including the old alcalde), whose duty was to open the road with their machetes when it was overgrown by branches.

First we forded a deep stream which flowed into the river on our right, and then by a good bridle path entered the forest. Here and there on the road-side were carefully piled up stone-heaps, on which were placed sculptured stones that had been found near. This showed me that the natives were beginning to take some interest in the preservation of their relics, a fact of which I had subsequent proof. I fancy this unexpected care was to be attributed to the intelligence and energy of our guide—Don Pedro. After passing on our left a "hacienda" which stood in a large clearing, our path turned abruptly to the right and we soon arrived at the first obelisk. In a small open space, covered with low brushwood and surrounded by forest trees, stood a richly carved monolith. Its height was over eleven feet, its width three and a half feet, its thickness three feet. The front represented the figure of a man—probably the deity in whose honour it was erected—with strange and complicated head-dress and breast plate; the knees shielded; sandals on the feet;

the hands pointing towards the breast. The whole was deeply cut and surrounded by florid carvings. The back of the monolith consisted of sixteen tablets, each containing emblematic figures. The sides, as well as the front and back, were also richly carved. In front of the idol stood an altar-stone about four feet in height, heavily sculptured, and with grooves on the top, probably intended for the blood of the sacrifice.

At short distances from one another were eight or nine other spaces containing similar monoliths, some erect, some fallen, some almost buried in the ground and partially concealed by weeds and underwood. Though the obelisks were similar in appearance, each idol differed in expression and dress, and the emblem and hieroglyphics varied greatly; the latter were in all cases beautifully and distinctly sculptured, but the lower extremities of the figures were unshapely and unfinished.

Our attendant Indians were very anxious to arrive at one of the monoliths, which proved to be engraven with the finest hieroglyphics, and to show my appreciation of their good taste I asked Don Pedro to find out from them if they could decipher the inscriptions. They shrugged their shoulders and laughed, as they pointed to the pedestal on which was carved in bold characters " J. Higgins." Leaving these "side chapels" as it were, we approached what may be called the main building which consisted of three large quadrangles, or amphitheatres. Here we had to dismount and climb over the fragments of the surrounding stone wall.

Entering the first, we saw numerous remains of sculptured idols ranged near the base of the pyramidal stone wall that separated the quadrangles. In shape this one was rectangular and its size about one hundred yards by fifty; large trees grew in it, but it was remarkably free from brushwood. The intervening walls sloped up in terrace-like steps to a height of more than one hundred feet. The stone work and masonry forming this vast mound was all broken and displaced by the bushes and huge roots of the ceiba trees that grew all over it. Assisted by the dislodged but finely cut stone steps, we ascended the wall and then descended into the second smaller quadrangle. Here were fragments of sculpture and a colossal head which at first looked very awe-inspiring, but on acquaintance gave the idea of a comedy mask. The Indians at this spot busied themselves by replacing and setting up several fallen carved stones, and one great head that we could hardly roll into position I christened after our guide, much to his amusement. The most curious object in this quadrangle was a deep pit, in the side of which was a small opening to a long narrow-covered passage which overlooked the river. At this point the wall which rises from the river bank is 70 or 80 feet in height, but like the others much broken and disturbed. The passage can be seen from the river, and on that account the ruined hill is called "El Cerro de las Ventanas"—the hill with the windows. When this pit was first opened and explored, it was found to contain a great number of red earthenware jars which held human bones buried in lime. A death's head beautifully carved out of the rare green stone—chalchinith—was also found in one of the funeral vases. From this quadrangle we passed into the third, which contained more and better executed pieces of sculpture than we had yet seen. The most notable was an altar six feet square and five feet high ; the top was covered with hieroglyphics and each side was adorned with four crossed-legged Egyptian-looking figures, seated on a hieroglyphic, and each holding something in his hand. Some enormous stone skulls formed steps up one of the sides of this quadrangle, and beside these were fragments of animals and reptiles. In a pit here were some magnificent maiden-hair ferns, and from the trees hung many creepers and twisted leaves.

Outside these rectangular areas were the remains of pyramids and terraces extending for somè distance into the forest, and indicating the probable enclosure at one time of the whole by stone walls. There was no ruined house, nor was there the smallest evidence that the ruins had ever contained a habitation. Copan, I think may be likened to a sculptured Stonehenge. It can hardly be doubted that this place was a great centre of priestly power, and used merely for sacrificial and other religious ceremonies. That the sacrifices were human is only too probable, as Prescott states that up to the time of the Spanish Conquest the practise of human sacrifice was so rife in Mexico, that scarcely any author pretends to estimate the yearly sacrifices throughout the kingdom at less than 20,000, and some carry the number as high as 50,000. As the ruins present no traces of a city, the question naturally arises where could the town of Copan have been that Hernandez de Chaves was sent to subdue in 1530. It seems to me highly probable that the ancient city occupied the site of the present village. The position answers exactly to the description given by a Spanish historian. " On one side defended by a range of mountains, and on the other by a deep fosse and an entrenchment formed of strong beams of timber with loop holes and embrasures." A high mound also which overlooks one of the rivers bears sign of having been used as a fortification. Altogether with the mountains, rivers, and ravine, the plateau would be a formidable stronghold. Fuentes, who wrote the chronicles of Guatemala, in speaking of Copan, affirms that "on entering the gateway there are two fine stone pyramids, moderately large and lofty, from which is suspended a hammock that contains two human figures, one of each sex, clothed in the Indian style. Astonishment is forcibly excited on viewing this structure, because, large as it is, there is no appearance of the component parts being joined together; and though entirely of one stone, and of an enormous weight, it may be put in motion by the slightest impulse of the hand."

I made many inquiries about this curiosity, but no one at Copan knew anything about it. Afterwards I was informed by a gentleman attached to the legation in Guatemala—Señor Gavarette—that he had seen fragments of this hammock in a now cultivated field among the ruins of Quirigua, which lie to the north of Copan, near Port Tzabal.

My scant description of these ruins can only give a general idea of their appearance, but their effect on the mind and imagination may be conceived. The mysterious idols carved by unknown hands, and standing in the midst of a forest as silent as themselves, impress the spectator with mingled feelings of melancholy and curiosity. The cold sculptured faces overlooking the cruel altars must have witnessed scenes so terrible, that even the intervening lapse of centuries cannot dispel the horror they inspire, and their grim features seem to mock at the efforts of man to reveal their written but unread secrets. The green and desolate walls, "all touched with the magic of the past," excite our interest and our sympathy, but that " past" is so buried and unknown, that our sympathy is without the reverence which mortals feel for most expressions of ruin and decay.

In the village of Copan are some more sculptured stones, but so timeworn and moss-covered that the hieroglyphics are indistinct; there is also a large monolith, fallen and broken, the carving on which appears only half finished, but the red paint with which it has been embellished is still apparently fresh. The altar that probably belonged to this column is circular, and stands on a carved pedestal behind a hut, whose occupant uses it as a mortar.

At Copan I made acquaintance with some of the

tolls that the traveller has to pay when journeying through the forests. The ruins were infested with that odious insect, the "garrapata." There are two kinds of these insects, the large and the small, and I think the latter are the worse; they abound in low, damp localities, clustering on the bushes and overhanging boughs from which they drop on the unfortunate passer-by. In appearance they are like minute crabs, and they clutch you firmly, not only with their legs but with two antlers. They do not sting, but the idea of being covered with these pests, which are difficult to remove even when seen, is so irritating that the thought of them works you up into a perfect fever.

Another annoying creature which is found everywhere in Central America, is the "nigua." This insect has an especial fancy for burrowing under the nail of the big toe, where it lays its eggs. Like the "garrapata," it does not hurt you, but a small black spot reveals its presence, and some care is requisite for removing the intruder and its bag of eggs. The depth of the hole made by this insect is often astonishing, and the best mode of healing it is to fill it up with the ash of a cigar. The people say that if the foot is put into cold water before the hole is healed, lock-jaw will ensue; it is much more probable though, that, with them, death would be brought about by the unaccustomed shock of the cold water.

A great deal of rain falls in the Copan valley, April being the only month in which it is quite free from it; the inhabitants say it is healthy, but their appearance belied the statement, and Don Pedro said that fever and ague was very prevalent in some seasons.

The young alcalde had been such a pleasant guide that I was sorry when the time for our departure drew near; he would receive no remuneration for his own trouble or for that of his Indians, and insisted on my acceptance of some strips of dried tobacco that had been grown on his own land, as a remembrance of the ruins of Copan.

CHAPTER XV.

HACIENDA — TIERRA CALIENTE — PASCUAL IN DIFFICULTIES — AZTEC MYTHOLOGY — HAT-BRUSH PLANT — JOCOTAN — SAN JUAN ERMITA — PLAIN OF CHIQUIMULA — RUINED CHURCHES — CHIQUIMULA — VISIT TO THE JEFE POLITICO — GIOTE — CHIMALAPA — SAN AGOSTIN — GUASTATOYA — MOTMOTS — A SPANISH DISH — LAGUNA — EL PUENTE — PONTE AGUELA — SAN JOSÉ — A SLIPPERY DESCENT — A CATARACT — ORIOLES AND THER NESTS — PLAIN OF GUATEMALA.

E had entered Copan from the south, and were now leaving it by a path running due west, our homeward path lying far north of the other.

The forest was damp and hot, and for that reason a wild garden of ferns, orchids, and creepers; parrots screamed in the high trees, and now and then a pair of macaws flew noisily over our heads.

At four leagues from Copan we re-entered Guatemala, and breakfasted at the very flourishing hacienda of Caparja, which is prettily situated in a valley. The family were all busily engaged in drying beef, long strips of which were hanging from lines in front of the house. This gave promise of some fresh meat, a luxury we had not yet tasted on our journey, but we were doomed to disappointment, as the provident folks preferred preparing all for the market rather than indulging in it themselves.

Farther on up the valley we passed some conical red hills covered with oak and fig, the road gradually descending into the "tierra caliente." It is impossible to define the limit that divides the temperate from the hot regions of the central plateau of Guatemala. On the Pacific coast the "tierra caliente" extends without interruption to the mountain range for a uniform distance of fifty miles ; but in the interior, the two zones so encroach on one another that you pass imperceptibly from one to the other, and not unfrequently, in a day's ride, pass in and out of the different regions two or three times.

The broad river on our left flowed fast, and from a rocky eminence about two hundred feet above it we had a fine view of the valley, where the stream formed a perfect horseshoe. The rugged features of mountain landscape were disappearing, and in the fertile lowland and on the hill sides were a few huts, peeping out from banana clumps and maize patches. On our right the high bank was covered with ferns and mosses, and below us the river side was fringed with a thicket of bamboos and creepers. The glassy current of the stream was broken in places by foam-crested rapids, and the swelling hills on the other side were diversified with forest, grass land, and a few feeble efforts at cultivation.

Here the "gazza ladras" were in force again, and cuckoos with long barred tails hopped about the low branches; but these were outnumbered by the lovely orioles—the chief delight of this country's bird-life—which from every bush and tree poured forth notes so sweet and wild that the very sunlight seemed brighter, and the valley itself more free and fair.

Soon we entered a village of which the houses were of poles and thatched with leaves; fan palms, mangoes, bananas, and ceibas bordered the road, which ran by the side of a mountain brook, on whose banks the houses were clustered. Farther on we ascended a hill and the vegetation changed again; on all sides were trees without leaves, but covered with flowers. Some of these blossoms were like the acacia, but of a rich pink; others were in form like a gloxinia, but grew in bunches or panicles; there were two species of the latter—a bright yellow and a pink. Presently we had to cross the river, and when I arrived at the bank, Pascual and the pack-mules were already in the midst of a swift, eddying current, that swept against the tottering animals. Some natives on the other side called to Pascual to go back, as the ford was higher up, but it was too late, and I had the pleasure of seeing my baggage gradually disappearing under the water. They managed to reach the shore without swimming, and when I joined them, Pascual, wet through, with a very pale face, was alternately uttering maledictions on the unlucky mules, and abusing the natives for not having warned him in time.

Following the river for some distance, we at last ascended a hill, and then commenced to cross a pine-clad mountain range. Long and steep were the ascents, but exquisitely fresh and fragrant was the breeze, as it swept gently through the whispering trees and across the emerald glades, which lay in bright sunlight far up among the dark masses of the pines, that crept higher and higher until they fringed the distant ridges. Under the friendly shade of these trees we lost our mournfulness, the atmosphere was clearer, and through the tapering points the sky looked of a deeper blue; the mossy carpet was so inviting that it was impossible to rest resting on it, and to watch the indefatigable woodpeckers as they listened and tapped on the tall trunks, or flew in sweeping darts from tree to tree.

The prettiest of these birds* was of a beautiful chestnut colour, spotted with black, with yellow head and red feathers under the eye. Then there was a black and white species, and also the great black woodpecker,† with its crimson crest and large ivory bill. The Spanish name for this bird—El carpintero—is very appropriate, as it never ceases to carpenter from morning till night.

A few large hawks were the only other occupants of these woods, and their harsh cries were the only inharmonious sounds that broke the stillness of the pine forest.

* Celeus castaneus. † Picus principalis.

It is curious that just as in Greek mythology the pine tree was sacred to Cybele, so among the Aztecs is the same tree sacred to the goddess Mattacueia, the mother of the gods, who fills the place of the Greek divinity.

From the top of the mountain range, where a small cross had been erected, we had a superb view of the distant peaks and of the valley through which flowed in the most serpentine windings the river we had lately crossed. High above its left bank stood the village of Jocotan, to which we were bound. Another valley pierced the mountain on our left, and in its centre was the village of Camotan with a large white church which looked almost as effective as that of Esquipulas.

The descent was long and only remarkable for the number of a curious kind of shrub whose flowers at a distance exactly resembled in colour and shape a green or red velvet hat-brush. On a nearer view we saw that the velvety appearance was given by short, closely set bristles.

Before entering the village we passed some hot sulphur springs, the stream from which crossed our road, and its bed was deeply encrusted with the deposits. Jocotan consisted of a number of tumble-down huts that had been set down promiscuously on the broken, hilly ground. On the highest part stood the church, plaza, and a large cabildo, in one of whose rooms we obtained a comfortable lodging. As our next day's journey was a short one we did not start so early as usual, and before leaving had an opportunity of witnessing the Indian mode of administering justice. The grave alcalde, with his silver-headed black official wand on the table in front of him, being ready to dispose of the cases, the culprits were brought in. Then began such a clamour as was never heard outside a Stock Exchange; prisoner, witnesses, alguazils and spectators all talking at the top of their voices, the men gesticulating frantically, and the women with their chemises held up in front of their faces, as is their peculiar custom. From out of this Babel the old alcalde appeared to gather some information, and after fining the prisoner, ordered the witnesses to be whipped, which put an end to the demonstration. In all villages a similar dispensation takes place daily, except on Sundays and feast days, when all the inhabitants, including the municipality, are drunk.

Our path, after leaving Jocotan, ran by the side of a very hot valley in which were large flocks of parroquets; the hills on the opposite side were red and bare, but on ours were well wooded. Now and then we crossed small tributaries of the large river that watered the fertile lowland, in which were a few palm-leaf huts surrounded by maize and sugar-cane.

A steep descent brought us into a village almost hidden in a palm-grove, at the end of which we crossed a stream and arrived at San Juan Ermita. This was a miserable little village of cane and mud-plastered huts, the whole of which might have been comfortably housed in the enormous church, that resembled one of those triumphs of art in sugar that usually adorn the windows of a confectioner's shop. Within the building all was dust and litter, an odour of decaying wood filled the entire place, and the dingy altars and discoloured walls proved the dire poverty of the expiring race.

At the hovel, where we dismounted for rest and refreshment, we received the customary answer to all our questions as to why the coffee was like mud, why there was no milk when there were plenty of cows, why there was no fruit when the trees ought to be bearing, &c.; the only response that came was, "Señor, we are so poor." I asked for some eggs if the hens were not too poor to lay—they certainly were to eat—and the old dame managed to find a couple which would probably never have been looked for.

When we left the village, another range of pine-covered hills presented itself. On looking back, the white Church of the Hermit, embowered in palms and bananas, and faced by two giant ceibas, appeared wonderfully picturesque; distance had deprived it of its plaster shabbiness, and all we saw was a beautiful sanctuary in a deep green vale surrounded by wooded hills. A narrow ridge, with a ravine on each side, conducted us for some distance across the pine range; then commenced tedious ups and downs with an occasional pretty peep of river, plain and villages. From the summit there was a far extending view of the plain of Chiquimula, with the town at the upper end and bounded by barren-looking hills. The plain of Chiquimula is situated about 1,390 feet above the level of the sea, and though fertile, is hot and dry, the average temperature being about 76°. A long zig-zag descent brought us to a river, which we forded, and again entered the "tierra caliente."

In a short time we approached the village of San Estevan, in which stood a large ruined church. A shady lane greeted us after leaving the village, and everywhere cultivation was in active progress. Ploughing, planting, and clearing land were being carried on all around, and herds of cattle were dotted about the green meadows of the broad flat plain. The hedges by the road-side were literally alive with small birds, and in the high trees were green parroquets, crow-black birds, and other larger kinds.

I could not help noticing, as I had previously done, that nearly all the smaller birds of this part of the country had striped heads, generally black and white; no matter what species, there was the invariable striped head. More numerous than any, was a bird very like our hedge sparrow, it had the same sober plumage, uttered the same sweet plaintive notes, and was of equally retiring habits, but the little head was barred with brownish and white stripes. In this lane we passed a regiment of soldiers moving at a swift trot on their way to Esquipulas; they looked very hot and dusty, and as most of their arms were being carried by Indians, who brought up the rear, I thought it would not have been a bad opportunity for an attack by the enemy of San Salvador. A little farther on we

o

saw on our right an enormous ruined church, roofless and desolate; it had been built by the Spaniards on the site of an Indian village, but a succession of earthquakes had dismantled the building and driven the inhabitants away. Since then it had been used as a burial-ground.

Chiquimula, though called a city, was the first and last place with any pretensions of a town that I saw between Guatemala and Copan. Here were paved streets, a large plaza with cathedral and municipal buildings, a market and shops ranged under the wide colonnades. A company of soldiers were performing some strange light infantry manœuvres in the plaza, the chief object of each individual apparently being to reach and remain under the shade of a large palm-tree that grew in the centre.

Thinking we might obtain some better accommodation than usual, I made some inquiries, and at last a chemist offered me the use of a house of which he possessed the key, as the owners were absent at Zacapa.

We were soon settled in the comfortable quarters which we had taken possession of, after the fashion of hermit crabs, and whilst Pascual sought a saddler to repair a broken stirrup-leather, I went out to see the sights. I had only gone a few steps when I received a message from the "Jefe politico,"—the chief of the Department—intimating a wish for my presence. As our entrance into the town had not been very imposing, I was at a loss to know how our arrival had reached the ears of the "Jefe." It turned out that he had been expecting us for some days, and at the request of the kind War Minister at Guatemala, who, imagining that we would visit Chiquimula before going to Copan, had procured a guide and prepared letters which might have been of use. That evening we renewed our stock of candles—most necessary articles—and laid in a sufficient quantity of bread to last until we reached Guatemala, forty leagues away.

When we had seen the last of the beautiful palms that surround the town of Chiquimula, the aspect of the country grew brown, rocky and dull. After crossing some ravines and a mountain-spur, we ascended a bold and precipitous range of hills. The ascent was so rocky and so covered with loose stones that we had to dismount and proceed on foot. The trees that grew on the steep sides were leafless; there was no point of colour in the landscape save a few coarse splashes here and there of red and yellow from some flowering but unfoliaged shrub, and an occasional flush of deep crimson and orange from the "hat-brush" plant, which lined the banks of the dried-up watercourses. Another wide plain spread out beneath us when we reached the summit of the range; a river flowed through it, and on the opposite side appeared the town of Zacapa, from which place an old and now almost unused road leads to the Bay of Honduras. The improving condition of the Republic was here shown by the deep cuttings through the woods which had been made preparatory to laying down a line of telegraph; but there was no work in progress just then, as the impending war had taken away all the available labour.

After descending the mountain we entered the department of Zacapa, which appeared to be a region of cactus and mimosa. Its entire length is traversed by the Motagna, the largest river in Guatemala, and which, rising in the mountains of Los Altos, flows in a northeasterly direction into the Gulf of Honduras.

Hitherto our road had run parallel with the Copan River, which near Chiquimula flows into the river of the same name, now we followed the latter in its northerly course until we approached the town of Zacapa, above which it falls into the Motagna. Before reaching the town, we turned off abruptly to the left and took the path that winds along the right bank of the main river. The inhabitants who live near these rivers, seldom call them by any other name than that which designates their own town, village, or even hut, and I was much puzzled at first by hearing what was evidently the same river called by a variety of appellations. We breakfasted at a collection of huts described as the "Llano de la Fragua," whose only beauty was in its name, and from there we proceeded along a hot uninteresting road.

From Chiquimula the vegetation of the lowlands was almost entirely of the cactus species. The fields were surrounded by cactus hedges, and the fencing of the road-side was made of cactus limbs. The fields so carefully hedged contained little else than cactuses, mixed with shrubs of cassia and mimosa.

Everywhere the grey green cactus was seen assuming the most fantastic shapes, round, flattened, and conical. Here rose a Cercus, like a gigantic candelabrum with a hundred wax-tipped branches; there stood in rows enormous tubes of the organ cactus, their tops foaming with snowy down, and painfully reminding the traveller of huge tankards of ale. Many of these giants were thirty or forty feet in height, and far overtopped the spreading "morro" trees, with their dark green leaves like mistletoe. Below them flourished the common "opuntia," whose fleshy and jointless cylinders seemed to grow at random out of one another, until stopped by the small orange-coloured flower or its pulpy fruit. Here were sufficient plants to stock a cochineal plantation if anyone had thought it worth his while. Hot, dry and barren was the appearance of these cactus forests, through which the unshaded road passed, orioles, parroquets, and blue birds giving them the only life and colour they possessed.

The night after leaving Chiquimula we slept at Giote in the verandah of a hut, whose mistress not only gave us a very good supper, but also cooked a tolerably plump chicken for our next day's luncheon.

It was still a cactus land through which we rode next morning, but diversified with trees covered with crimson and lilac blossoms. After a hot ride along a white limestone ridge, we descended into the village of Chimalapa which was buried in palms and dracœnas. Here we crossed a tributary of the Motagna, and then followed the course of the latter river for some distance. Small Indian settlements were on its banks, and the inhabitants were mostly occupied in fishing, bathing, and clothes-washing. Cranes and herons stalked solemnly about the shallows, and large kingfishers* skimmed swiftly over the deep pools. On the bare hills on the other side of the river stood the church of San Agustin, a great pile of masonry, by whose side the village houses looked like grave stones.

Near the straggling village of Gicaro we turned away from the river, and after a few more leagues of hot, dusty travelling left the cactuses behind, and entered a dark shady gorge. In the rainy season this long narrow ravine must be very picturesque when the mountain stream flows through it, but now the sleepy river had indeed gone to bed, and we toiled over rocks and boulders as if they had never known water.

The day's journey had been very hot and long, that it was dark when, after ascending a hill, we arrived at the town of Guastatoya situated in a narrow plain surrounded by high hills. A native offered us the use of his cottage which he said was the most desirable in the place; when we arrived there we found it contained nothing else but the picture of a saint and a quantity of Indian corn pods. The latter were very welcome, for the mules, and we at once set our host to work at husking and shelling.

Our path from Guastatoya was through an intensely hot and dry country; here we saw a great number of mot-mots,† a small handsome species with long thick

* Ceryle torquata. † Cumomota supercilieris.

silvery green eyebrows, and with the two long tail feathers much unfledged. The natives call it the "pajaro bobo" foolish bird—on account of the melancholy low note it continually utters, even when you approach close to it. A succession of ravines and stony hill ranges, intersected by valleys cultivated with sugar cane and bananas, brought us to Florido, a village about five leagues from Guastatoya. With the expectation of obtaining breakfast we dismounted before a very clean-looking cottage, in the verandah of which a couple of hammocks were suspended. We were received by a pleasant matronly woman, whose numerous children were far cleaner and neater than any we had before seen ; the eldest daughter—a young bride—was extremely fair, and had most delicately cut features, and there was an air of refinement about the whole family which was most remarkable. The children soon caught a bird that was certainly "no chicken," but it answered the purpose, and was speedily turned into very good soup, and tough, but, for hungry people, palatable fowl. Some eggs, the produce of the same bird, were added to the repast, and our hostess laughingly remarked, as she placed an omelette on the table, that the old hen had done her duty towards our entertainment. In addition to these luxuries, there was a dish of meat that the good lady called "duelos y quebrantos" the meaning of which I did not discover until later. It appears that when a farmer loses an ox or a sheep by accidental death, he cuts it up and distributes it among his neighbours, keeping a few odd bits for his own table, hence the name—"grief and broken bones."

When we left Florido our road was uphill, then through a delightfully shaded ravine we reached a village surrounded by well cultivated land ; the houses here looked better cared for than usual, and one hacienda we passed on our left near Laguma had all the appearance of a comfortable farm-house. Soon the ascent of a steep mountain commenced, and when after a laborious climb—for the mules—we reached the top, we found we had to descend by an equally precipitous path into a narrow valley that lay deep down below us, and in which was the village to which we were bound—Puente.

At the bottom of the descent we crossed a bridge of stone and cemented brick, standing on a rock foundation. One arch spanned the stream, but at the side there was a supplementary one to carry off the water in time of floods. An inscription on the bridge stated that it had been commenced in 1826, and after various delays was finished in 1840. The view up the gorge, close above the bridge, was very wild and picturesque. The mountain torrent rushed down in falls of white foam between massive walls of rock hundreds of feet in depth, until it almost reached the bridge where it subsided into deep clear pools, and shallow rapids. Above, the mountains were clothed with pines and oaks, the jutting points were hung with flowery creepers, and below there was a green mass of bamboo and broad-leaved arums.

The valley was so narrow that there seemed to be no room for more than the stream, which when it had passed the bridge widened out into a river; at the far end a chain of mountains closed it in, and beyond that again other ranges lorded it over all, their green crests meeting the blue of the overarching sky. The village, which was close to the bridge, consisted of eight or nine houses, and in the verandah of one of these I established myself for the night. Pascual, as usual, sheltered himself on a bench near the entrance to prevent the intrusion of pigs and dogs, which wander about at night in search of stray morsels. On this occasion his precautions were not wholly successful, as in the morning I discovered that an old hog had run off with one of my boots, and a cow had swallowed my soap which was wrapped up in a leaf of maize, and carefully deposited on the wall of the verandah. The ancient Greek, when he had his shoes stolen, lifted himself up and said, "May they fit the feet that they ran away with!" Pascual said nothing of sort, but with very forcible language and a stick pursued the pig and brought back the property.

On a few previous days I had been obliged to make my toilet in the presence of the family in whose house I was lodging, but never until now before the entire village population, who regarded with the greatest curiosity such novelties as brushes, &c. Fortunately even the most embarrassing situations have their limit, and making as dignified an exit from the village as circumstances would allow, we commenced the long ascent of the mountain which rose abruptly behind it. Soon after arriving at the top, we caught a glimpse of Agua and Fuego over a distant mountain range; continuing along a narrow ridge we passed the village of Ponteazuela, most picturesquely situated and commanding on both sides lovely views of the deep-lying valleys. Leaving behind us the rich pastures and well cultivated lands round San José, we descended into a hot vale by a very steep road paved with cemented stones, and so slippery that we had to dismount and allow the animals to slide down as best they could. Sugar cane, oranges and bananas grew plentifully here, and we breakfasted under a fine ceiba tree that grew near a pretty hacienda overlooking a stream. At this point we were five leagues from Puente and seven from Guatemala. When we again reached the table-land, we recognised once more our old friends the barrancas. Near one of these Pascual, who was ahead of me, suddenly stopped, then turned and rode back in great excitement; I imagined that he had seen a deer or perhaps a congar, and hastened to meet him, when he informed me that if I rode quickly to the spot I might have the fortune to see the beautiful creature that he had disturbed—" un conejo grande"—a big rabbit.

Near a village where there were some stone quarries, we crossed a stream which was fed by a cataract that rushed down a deep hill cleft. Here grew palms, dracœnas and heliconias forming a pleasant green nook, in contrast with the dazzling white of the hot unsheltered road. One of the rarer species of orioles,*

* Icterus wagleri.

with black head and breast, we met with in this locality, and from one of the neighbouring trees depended two of their beautifully worked pouches. A few days before we had ridden under a similar oriole's nest, which was so near the ground that by standing up in my stirrups I was able to look into it by pulling the branch from which it was hanging; it proved to be an old one, but it was strange that the bird should have built it in a spot almost within reach of every passer-by. I know of no object, except a bird's nest, that ingenious mortals have not reproduced with more or less success, and probably there is nothing more wonderful.

> "Of birds how each according to her kind
> Proper materials for her nest can find,
> And build a frame, which deepest thought in man
> Would or amend or imitate in vain."

Winding round barrancas, ascending and descending hills, we gradually approached the city. The indifferent road suddenly changed into a broad highway, which had lately been made, the old path running far below it; market-women, mule teams and droves of cattle gave a lively appearance to the scene and looked especially gay to us after the solitary tracks we had been traversing. At a turn in the road we saw the plain of Guatemala below us, and beyond the city rose the great volcanoes, touched by the setting sun but standing out as clearly and grandly as when we had said farewell to them in full noon. We had quitted the plain by the south, we now re-entered it by the north-east, and by one of the prettiest roads in the neighbourhood. Descending by a deep cutting in the wooded hills, we crossed a brawling stream and ascended by a paved road to the green table-land. Orange, mango, coffee, sapote trees and an abundance of foliage adorned the gardens in the outskirts of the town; passing through these we wended our way through the district of Candelaria, leaving the hill of Carmen on our right and in a very short time drew rein in the patio of the Gran Hotel.

That evening instead of eggs and tortillas, I indulged in a repast which an elegant Californian mining phrase would describe as "a hunky old spread, with all the express French frills."

CHAPTER XVI.

MILITARY SERVICE—STRENGTH OF ARMY—EQUIPMENT—FOREIGN OFFICERS—EL POLITECNICO—CONGRESS—A FEDERAL UNION—JUSTICE—FALSE WITNESSES—JUSTICE IN SALVADOR—RIGHTS OF FOREIGNERS—INHABITANTS OF CENTRAL AMERICA—A PROBABLE FUTURE—PETEN AN UNKNOWN LAND—DEPARTURE FROM THE CITY.

THE aspect of the city at this time was very war-like. Drill was continually going on in the plaza, and small bodies of cavalry meandered through the streets in single file to create an effect of numbers. At parades, and when mounting guard, these soldiers pay some attention to uniform and general smartness, but a regiment on the march presents a sorry appearance. Men in dirty white trousers and red shirts, others in blue jackets and with trousers tucked into strange boots; many with no shoes on at all, and most wearing two hats—a straw one, with shako or forage cap on the top. Short in stature—a man of five feet six inches would be a grenadier—and with not very prepossessing countenances, but active and hardy, they make up an army superior in numbers and in ability to carry on undisciplined warfare to any that the other small Central American Republics might place in the field against it.

Military service is demanded for a certain period from all men between eighteen and fifty years of age, with the exception of Indians, priests, students and those who prefer paying an annual tax of fifty dollars. The distinction between an Indian and a ladino is sometimes so minute that the question of military service has to be decided by the fact of wearing shoes; if the individual wears them he is a ladino and consequently has to join the army, if he does not wear them, he is an Indian and exempt. As for the Indians they carry on the transport service for the officers, and in times of necessity act very well in fortifications and barriers. The strength of the army in war time is estimated at about 16,000 men, though more could be raised, if necessary, and if arms were forthcoming.

The pay of the soldiers—when they get it—is three réals—1s. 6d.—per day, and out of this they clothe and support themselves. Thus the quartermaster's department is not difficult to manage as the men carry their own baggage, which consists of a woollen serape in which they wrap themselves when they lie down on the ground to sleep; washing utensils are not required, and for food they take whatever they can find.

At the present time the expected war was popular, and though in some cases coercion was necessary, yet on the whole the country responded well to the President's appeal for soldiers. Just then, however, they were not called upon for active service, as the trouble with Salvador was arranged, and after a review of the troops their arms were collected and they were disbanded. The President in a touching address, which was freely circulated throughout the city, thanked the soldiers for their loyalty in answering so promptly to his summons for the maintainance of the honour of the country, and dismissed them to renew their peaceful occupations in the bosom of their families. It was an amusing scene to see the regiments marching out of the city on returning to their respective districts ; there were men carrying bird cages, others dragging horses and dogs, officers with drawn sword in one hand and a game cock in the other, and all in fancy costumes and with the air of heroes.

Two months later, war was really commenced between Guatemala and San Salvador and after some severe battles, in which the former was always victorious, President Barrios entered Salvador, and finally dictated the terms of peace. Not only did the army of Guatemala outnumber that of its opponents, but it was better armed with the best American breech-loading rifles, and the artillery was equipped with Gatling guns and Krupp cannons.

To both sides foreign officers had given their services, but the native commanding officers on the side of Guatemala were superior in skill and tactics to those of Salvador. Besides General Barrios himself, there was General Lopez Uraga, an astute strategist, and well known as being an able organiser and good officer; his text-books on military art and science are extensively circulated throughout all the States of Spanish America. General Solaris, too, is another soldier of experience and capability.

Guatemala is progressing in military as well as in civil matters, and its college—Politecnico—is a well-conducted institution; the young cadets are quick and smart, and most of them can drill a company in a very efficient manner. Good instructors in mental and physical exercise are provided, and no pains are spared in expanding the intellect and improving the condition of the youth of the country who aspire to military honours.

Between the first threatenings of war and its final outbreak, a Congress was held in the city of Guatemala, to discuss the propriety of forming a Federal Union. Plenipotentiaries from the five republics met, with the ostensible purpose of conferring upon the means of uniting as one nation. If they were really to unite, there would be some reason to hope that progress would be made in civilisation, and the development of the resources of those regions. It was feared, however, that the proposed Union was merely intended to be a loose confederation, possessing no central powers, capable of accomplishing nothing but the creation of offices. A similar Union had already been tried more than once, and by those very States, and each time had been soon abandoned, therefore there was small reason to hope for better success this time.

I left Guatemala during the Congress, and so do not know what took place, but as war shortly afterwards broke out, much good could hardly have been effected.

The government of Guatemnla is called republican representative, and consists of a President, Ministers of the Interior, Exterior, and of Public Instruction, and also a body of fifteen members, charged with the execution of justice and public interest.

A visitor to this country cannot help noticing the contrast, between the administration of justice and that of the other wheels of government. In the latter case, there is exhibited not only talent and a painstaking zeal, but also a brilliant executive power, whilst in the former there seems to be much incompetency and sometimes a disregard for individual rights. In the town as well as in the village, complaints are heard of the difficulty of obtaining redress for the most barefaced acts of injustice.

The following story, told me by the sufferer himself —a gentleman of high position in the city—will illustrate the faults spoken of. This gentleman advanced one thousand dollars to an army officer, on account of corn which was to be delivered. Time went on, and as he neither got the corn nor the money back, he sued the officer. To his astonishment, he was himself sued for damages amounting to five thousand dollars. The officer said that he had offered the corn—which he had never done—and it had been refused, and he had thereby suffered losses to the amount stated. He owned at first that he had received the money in

P

advance, but afterwards disputed the point, and when, after some weeks' continued postponement, the case was resumed, the judge was referred to the previous admission as being set down on a certain page of the documents, which would go far towards proving the rights of the affair. When the judge referred to the page mentioned, nothing could be found bearing on the subject, and it was subsequently discovered that the pages had all been purposely re-numbered. After some months' litigation, and finding himself as far from redress as ever, the gentleman went to the Minister, but it was of no avail, and he fully expected to lose his thousand dollars and also some more in damages.

One of the difficulties in the way of justice is the ease with which false witnesses can be obtained, and their constant use. Not long ago a mother wanted to obtain the care of her child from the father; she was asked if he ill-used it, and replied, "No; but I can get plenty of witnesses to prove that he does."

Owing to this system, a case occurred a short time back in Salvador which might have terminated very seriously. A young foreigner of good standing saw a woman enter his warehouse and steal a roll of cotton; he followed her and took it away. Next day he was arrested, and accused of having stolen a diamond necklace from this woman (many of these people have old jewelry), and five or six witnesses swore that they had seen him take it. He indignantly refused to plead, and after some months—he had of course obtained bail —-the President, who was a friend of his, came and

Inhabitants of Guatemala.

informed him that he had been found guilty, and would be sentenced to five years in the chain gang; why did he not follow the custom of the country (which he had been long enough in to know), and contradict these witnesses? As he steadily refused to employ false witnesses on his side, the President at last said that the only way of settling it would be to make him an officer, thereby necessitating a new trial. He was consequently made a colonel, and nothing more was heard of the transaction.

But after all, an isolated case of injustice does not prove its habitual adoption, and may arise from absence of ability rather than the want of will to judge rightly; and though a native may occasionally have cause to complain, yet so far as my observation goes I should say that the rights of foreigners in Guatemala are respected by the authorities.

Regarding the inhabitants themselves of Central America, it is commonly stated that they are so quiet and peaceful that there is no necessity for a traveller to carry, much less to use, a weapon of any kind, either offensive or defensive. My knowledge extends only to Guatemala, but I can say that in my journeys through that State I never heard a rude remark, nor did I ever see any one that the most timid imagination could regard as a dangerous character.

This speaks well not only for the people but also for the Government; only a few years ago, comparatively, it was dangerous to traverse the city after nightfall, now the *serenos*—watchmen—have but little else to do than sleep in some comfortable corner, or mournfully chant forth the passing hour. How different this from Mexico, where everybody is armed, and when on the road is continually on the look-out for robbers!

Everything points to a future for Guatemala; exports are increasing, modern improvements are being introduced, agriculture is extending, and, above all, the government is attending to public instruction. Education will create a new class of worthy citizens, and will lead to the intellectual and material prosperity of a true Republic.

It often happens that people who live in a country have never seen and care but little for places that are of great interest to a stranger. I had been surprised that so little was known in Guatemala about Copan, but was not so much astonished that nothing at all was known about the distant regions of Peten. No one had ever been there, and all sorts of difficulties and dangers were predicted in my intended journey thither, and from thence to the Gulf of Mexico. No muleteer even had reached Peten, and Pascual was warned about the utter impossibility of travelling on the road to that place. Fortunately he paid no attention to the croakers, and agreed to accompany me, knowing that we should find an Indian guide at Coban—a town in Vera Paz, and about thirty-five leagues feom the city of Guatemala.

I had been greatly disappointed, on my return from Copan, at finding that the Italian minister—the Duca di Licignano—had left for San Salvador on official business. He had been very anxious to accompany me to Peten, and by his departure I lost a very charming companion. It was no use complaining, but the journey before me did look more lonely, and when I bade a cordial farewell to my kind friends it looked lonelier still, but the thoughts of a new and strange country soon dispelled unavailing regrets, and shed upon me a glamour of hopeful anticipation.

It was a thorough Guatemala morning: fresh, clear, and with a silvery blue sky, when the mules tramped steadily through the gateway, and in a very short time we had lost sight of the plain and city, and were on our way to the north.

CHAPTER XVII.

SPIRITUAL RELATIONS—CARRIZAL—VUELTA GRANDE—THE RIVER MOTAGNA—HOT SPRINGS—LLANO GRANDE—A SUGAR PLANTATION—MOUNTAINS OF CHOACUS—AN INVALID CARRIAGE—SAN GERONIMO—SALAMA—FLOWERING YUCCAS—MOUNTAINS OF QUILILA—SANTA ROSA—VALLEY OF PURULA—CABILDO.

ROAD is such a familiar object that the effect it gives to a landscape is often overlooked, but I think that just as a castle on a hill or a cottage on the hillside enhances the natural beauty of a scene, so does a road render more attractive the country through which it winds.

Who has not looked with a sort of wondering pleasure even at such an unromantic affair as a railway-train, when in a hundred curves and grades it reaches gradually the white speck of road that once seemed so far above it! apparently motionless, yet always moving, sometimes in full view, then twisting snake-like out of sight, leaving no trace behind it except a soft white cloud that clings for a moment to the green mountain bank. Perhaps it is only the imagination inspired by the mystery of the road that gives it beauty—I know not ; but whether silent and deserted, or when alive with the freight it bears, I always fee grateful to the road for its attractive utility.

Had it not been for the broad white road which connects the city of Guatemala with the village of Chinautla, the ravine through which it runs would have lost half its charm. As it was, it formed a very picturesque feature as it wound round the hills, on one side a rocky wall and on the other a sloping bank, along the bottom of which flowed a stream. In many places the roadside, overhanging the ravine, was strengthened with upright logs of wood arranged in terraces; on these flowering shrubs had grown, and the many-coloured blossoms produced an effect that could hardly have been surpassed by a landscape gardener.

The village of Chinautla is about three leagues from the city and is a favourite watering-place. It is prettily situated, and a broad but shallow stream flows through it. The cottages are perched about on the rocks and on the river banks, half concealed by mango and other fruit trees, and having little gardens in which the Poinsettia* with its crimson-leaved coronet is very conspicuous. The old road from the city here descends into the village by a steep path cut out of the sand-stone; the scenery on this road, which lies far above the new one, is wild and picturesque, and affords some magnificent views of the barrancas.

On a former visit to Chinautla I had witnessed a

* Flor de Pascua.

curious Indian custom. Two very ragged old Indians met and at once commenced to salute one another; first they solemnly removed their tall black straw hats, then they kissed one another on each cheek, and finally one knelt before the other and kissed his hands and knees, all the time uttering benedictions. I thought one of them must have been a priest, in spite of his unclerical aspect, but I was informed that these men regarded one another in the light of "spiritual relations." I could not learn what constituted this relationship, but those who are thus connected are bound by oaths and custom to treat one another with the greatest reverence and respect.

The Indians of this country are deeply imbued with superstition, but are harmless enough when their prejudices are not interfered with. Among other strange ideas, it is a popular belief that foreigners eat children. In Salvador, not long ago, two foreigners were at breakfast, and for a joke showed a ham bone to an Indian child, saying that that was what naughty children changed to. The child ran and told the people that white men were eating children, and the fanatical Indians were on the point of killing them, when the padre said that of course it was right to kill them, but it would be better to try them first and shoot them after. In the meantime he sent a messenger for some soldiers, who arrived just in time to save their lives.

The Indians who live near the Volcano of Pacaya resent any attempt by a foreigner to ascend the mountain, as they say he is only going to poison their river. This water poisoning is another very general superstition, and it is related that a few years ago a foreigner was killed on the spot because he was seen mixing a seidlitz powder in a glass of water.

After Chinautla the fantastic rock formations disappear, the valley is more open, and at San Antonio the great highway—which is eventually to extend to Izabal (which is connected by water with the Bay of Honduras)—stops. The prospect of war had caused work on it to be suspended. About seven leagues is the length of the road that has been made up to the present, and it is very doubtful when the remainder will be accomplished. Here we branched off to the left and commenced the ascent of the mountain. After we had reached the top, we followed a convenient ridge and at last reached Carrizal, where we stopped for the night at a clean and comfortable hacienda, whose proprietor —a queer old fellow with the most enormous bushy eyebrows—owned the plantain and coffee plantations in the valley below the house. A neat little chapel was attached to the building, flowers adorned the patio, birds sang in cages, cows were milked, and altogether our quarters were very pleasant ones.

When we continued our journey at daybreak on the following morning, the path still followed the ridge we had been traversing the previous day. The trees that crested the mountains and bordered our broad ledge of turf and moss were all festooned with the tillandsia, and as the sun rose behind them, it was very beautiful to see the sparkling brilliancy of the dew-covered moss. We might have been riding through an avenue of crystal, so sharp and transparent were the drooping stalactites of the over-arching boughs. For the moment the trees had thrown off their funeral garments and had decked themselves in bridal robes of silvery lace; nothing was wanting but a few forest fairies to realize a poet's words :

> "A million little diamonds
> Twinkled on the trees,
> And all the little maidens said,
> 'A jewel, if you please ?'
> But while they held their hands outstretched,
> To catch the diamonds gay,
> A million little sunbeams came
> And stole them all away."

Further on, our ridge ran due north for some distance, then suddenly turned off at an abrupt right angle to the east. At this corner, appropriately named Vuelta Grande, was a picturesque little village, each house of which crowned a separate cone-shaped hill and commanded magnificent views of the surrounding ravines and distant mountain ranges. Presently we caught a glimpse for the last time of the city of Guatemala, which lay far away to the south on the same level as our own; between us was a tossed and broken valley, bounded by wooded hills that stretched towards the distant plain.

During our descent of the Sierra, which was extremely hot and tedious, we noticed that the soil in many places was interspersed with breadths of a shining sandy material that at a distance looked like wet mud; wherever a stratum of this substance crossed our path the adjoining hills were entirely composed of it.

At a cottage that we passed, we were regaled with some armadillo soup, which was very refreshing, and far preferable to the native coffee. Soon afterwards we reached the river Motagna, or as it is here called the Rio Grande, and which separates the department of Guatemala from that of Lower Vera Paz. We crossed by a strongly-built wooden suspension bridge, the entrance to which was under lock and key. The object of this precaution I could not discover, as no toll was demanded by the gate-keeper and it entailed unnecessary trouble on everyone.

At some distance from the river we passed hot sulphur springs near the village of La Canoa. The ground all round them was stony and bare, but appeared to have great attractions for sand-pipers, turnstones and birds of that description. Hard by this place we once more were attracted by the strange growth and forms of tree roots. On the banks of a tiny stream were the remains of a bridge, and through the stones ran the roots of lofty trees hanging bare and exposed, and extending for thirty and forty feet on either side of the ruined buttress. Enormous blocks of milk white quartz stood in the water-bed each bearing a large shrub on its summit, the roots vainly endeavouring to attach themselves firmly to the smooth surface. But the most curious appearance of all was that of a fine wide-spreading tree about fifty feet in height that was perched on the top of a pyramid-shaped stone, ten feet high. The trunk of the tree—three feet in diameter—overlapped its support, but was retained in position by the slender roots, which had encased the stone as with a net, and then, burying themselves in the ground, had made a close prisoner of the huge block. In the same village were other similarly caged stones, but on a smaller scale. We stopped for the night at a large hacienda in the Llano Grande valley, where there were extensive sugar-cane plantations.

Some people might imagine that in a plantation where some hundred labourers were employed, sugar would be obtainable as an adjunct to coffee, but it was not; there was nothing but the usual honey syrup. There was not even the black brown "panela," or "poor man's sugar," as it is called, which is made by merely boiling the juice so that it will harden in cooling. Perhaps the absence of the proprietor accounted for the scarcity of provisions. At the far end of this valley we crossed the Caña Brava—a pretty stream lined with feathery bamboos and other shrubs—and then commenced the ascent of the mountains of Choacus. Here the scenery was very grand, our road winding up the steep side of a pine-clad mountain, and high above a narrow vale, on the other side of which rose almost perpendicular rocky walls. A few trickling silver threads, which in the rainy season would be foaming cataracts, sparkled over the hanging cliffs, and imparted a deeper green to the rank foliage at their base. The air was scented with the delicious odour

of a small white flower that grew on the bushes on the
road side, and amongst these blossoms the bees and
humming birds kept up an untiring revelry. Mingled
with these plants were shrubs whose leafless and
straggling boughs were redeemed from positive ugliness
by rich creamy flowers. Yellow was no longer the
prevailing colour as it was in Los Altos, but flowers of
a silvery white or delicate pink were interspersed with
lindenias, fuschias and rose-coloured dahlias.

During our descent from these mountains we met a
most primitive conveyance drawn by two oxen, that
were toiling up the stony path where probably no
vehicle had ever been before. Some rough planks had
been placed on a frame work, underneath which were
four solid blocks of wood as wheels. The body of the
carriage consisted of a large iron cauldron; this had
been half filled with straw and on it lay a poor sick
woman who was being taken to the hamlet we had
that morning left. A few green boughs fastened to
four upright poles formed a shade from the intensely
hot sun.

The plain which we at length reached was cultivated,
and hedges broke the uniformity of the fields, but it
looked arid and treeless. A few farm-houses were
scattered about, and cattle wandered listlessly among
the boulders and on the barren hill-side where there
was little else than cactuses and Indian figs. In the
eastern corner of this plain, and surrounded with fresh
verdure, stands the old Dominican convent of San
Geronimo, which now belongs to a Spanish company

who have there built a sugar refinery and cultivate the cane to a large extent. A recipe for liqueur that the ancient proprietors left behind is still used, but I was not impressed with the quality of the beverage when I tasted it in Salama. This town, although the capital of Vera Paz, is a melancholy looking place and reflects the dullness of the surrounding plain. It boasts though of an hotel—the Vera Paz—which we comfortably filled, as fortunately there were no other travellers.

In the evening when I visited the plaza—in which was a magnificent palm tree and a fountain ornamented with some painted mermaids—there were sounds of music issuing from the church, and on entering I found that a child was being baptized. The ceremony was performed to the accompaniment of a harp and piano, respectively played by an Indian and a ladino; polkas and jigs were the favourite tunes and they were executed with as grave an air as if they had been the most solemn hymns. Near the church was a row of tall yuccas in full bloom, and in the bright moonlight the panicles of white bells gleamed like silver, the long leaves standing out clear and strong. It is said that the flowers of these plants close in the day time, but I went to look at them once more before starting the next morning; I could not see any difference in the blossoms, but the leaves were slightly drooping.

We left Salama early, and after crossing the Rio Rabinal by an ugly covered bridge with white buttresses, traversed a barren plain and then commenced the zig-zag ascent of the mountains of Quilila.

Vale of Purula.

Looking back we could see a green thread winding round, the lower hills marked the course of the stream we had lately twice crossed, and adjoining patches of cane and maize alone diversified the brown and arid soil of the plain of Salama. When we arrived at the summit of the first range we had at once to descend, and then after crossing streams and ravines finally ascended the heights which mark the highest point of the Cordilleras between Guatemala and Coban. The sides of the hills were here clothed with thick underbrush, amongst which grew dwarf palms and flowering dracœnas. Forests of pine and oak covered the slopes of the adjoining mountain ridges, and in the recesses of the dark ravines an occasional light gleam marked the corn or cane patch of a poor native.

A narrow, rocky gorge introduced us to the valley of Santa Rosa in which stands the village of the same name, prettily situated on rising ground. Here we branched off in order to visit what I had heard described as the "celebrated grottoes of Purula." At the extremity of a long narrow stretch of pasture land we passed a comfortable farm-house, and then ascending a short hill looked down into a valley. One could not wish to see a more delightfully romantic spot than this vale of Purula. The green meadow-land through which a stream flowed was surrounded by lofty peaks, some shapely and soft, others wild and fantastic, but all covered with thick forests, out of which masses of beetling rock hung over the ferny slopes and the cool glens that lay between them. The crest of each isolated cone was hidden in white clouds, and the grey mist that drifted across the black crags and down the green passes changed to a drizzling rain as we rode into the valley. On the path-side were wild raspberries and blackberries, which grew under the shining leaves of the liquid amber trees, showing in their rank luxuriance a proper appreciation of the incessant rain that falls in these parts.

At the upper end of the valley, in which we saw some purple lobelias, we entered the village whose population is almost entirely Indian, and as each house stands in a large garden it is necessarily of some extent. Mango, orange, sapote and other trees here mingle with tree ferns, palms and ceibas on the sheltered hillside, above which are pines and oaks, and below a tangled growth of cane, maize, bamboo and deep grass. Towards evening it became bitterly cold, and the rain which fell in torrents poured in through the roof of the crazy cabildo where we had to pass the night. Opposite our domicile a fine new cabildo in brick and stone was in process of erection, but at present its rooms were too full of lime and rubbish to admit of habitation. The alcalde could not make out the object of our visit; as for grottoes he knew nothing about them, and I began to suspect that we were on a wild goose chase. No one in Guatemala had ever seen them, though many were ready to speak of their beauty. At last a man appeared who said he knew where there was a cave in the mountains, and promised to take us there next day.

A Tea-party.

That evening to pass away the time I gave a tea party to the head-people of the village, and as none of them had even heard of such a thing as tea they were pleased with the novelty. My visitors were few but select, and consisted of the alcalde, three alguazils, and two old ladies. None of them wore shoes or stockings, and the chief dame was dressed in a brilliant coloured calico and carried a man's hat upon her head. She was very voluble and laid great stress on the fact of her having once been to Guatemala, a journey which had made her famous. The men were grave and taciturn, each one merely remarking, as he deposited his black staff on the table, that such weather was unprecedented even in rainy Purula. The entertainment concluded with an exhibition by Pascual of such of my effects as would amuse them, the camp-bed and rubber-bath coming in for their usual share of astonishment and admiration.

"How are such things made!" they said, "and what money he must have to possess such things!"

CHAPTER XVIII.

GROTTO OF PURULA—STALAGMITES—SANTA CRUZ—VALLEY OF COBAN—CAJABON RIVER—CURASSOWS—PACAYA—THE QUESAL—NEST OF TROGON—SAN CRISTOVAL—CROSSES IN WOODS—A "MILPA"—INDIAN LABOUR—MOZOS—COBAN COFFEE—PASION RIVER—DEPARTURE OF MOZOS—AN ANCIENT CITY UNDISCOVERED.

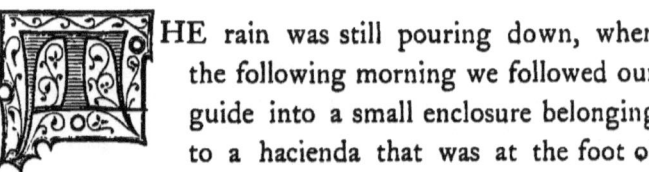HE rain was still pouring down, when the following morning we followed our guide into a small enclosure belonging to a hacienda that was at the foot of the mountain in which was the wonderful grotto. Dismounting, we sheltered our animals as much as possible under the eaves of the cottage, and with the aid of its proprietor commenced the ascent. There once had been a path, but it was so overgrown with thick bushes that it required great exertion on the part of the Indians to cut a way through with their machetes.

At last, when about half way up the mountain, we

arrived at the entrance to the cave. An oval aperture admitted us into a semicircular cavern about 200 feet in diameter and 100 feet in height. The sloping entrance was covered with ferns and begonias, some of the latter being of great size; one leaf that I measured was 19 inches from stem to extreme point. In the interior, stalagmites of very quaint and regular forms rose up towards the ceiling; some of them resembled the trunks of palm trees, others, like fluted pillars, seemed to serve as supports to the fretted roof, from which depended fine needles and sharp stalactites, varying in size from a tear-drop to a reversed spire. Here the petrifractions approached one another so closely that a hand could scarcely be introduced between the gradually approaching points; there the ascending and descending crystallizations formed a palisade with bars a foot apart.

I looked in vain for anything here that surpassed or differed from most caverns, and saw nothing out of the common except a grander foliage and some enormous centipedes. As for the rest, the grotto was neither large enough to astonish, nor dark enough to show off the sparkling crystals, and hardly compensated for a muddy climb and a thorough drenching.

The mules were greatly disappointed at our speedy return as they had imagined a day's holiday, but we had to reload them and go on with our journey. In our morning's ride we had partly retraced our steps of yesterday, and now we continued the path through the beautiful vale in the opposite direction to the village.

The valley, which here varies from quarter of a mile to half a mile in breadth, is too swampy in its centre for cultivation, but it affords pasture for cattle, and the mountain slopes and lower hills are occupied by a few haciendas and clusters of cottages.

Shortly after we had recrossed the valley, the road we had yesterday quitted joined our track and pursued its winding way with a deep stream on one hand and a high mountain on the other. In fine weather this place must be a perfect Paradise, and in spite of the terrible down-pour and the mud I enjoyed the ride very much. The wild flowers were in greater variety and quantity than in any place I had before seen in Central America, and the numerous ravines that cut through the hills were filled with rare shrubs and trees. The high bank on our left was clothed with ferns, among whose delicate fronds the water trickled in diamond drops; pink and white begonias clustered over the jutting rocks, which shone like polished granite from the moisture; fuschias and Indian pinks, overrun with garlands of purple glycine and creepers, formèd a canopy above the golden mosses and feathery grasses, while over all spread the shade of the forest trees whose various kinds stretched up to the misty pine crests. The branches which arched the deep stream on our right were loaded with orchids and parasites, over whose blossoms a few humming birds hovered as if in defiance of the rain which had extinguished the spirit of the cuckoos and blue-birds.

On the other side of the valley a fine cascade fell

from a height of 200 feet, sometimes visible in a sheet of foam and sometimes hidden in the dense foliage that clothes the towering cliffs. Dell, stream and gorge, heights and lowlands all formed a picture which on a fine day and in sunlight would have delighted an artist, and which in spite of the ceaseless patter of the rain was attractive enough to reward the visitor. Gradually the valley narrowed, and when we issued from it we found ourselves close to Tactic, a large clean-looking village about five leagues from Purula.

Here again were large gardens and fruit trees, but instead of having to lodge in a cabildo, we were welcomed to the new and comfortable house of Agapita Flores. This good dame—a bright, cheerful little body —had for years been cook in the family of the gentleman with whom I was about to spend a few days at Coban. After the manner of cooks, she had married, not exactly the coachman or butler, but a carpenter employed by my friend, and forthwith they had determined to set up in business for themselves in Tactic— eight leagues from Coban. It was an agreeable change to see clean linen on the table, and crockery and glass, to say nothing of a coffee and tea-pot, and a bright fire soon made me forget the discomforts of mud and damp.

When we rode away next morning the sun was shining, birds were singing, and a large bunch of roses that I had picked from Agapita's garden was as fresh, and almost as sweet as if it had been plucked in England; butterflies—for which the region around

Tactic is famous—sped along in hurried flight, only pausing for an instant to touch the moist flower bells, or to rest on the damp road; the open valley looked green and fertile, and on all sides there was the bright joyousness of sunshine, rendered doubly grateful after the gloom and chill of the preceding day.

The next village we came to was Santa Cruz—well named, as small chapels and crosses are seen at every turn; then by a continued winding ascent we reached an elevated point in the Sierras, and looked down into the fertile valley of Coban.

The town is beautifully situated in the centre of the valley, through which flows a river winding through cultivated fields, green pastures, and rich coffee plantations. Hills and gentle slopes break the monotony of the plain, and among them peep out the houses and cottages of the industrious inhabitants. The town itself gleams like marble in an emerald setting, so white and pure are the churches and houses, and so green the mass of verdure in which they lie. In their midst rises a hill crowned by the cathedral, the Dominican cloisters, and a high two-storied gateway which leads into the plaza. On another eminence to the left stands El Calvario, a long and broad flight of steps conducting to the picturesque façade.

At the foot of these hills, and scattered in fanciful confusion, are the houses, so low and so hidden among the trees that only their long white walls reveal their presence. Green, undulating hills thickly wooded, and with here and there black notchy crags overhanging the dark ravines, enclose the broad valley, and they in their turn are backed by pine-clad ranges that extend as far as the eye can reach. After crossing the river Cajabon we approached the outskirts of the town, and soon found our way to a house that was indeed a home during our sojourn in Coban. Our host—Mr. F. Sarg—was a well-known naturalist, and as Dr. Berendt, the celebrated ethnologist of Central America, was also at that time living with him, I looked forward with no little pleasure to my visit.

The first glimpse of the garden that was laid out in the patio, three sides of which were surrounded by the verandah, was a delight; here were all the Old World flowers—roses, violets, mignonette, heliotrope, sweet peas, verbena, geraniums, &c., &c. Palms and a few other tropical plants occupied the centre of some of the borders, but they only showed off their hardier companions to greater advantage.

Outside the garden a handsome pair of tame curassows* wandered about. These birds are a little smaller than a turkey, and the male has a shining black plumage on the upper part whilst the abdomen is pure white; the bill is yellow and very strong, and the crest, which it can raise or lower at pleasure, is composed of curled feathers. The female of this species, which I was told varied from the Crax alector, is of much lighter colour than the male, the upper parts being speckled, the lower of a rich tawny brown, and the crest tipped with white. Their large and

* Crax Blumenbachii.

beautiful eyes give them a very gentle appearance, and if it were possible to acclimatize them they would be great ornaments to an English farm-yard. The male bird here was named Moses, and it was very amusing to see with what alacrity he answered to a call and pecked at your hand to gather its contents.

The city of Coban, which is situated about four thousand five hundred feet above the level of the sea, was founded by Bishop Las Casas, who for many years devoted himself to the task of civilising the savage tribes of the Tierra de Guerra, as this part of the country was then called. In 1560, the Emperor Charles V. named it the imperial city, and though for political reasons Salama has been made the present capital of the Department, yet Coban still outnumbers it in population and exhibits more life and industry.

This region abounds in interesting objects of nature, such as birds, flowers, shells and butterflies. The streets even in the environs of the town are very rich in vegetation, as they are lined with gardens whose hedges are composed of a species of Euphorbia with stinging leaves. The stem of these plants grows so rapidly that in a short time they form a compact wall on which grow ferns, orchids, mosses and various grasses. In the gardens themselves, besides a variety of fruit trees, pepper, allspice, roses and wild dahlias, the most conspicuous plant is the Pacaya—a straggling sort of palm that produces a long pod which makes a very good vegetable. In the deep recesses of the surrounding forests is found that most superb bird the

The Quesal. 233

Quesal.* The plumage of the male is I think of more brilliant colouring than that of any other bird. The crested head, back, and long tail feathers are of a bright metallic green shot with gold, the breast is a rich crimson and in all parts the plumage is very silky and fine. The drooping tail feathers, four or five in number, are usually about three feet in length, but sometimes they reach four feet and over. They are very vain of them, and Juarros says that they "are aware of the value of their tails, for they take great care in providing two issues to their nest, entering it by the one and quitting it by the other, in order to avoid any accident to the most precious portion of their plumage." If they build inside the trunks of trees it is extremely probable that they have two issues, but if they build after the manner of the common trogon,† one of whose nests with eggs I afterwards found at Palenque—the issues would be unnecessary, as the one in question was merely an indentation in one of the forks, and the bird was almost entirely exposed to view.

A few years ago it was feared that the great demand for the skin and feathers of these birds would rapidly extinguish the species, but lately, as their novelty waned, they have not been so much sought after, and probably if fashion will permit, they will haunt the forests for many years to come. Mr. Sarg once had one of them in captivity and it was a very uninteresting bird, taking no interest in anything and paying no attention to anything except its food, with which, if allowed, it

* Trogon resplendens. † Trogon mexicana.

would completely gorge itself. This beautiful freedom-loving bird is a worthy emblem of a republic, and just as Africa has the ostrich, Ceylon the elephant, Algeria the lion, India the tiger, and the natives of the Andes the condor, the United States the eagle, and Australia the kangaroo, so, since 1871, has Guatemala adopted the quesal, which now figures on her shield.

Another pretty bird found in Vera Paz is a small brown fly-catcher* with a yellowish breast and long flat bill. This species is peculiar from its beautiful fan-shaped crest; in some the crown feathers are red with black spots, and in others they are yellow or brown with black spots and all have a blue fringe. Singing birds are greatly appreciated in Coban, and there are few houses that have not several cages of different songsters.

Besides the saints and shrines that are seen in all the native houses here, there are many Indian chapels known as "Saints' Houses," which are used for feasts and ceremonies. Some of them bring in a very good revenue to the priests, that of San Domingo affording about three hundred dollars a year. Life size figures and altars fill these chapels, and before them are lighted candles and offerings of fruit and flowers. A favourite plant is a very beautiful Bromelia that grows in the hot regions; its stem is about three feet in height, forming a panicle of flowers whose leaves are of a delicate rose pink, shaped like shells out of which springs a yellow thyrsus.

* Muscivora mexicana.

The Indians here, in addition to other superstitions, have their wise men and sorcerers. A ludicrous incident occurred shortly before my arrival in Coban in connection with one of these soothsayers. The commandant, who kept a very tight hand over these people, had lost a cow. He therefore sent for one of the sorcerers and asked him whether he could find out where the cow was. Taking a glass ball from his pocket he examined it attentively, and at last said he saw the cow, but it was very ill, and in a few moments it was dead. " And now," said the commandant, "can you divine your reward for this information?" " Yes," answered the sorcerer, " the lines in the glass mark twenty five dollars." " Then take him," said the commandant to his officers, " and administer twenty-five lashes, which is what I can trace in the globe." The animal had been found and brought back just before the arrival of the sorcerer.

The women wear their hair in a long tail which they braid with red woollen cord, the amount of which is an unfailing tell-tale of the scantiness or profusion of the tresses with which it is interwoven. These plaited tails give a youthful and school-girlish appearance to their owners, but a front view often reveals a wrinkled countenance whose only light is that of a never absent cigarette.

Of late years Venetian glass beads have been introduced, and they make quaint necklaces of these and old coins. Certain colours alone are in fashion, amber being in the greatest favour, as they declare it preserves them from illness.

In times gone by the good ladies of San Cristoval—a village which lies a few leagues south of Coban—used to take rather a mean advantage of one another in the following way. During a ride we once had there I noticed that the usually spotless chemises were almost invariably stained with a yellowish red colour. Inquiring about it, I learnt that they make here a very favourite beverage of cocoa and some other ingredients, which after drinking leaves a reddish stain on the mouth. As the preparation costs money (and napkins had not been introduced) the indelible stains on the chemise showed that the owner had been drinking the expensive beverage, and of course the more stains so much the wealthier was she who showed them. Now that money is more plentiful, this old sign of riches is unconsidered, as while few formerly were honoured with the marks, now they may be seeen on all.

There is a large lake at San Cristoval, and at a certain place on its banks an orchid grows which has not been found in any other part of the world ; it is terrestrial, small and of a white colour. Another peculiarity of San Cristoval is that the Indians there speak a different dialect from that spoken at Coban. But in the whole of Vera Paz there are many different dialects spoken ; for instance at Coban it is Kaechiquel that is spoken; at San Cristoval and at Tactic—Pocomehi ; and at Rabinal it is Quiche. North of Coban dwell the Lacandones, Manches, and other branches of the Maya family. It is related that at Rabinal (which has just been mentioned) there lives a little animal called the "carbunco," from having a precious stone in its forehead which sparkles in the dark. It lives in the mountains, and only comes down at night to drink at the river. A certain official—a ladino— at Coban declares that he has seen it.

On our return to Coban from our visit to this village of San Cristoval we left the main road, and followed an Indian path through the woods; here among many other splendid orchids we saw a very beautiful one— Barkeria Skinneri—in each of whose deep rose-colored flowers was seated a little white nun.

In these silent woods, hidden away in sequestered nooks and under thick foliage are continually seen crucifixes and chapels; these are always adorned with fresh orchids and flowers, showing that the old Dominican teachings have left their impress on the habits and customs of the natives. Maize plots, too, are frequently met with in the most unexpected places. An Indian loves his *milpa*—maize plot—better perhaps than anything else except aguardiente, and regards with fear the approach of any foreigner to his domain. He is haunted by the belief that passing strangers must be on the look out for good coffee-lands, and that his little ewe lamb may be taken from him by wealthier white men. The proprietors of very isolated *milpas* seldom live on them except during the seasons for planting and reaping; at other times the huts are empty, and their owners employed in town or village.

It used to be no uncommon event to meet in the

woods a grave Indian stalking along with a strange burden slung to his back and attached to the forehead by the usual strap. This burden was a corpse, wrapped in mats, and with hands exposed and clasped in front, which a relative was carrying from the *milpa* for burial at the nearest church.

As Indians are not fond of working more than they can help, the authorities of Coban have adapted a measure which compels all Indians to work when required. When labourers are wanted for the plantations, &c., or porters are required to transport goods, a requisition is made to the alcalde stating the necessary number and for what time and place. A fixed price is paid and at the time appointed the *mozos* appear. This system works extremely well on the whole, although it may have a few drawbacks. For instance, as they work out their time when they like, it frequently happens that on some days there are no labourers on a plantation, and on others there are too many. Their pay is about ninepence a day, which is much less than in other parts of Guatemala. A Trades Union would be troublesome here, but fortunately Indians never co-operate and seldom agree. In spite of their courtesy to each other, they are not averse to backbiting and enhancing their own merits at the expense of another, and scarcely one among them is graced with "a hamely way o' standin' by his neighbour." As porters they are admirable, being honest strong and willing, and though the wages they receive seem inadequate, yet they appear contented and happy. They are chiefly employed in the transport of goods between Coban and Panzos, from whence shipment takes place down the Polochie river to Port Tzabal.

A cart road is now being made by the Government from Coban, which will greatly " open up" this part of the country and probably induce many foreigners to settle here. At present there are very few foreigners indeed at Coban, but as its fine climate, rich coffee land and agricultural wealth become better known, it cannot long remain neglected. Coban coffee has a peculiar delicate flavour, and the fine plantations that are gradually arising point to a prosperous future for this section of Vera Paz. A melancholy example of an unwise choice of site for a coffee plantation may be seen here. Underneath the hill of Calvario lies an extensive property, which some years ago was cultivated with coffee. The situation was so picturesque, with its undulating slopes and varied scenery, that the proprietor determined to make it the fashionable drive. Broad and level roads were cut through it, side avenues for equestrians were turfed, sign posts directed you to interesting points, and above all there was a most exquisitely laid out garden containing a grand collection of rare trees, flowers and orchids. To-day, the once handsome residence of the owner is a ruin, the garden is a wilderness, the fountains are broken, the walks and drives are utterly neglected, and the " finca" of " Nuestra Señora de las Victorias" is a failure. Too late it was discovered that the soil and situation were unsuited for coffee, and the plantation was left to look after itself.

For some days after our arrival in Coban we had been anxiously expecting the Indian mail-carrier from Peten, so as to learn whether the intervening country was flooded—as is often the case—or not. As he did not appear, it was supposed that he had fallen a victim to the seductions of the marimba feasts, which are very prevalent at this time of war and are considered of far greater importance than the mails. The usual route to Peten, and that which M. Morelet travelled on his journey to Coban in 1848, is by way of Cajabon, San Luis, Dolores, &c. As this road makes a great curve eastward and is long and tedious, Doctor Berendt suggested that I should make my way direct to Peten by a path which, though almost untraversed, he was certain was practicable. His plan was for me to cross the Chama range of mountains to the Pasion river, where I was to take a canoe and travel down the river to a point called the " Paso de Sacluk." Here I should be only a few leagues from Sacluk, which place was to be my head-quarters as long as I remained in Peten. So little is known of the region of Peten that, in the new Government map of Guatemala, the Pasion river is in such a position that by no possible means could Sacluk be reached from the south by water, without ascending one of the small tributaries of the main river. Doctor Berendt said that instead of going up stream, I should have to descend the river for about three days before I reached the Paso de Sacluk from

Arrangements for my Journey.

Concuen which was situated on the river itself. Events proved that he was perfectly right, although he had never visited Concuen, but was well acquainted with Sacluk. And here I cannot refrain from thanking the kind Doctor for his thoughtful attentions. No trouble was too great for him in his endeavours to make my journey as pleasant as possible ; he furnished me with letters to all the places where I might want assistance, not only on the road to Peten, but also to Palenque and the Gulf of Mexico ; with maps—drawn by himself—showing the exact course of rivers, &c., and also with many useful hints as to the avoidance of difficulties and troubles that might occur. Nor was Mr. Sarg less helpful to me. He took care that the best Indian porters that were available should be engaged, and procured from the commandant a soldier who spoke the Indian language, could prepare bird skins, and was to take the place of Pascual when the latter returned from Concuen. In fact, my path, which might have been one of thorns was strewn with roses by my good friends at Coban. The most doubtful point was whether the mountain path could be traversed on horseback ; nobody had been to Concuen, and consequently there was much discussion on the subject. Finally it was settled that the road was practicable for four-footed animals, as Pascual was to ride one of his mules, and I the wiry little horse that he had hitherto been riding. Thus everything was ready for a start, and one fine afternoon—there had been a good deal of rain previously—my five Indians, under the command of

José Maria—the soldier guide, set off for their first night's halting place, leaving Pascual and myself to overtake them on the following day.

I had been rather disappointed at finding that the ancient deserted city that the padre of Quiche told Mr. Stephens in 1840 he had seen with his own eyes, and which was situated four leagues from Coban, was a myth, but the most searching inquiries failed to produce the slightest evidence that such a city had ever existed. Mr. Stephens in his delightful book on Central America says when speaking of the padre: " His first curacy was at Coban, in the province of Vera Paz ; and he told us that four leagues from that place was another ancient city as large as Santa Cruz del Quiche, deserted and desolate, and almost as perfect as when evacuated by its inhabitants. He had wandered through its silent streets and over its gigantic buildings, and its palace was as entire as that of Quiche when he first saw it." If any such ruins had been anywhere near to Coban it is improbable that their existence would be unknown at the present day. Mr. Sarg employs many people in collecting birds, butterflies, &c., from all parts of Vera Paz, and it is unlikely that such a city would have escaped their notice. A short time ago they discovered a cave in the hills at some distance from the town, and in it were some curious and valuable pieces of pottery, masks, &c. But there was plenty of interest in Coban without ruined cities, and I was very sorry when my pleasant rides, visits to the coffee plantations, strolls through the market and searchings

Farewell to Coban.

after birds and plants were over. The last visit I paid was to the house occupied by M. Morelet and the fair Juanna; in it dwelt an old lady who remembered the traveller, but whose memory was now getting so bad that she invariably mixed him up with Cortez, the Bishop of Coban and Montezuma. With many a wistful glance back at fair Coban we rode away, and as I thought of the kind friends just left, I remembered the words of Rowe:—

> "But though my mouth is dumb, my heart shall thank you,
> And when it melts before the throne of mercy
> My fervent soul shall breathe one prayer for you,
> That heaven will pay you back, when most you need,
> The grace and goodness you have shown to me."

CHAPTER XIX.

LIQUID AMBER TREES—SAN PEDRO CARCHAH—BARRICADES—
A CENSER—ARRIVAL OF MOZOS—EUPHORBIA—A BEAUTIFUL
RIVER—LA TINTA—MATCHES—ACCIDENT TO MULE—NIGHT
SOUNDS—A DESCENT—STRELITZIA REGINA—ANTHURIUM—BROAD
LEAFED PLANTS—ESPIRITU SANTO—THE CABILDO.

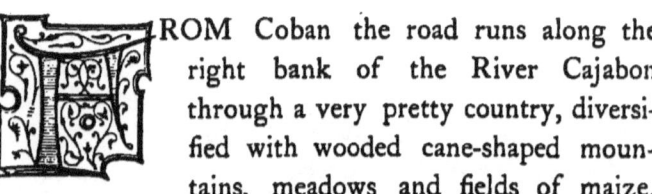ROM Coban the road runs along the right bank of the River Cajabon through a very pretty country, diversified with wooded cane-shaped mountains, meadows and fields of maize. The cottages were all bright with balsams and roses, and on the hill-side grew tree-ferns and liquid amber trees. These trees are so named on account of the yellow gum that oozes from them; this the Indians collect in small cylinders and burn as incense. At a league and a half from Coban we arrived at the town of San Pedro Carchah which contains a population—nearly all Indians—of about 36,000. This total is

larger than that of Salama and Coban together. It is a place of importance and far superior in its houses, public buildings and general activity to an ordinary Indian town. The principal men wear a broad band, ornamented with little silver sprigs, round their tall black hats. We were informed at the cabildo that our Indians had resumed their journey some hours before, but after crossing the river it was not long before we came up with them.

Shortly after leaving San Pedro we entered the mountains by a narrow and stony path, the hills rising directly from it on each side. The hills, like those at Purula, were softly rounded and crowned with virgin forest, whilst lower down the brushwood and broad patches of yellow flowers showed that the woods had been burnt and planted, and were again overgrown. Now and then high up on the sides might be seen a *milpa*, and the form of its owner moving about in the act of planting his maize. Ferns and flowers of various kinds bordered our path, luxuriant fuschias, delicate petunias, and the pink-tinted oxalis clothed the banks, and occasionally a dark purple passion flower that had twined itself round some stronger stem hung like a star from the overarching boughs.

About three leagues from San Pedro we reached the "Ermita de Caqueton," a small shed under which was a shrine decorated with fruit and flowers. Shortly afterwards we left the main road to Cajabon, and turned off by a narrow path to the left into the heart of the mountains. Here the track grew more rocky, but the views from the different heights were very fine. Curious hills ran up to a sharp point which was crowned by a single pine tree, and looking back from our eminence the whole country as far as the horizon appeared to be a series of giant ant-hills lying close together. Already I had noticed that the path was not intended for fourfooted aminals, as every now and then our progress was impeded by a barricade of poles slanting down to a single log for people to cross on foot. Probably these obstacles were at one time intended to prevent cattle from straying, and had been replaced after the last animal had departed.

At two leagues and a half from Caqueton we arrived at Chirrequiche, where we intended to pass the night. This place was merely a hermitage like that at Caqueton, and a glass case containing the figure of a saint stood on a few boards at the extremity of the shed. In front of the saint was an earthen censer in which were two figures of ducks or dogs—I could not determine which—evidently moulded with the dish as they were not fastened on, but were part of the dish itself. Afterwards I saw similar censers before every shrine. When José Maria and the Indians arrived two or three hours after us, they at once proceeded to unpack themselves, then swung their hammocks to the rafters and made a fire on the ground in the centre of the hut. Indians always warm water before drinking it, and even when they stop in the middle of the day for a short rest they always light a fire. Each man carries his own provisions, which consist of coffee, beans, tortillas, toste-poste—which is merely tortillas baked hard and broken up into fragments—and sometimes strings of dried meat. They are also very fond of meal, a handful of which they often put into their drinking water. As I had biscuits and tinned meats for my own consumption, hot water was all I required to make tea, a beverage that I found far more refreshing and more wholesome during my journey than coffee or chocolate.

If the water during the rest of our journey was to be no better than the present, I was not surprised at Indians preferring it boiled. A hole in a deep valley supplied us with a brown fluid which they declared was water, and I had to take their word for it. I subsequently found that the scarcity of water was another great obstacle to the route I had chosen. However willing these Indians may be they are not fond of early rising, and after they have got up they like to dawdle over their coffee and are never in a hurry to set off. When on the following morning we finally did start it was later than it ought to have been, considering the distance we had to travel. We must have formed an odd looking party as we wound along the narrow path in single file. The Indians led the way, each man naked to the waist, bare-legged, and carrying on his back a portmanteau, or wooden box, whose weight was supported by the forehead strap. Staff in hand, they stepped along bravely, encouraged by José Maria, who with no bundle or impediment of any kind was well able to hasten on a lingering step. Pascual followed, giving to José Maria the full benefit of his fluent tongue, and I brought up the rear on my wiry steed, whose size did not correspond with his proud amblings.

In a short time we entered a thick forest where the trees bore crimson euphorbias, whose delicate little blossoms covered their thick limbs; a yellow epidendrum hung its waving panicles from lofty oaks, and another pink orchid, like a hyacinth, grew on many of the boughs. Several of these were collected for me by one of the Indians, and also some specimens of "Odontoglossum grande," whose spreading handsome blossoms. were as fragrant as violets. Soon Pascual and myself went on in front, and after a steep descent which was a vast fernery, between the rock-work of which we had to pick our way, the path became exceedingly bad. Here we had to dismount, and the greater part of our journey to Concuen was henceforward pursued on foot. The track was a quagmire, through which the animals floundered up to their girths in mud. Dotted about were huge slippery boulders, and now and then the only means of ascending or descending the steep hills was by a series of single logs in which notches had been cut to afford foot-hold. Sometimes there was a space between these high steps of nearly six feet, and often and often I gave up the idea of the animals being able to overcome these difficulties, but whenever I looked back there they were bravely following, and urged on by Pascual accomplishing feats worthy of mountain goats. I do not think it would be possible to exaggerate the badness of that road. Pascual, who had travelled a good deal with his mules over Central America, said that he had never seen anything approaching to it. I was wondering whether the Indians would be very late, but at seven o'clock, that is two hours after our own arrival at Tzibal—where we were to pass the night—they appeared.

Tzibal, or the " Rancheria " as it is also called, was another hermitage, and only differed from the others in having a more open roof. The only water we could find was in a small pool at some distance from the shed, but soon we had plenty, as shortly after the *mozos* had arrived the rain fell in torrents and continued all night.

A number of Indians, who were proceeding to Coban, dropped in by twos and threes until at last the shed was crowded. Counting our own party there were twenty-two where there was barely room for ourselves. Our poor animals were very tired, and we were afraid they would find but scanty provender outside ; fortunately one of the guests had a quantity of maize in his pack, and he was glad to dispose of it to me, so they got a very good feed.

The rain came at a very unlucky time, as we understood that to-morrow's journey would be over a far worse road than to-day's, and every drop of rain increased the mud and slipperiness of the track. The morning broke cold and wet, and the porters enveloped themselves and their burdens in their palm-leaf cloaks previous to starting. The wet weather did not last long, and sometimes we caught a glimpse of the blue sky through the thick leaf ceiling overhead; but the sun's rays cannot pierce the foliage of these woods, consequently the ground is never dry and the vast extent of the mountain and forest forms a condensing apparatus which is almost ceaseless in its operation.

At a league from Tzibal we crossed a tiny stream—the first we had seen in the mountains—and a little farther on we came to the river Tual. Such a beautiful stream! the sight of it was worth the mud and wet we had been struggling through. Through a green gorge it came in white foam and hurrying rapids, then tinkling over stony shallows, deepened into dark still pools, which broadened out into a clear silvery stretch, finally disappearing in the black forest with a tremulous music as it rippled over the pebbly falls that sloped gently out of sight. Overhead the high trees arched but could not span the broad stream, and the sun touched the ferns and mosses with many a bright ray, and cast golden hues in which the rare butterflies and birds that hovered over the water gleamed like burnished metal. Most of the butterflies were of an ultramarine colour, but a few larger ones were of a lovely pale green and had a conspicuous crimson spot on the wings. Of birds, there was a glossy green jacamar who did not seem in the least afraid of the intruders, a trogon, a small king-fisher and a few humming-birds. It was a fresh and charming scene, continually changing from utter quiet and repose to life and sound; even the river would sometimes cease to speak, then suddenly it would accompany the forest voices with varied melody; the trogon would utter its melancholy note, the humming-bird would find something to tell to the creepers, the trees would whisper to one another, and

> ". . . . . . the squirrel gay
> Amid the branches green did seem to say,
> With wild bright eyes and bushy tail upcurled,
> 'Come up! come up! come up and see the world.'"

Hitherto the road had not been much worse than that of the previous day, but as soon as we crossed the river and commenced the ascent of the steep hill on the opposite side, we admitted that the business of yesterday was but child's play. We crawled up slippery rocks only to descend into a sea of mud; we clambered up banks by the aid of tree roots only to let ourselves down on the other side by their branches, and tore our clothes off in the thorns so as not to break our limbs over the rugged boulders. Some of our feats of "ground and lofty tumbling" were worthy of professional acrobats, and especially in one long and narrow incline where square blocks of granite stood on their edges, and the only means of progression was by jumping from angle to angle. At the summit, which was crowned with pinnacles and curious rock formations, we observed very deep circular wells almost as even and rounded as if cut by human hands. By listening attentively the sound of running water might be heard, as if a river was flowing through the mountains underneath our feet.

The descent was very difficult for the animals, as it was so encumbered with rocks that there was often barely space for them to pass, and the steps so deep that it required a jump to reach them. At one place there was an almost perpendicular fall of about fifty yards, made up of broken rock and stones. Wondering how the plucky creatures were going to manage, I looked round and saw the horse coolly sit down on its haunches, and in a moment it had slid past me and was up again picking its way among the rocks.

Late in the afternoon we reached La Tinta, which was an open shed and where we had intended to pass the night. The day had been intensely hot, and after our exertions we were very thirsty; after careful inspection, as we could find no water, we determined to go on in the expectation that we might find a stream. We had only accomplished three leagues that day, so hoped to get over another before dark. I therefore fastened to a pole of the hut a sheet of paper informing José Maria that we had gone on, and again took up our journey. After an hour's walk we thought we were getting clear of the mountains, but we found that the light was only from a narrow valley at the other side of which rose another chain. Before we had ascended very far night closed in, and we could not see a yard in front of us. By the aid of a box of matches we still kept on, but at last I was so completely tired and worn out that I could go no farther, and made use of the few remaining lights in seeking a block of stone less damp than the rest on which to pass the night. Pascual, whose motto ought to have been "Excelsior" and who was not to be beaten, said he would go a little higher to see whether the prospect improved, and before he had proceeded ten steps he came upon a small palm-leaf hut about six feet square and under this friendly shelter I flung myself with delight. Of course we had no food and worse than all had nothing to drink, as we had found no water, and Pascual, who till now had always carried a flask of horrible aguardiente, had not even that luxury to assuage our thirst, as he had poured all that was left down the throat of the mule which had met with an accident. In one of the rocky ascents its off hind leg had been firmly wedged in a hole between two rocks. It was in a very dangerous as well as painful position, as the least struggle would have caused it to roll over the precipice and have broken the limb. Evidently knowing this it lay perfectly still with its head over the bank, eating the rank grass and any leaf that was within its reach. With difficulty we removed the rocks and found that the poor animal was very badly cut.

The various events of the day, ending with the mule drinking the brandy and our attempt at ascending the mountain by the light of a box of matches, made me laugh so heartily that I forgot thirst and hunger and soon fell asleep. It was difficult though to sleep long on account of the cold—the Indians having all our rugs—and the weird sounds that issued from the forest. Now there was the steady stroke as of a hammer, now the mournful cry of some night bird, or the moan of a panther; occasionally the patter of feet and a rough grunt announced the presence of wild pigs, or an angry snarl betrayed the neighbourhood of a prowling wild cat.

> " Sweet scents wax richer, freshened with cool dews,
> The whole vast forest seems to breathe, to sigh
> With rustle, hum and whisper that confuse
> The listening ear, blunt with the fitful cry
> Of some belated bird."

At daybreak, and in a drizzling rain, we proceeded on our way.

I had been constantly wondering how Pascual and his two animals were going to make their return journey, as we had been frequently descending places, which to ascend would be very difficult. Our journey this morning convinced me that they could not return this way. In a very steep descent, down which the path ran amidst a confused mass of slippery rocks, we came to a sheer fall of between five and six feet. How the animals got down I know not, but I am sure they could not have got up again. At the bottom of this hill there was a clear running brook, and I think the sight or smell of the water alone induced the thirsty creatures to make the effort.

Soon after we had crossed this stream, after ascending its bed for some distance, the horizon expanded, the atmosphere became fresher, and we knew that we had overcome the worst part of the mountains of Chama or Chisec. There were still the grand forest trees, but the smaller plants were more luxuriant and of more variety. Here were marantas, with their long leaves of dark green velvet; and the curious horned flowers of the anthurium; and a fine shrub,* whose handsome leaves changed from green to rich purple as the breeze tossed them up and down. There were also climbing ferns and crotons of various sorts. The most conspicuous plant and the most frequently seen, was the Strelitzia Regina, whose fleshy leaves and yellow bird-shaped flowers formed a very attractive feature in the scene.

At last we entered a broad valley full of plantains, whose enormous leaves were so overgrown with creepers that it was impossible to walk upright along the narrow pathway. It was very hot indeed, but as at every step we received a shower-bath from the wet vegetation we could not complain. Presently we heard the gobble of a turkey, then a cock crowed, and we knew that we were approaching the village of Espiritu Santo.

This is a comparatively new village, as its inhabitants formerly lived at Chisec, a few leagues away, but the situation was so unhealthy that it was deserted for the present site. It is a picturesque spot, but entirely shut in by virgin forest, which is gradually being cleared. The cottages are made of thin lathes of wood and thatched with palm leaves; each one stands in its own garden, and all are dotted round a large green, in the centre of which stands the church.

The road skirted the village, and opposite the

* Sphærogyne latifolia.

church we dismounted at a long bird-cage building, which was the cabildo. This was divided by sticks into six or seven compartments, into the largest of which I was ushered by the alcalde. It contained a table and chair, and as a pedlar, who was hawking his goods in the verandah, had a hammock, I bought it, and thus comfortably awaited the arrival of José Maria and the Indians.

CHAPTER XX.

A VILLAGE SCHOOL—STRANGE NOCTURNAL VISITORS—A SWAMP—FOREST PLEASURES—CANDELARIA—A DESERTER—INDIAN VOICES—A NIGHT JAR—CHACHAS—INDIAN POST-MAN—A RIVER CAVERN—LOST IN THE FOREST—SAN DOMINGO—PALM GROVES—SAN ANTONIO—INDIAN FREEMASONRY—TALPEMIX—CONCUEN—DON RAMON.

E had reached Espiritu Santo shortly before noon, and to my delight and astonishment the mozos arrived the same evening. As the journey had been rather hard, I determined to rest for a day where we were, and then resume our march to Concuen. The alcalde and his wife were very civil, and furnished us with very good food, the village being by no means deficient in the necessaries of life. One of the compartments next to mine was the village school, and as the division between the two rooms consisted merely of sticks or poles some inches apart, everything going on in one room was plainly visible from the other. School went on three times a day, and the scholars—about thirty in number—were neat,

clean little Indian children, all striving to learn the elements of Spanish. They all sang their lessons together in a high key, and it must have been constant repetition alone that taught them their words, as they never appeared to pay the slightest attention to what they were chanting. Their teacher was a boy of about twelve years of age, and always carried a baby in his arms, I suppose as a sign of authority. It was remarkable in what good order he kept them, and as he sat on a high stool, surrounded by the children, there were none of the pranks and jokes which, under similar circumstances, would probably be played in a white school. So sedate were they that, when I caught them peeping shyly at the stranger, I tried in vain to make them laugh, not a smile was to be extracted.

When school was over they all trooped in single file into my room, came up to me, and with a low bow raised my hand to their forehead, and with a grave "Buenos dias, Señor," departed. The first time they did this I thought it was a village welcome, but whenever school was over they repeated the same performance, only changing the words to suit the time of day. When they left me, they all knelt in a row outside the church and repeated a prayer after their master; probably they were returning thanks for school being over. They were kind-hearted little creatures, and brought me many a land shell and butterfly, which they would timidly put down beside me and then walk demurely away.

Land and fresh-water shells are very plentiful in

these parts, and the natives are fond of them for food. Here is the menu of my last dinner in the village :—

Soup.
Parrot.
Fish.
Fresh-water shells, and preserved salmon.
Entrée.
Omelette del Espiritu Santo.
Roast.
Two trogons.
Dessert.
Bananas, oranges, tortillas and frigoles *ad lib.*, maize water and coffee.

The trogons I had shot for their skins, and were certainly most ill-flavoured birds on the table, almost worse than the parrot.

During our stay in the village the lame mule grew worse and worse, and I soon saw we should have to leave it behind when we proceeded to Concuen. This, however, would not matter much, if the road was as impracticable as hitherto. But Pascual did not at all like having to leave his animal here, and once, when I was in my room, I heard him eulogising its various qualities to the wife of the alcalde; suddenly he was struck by the idea—which had occurred to me some time previously—how was he going to return to Guatemala? A sound mule could not accomplish the journey by the road we had come, much less a lame one. Appalled by the prospect of having to pass the rest of his days in Espiritu Santo, he lost all control over himself and burst into tears, exclaiming, " O Benita! Justina! my pretty creatures, shall I never see you again?" (The ladies in question were not his children, but only two of his mules.) The alcalde's wife possessed a keen sense of the ridiculous—and it really was very ludricous to think that here, within a few days of a civilised town (Coban), we had placed ourselves in such a position that it seemed highly probable Pascual would either have to lose his mule or remain with it until it died; and nothing would induce him to part with it. The absurdity of the situation struck her so forcibly that she positively screamed with laughter. I could not help joining, and at last had to retire to my hammock, poor Pascual walking off in high dudgeon.

He soon recovered his spirits, and the alcalde promised to take great care of the animal during his absence, saying that he would find an Indian to guide them back to Coban by a longer but easier route which was known only to a few. I may say here that this was eventually done, and Pascual arrived safe and sound at the house of Mr. Sarg, full of his adventures, and not at all displeased with his journey.

That evening, after I had retired to bed, my door was opened very quietly, and two or three people entered carrying a large bundle. As my head was toward the door I could not see well what was going on, but imagined that, as the stocks were in my room, the authorities were going to place some refractory native therein. In a few seconds, however, all was quiet, and on looking up I could distinguish in the dim light the figure of a man dressed in black, kneeling before a cross. By his side was the dark bundle.

Could it be a dead body by which a priest was watching, or what? Whenever I looked up, there was the bowed and motionless figure in front of the cross, which had been set up for the occasion, as it certainly was not there when I first entered the room. At last I fell asleep, wondering who and what the visitors were, and when I awoke in the morning, watcher, cross, and bundle had vanished. When I made inquiries about them, the answers I received were very unsatisfactory, and all I could make out was that they were holy men bound on a pilgrimage, and that one of them was very ill.

From Espiritu Santo the path we followed was level as we wound round the hills, instead of crossing them, but it was a quagmire nearly the whole distance. Where the water was not up to your knees it was slimy and treacherous; you place your feet on a prostrate log and it turns over; to save yourself you catch at an overhanging branch, and the punishment is prompt and severe, as probably you have clutched a stinging creeper or the still more painful and thorny palm— Dæmonorops plumosus. There is no scarcity of water now; streams flow at the bottom of deep gulches, which have to be crossed either by a fallen or slippery tree, or by descending and ascending through knee-deep mud The branches of enormous trees meet overhead, forming an impenetrable shade, and rendering the damp heat more intense. But there is a bright side to the picture that far overbalances the dark. The scenery is splendidly tropical; vines and orchids festoon the trees, from which you are saluted by the merry chatter of the parrots, and amid whose dense foliage you mark the crimson breast of a trogon. Silvery cecropias gleam under the white inga blossoms, and among them dart little black birds* with bright crimson heads and necks. On the broad shield-like leaves of an alocassia rests a brilliant sulphur butterfly, with long swallow-tails edged with black velvet; others of a light blue sheen float lazily along, knowing that pursuit is impossible over the marshy soil. Palms in variety, new plants and flowers, birds and insects, all are there waiting to teach you something, to give you a thought, a lesson in woodcraft, and certainly to brighten and render companionable the solitude of the jungle.

After two leagues we reached a circular clearing of about seventy yards in diameter. In the centre were two large and well-built thatched sheds; one of them was occupied by an old Indian couple, the other was the usual traveller's shelter, and contained a shrine dedicated to Our Lady of Candelaria. The altar was decorated with a vast quantity of small yellow gourds, which had been strung together, forming a sort of canopy, with tassels of the same fruit. The offerings were very numerous, as besides orchids, fruits, and flowers, there were the skins (roughly preserved) of some gorgeous little humming-birds, bunches of feathers, green mosses, two earthenware dishes, and some strips of linen. Despite the superstition and the absurdity of some of the gifts, there is something very

* Pipra mentalis.

touching in this custom of the poor Indians. Whether the offering is a garland, a cross, or even a few flowers, it has the merit of humble sincerity, and inspires a pathos in these lonely forests that would be mere sentiment in a crowded church.

After waiting some time for the mozos we began to fear that something had happened to them, or that we had taken the wrong path. Towards dark they appeared, but José Maria was not to be seen. As I had given him my gun to carry, I thought he might have lingered on the way after some bird, but the last Indian who arrived brought the gun, and complained by signs and the few words of Spanish with which he was acquainted, that the gentleman in question had run off. He had told the Indian to take the gun, as he was not going to travel on such a road any longer. Pascual then told me that he had noticed a very ill-countenanced ladino talking very earnestly with José Maria at Espiritu Santo, and doubtless this man had induced him to leave me—more especially as I had paid him his wages in Coban—and join in some other enterprise. It was a very foolish thing for him to do, as being a soldier, and living with his family at Coban, it would be impossible for him to avoid being captured at some time or other. Eventually he was taken, and in a recent letter I have received from Mr. Sarg, he tells me that he was then undergoing severe punishment, not only for deserting me, but also for being absent from his duties as a soldier.

In the meanwhile we were in a dilemma; neither

Pascual nor myself could understand a word of the Indian language, and the brightest of the mozos knew little more than "yes" and "no" in Spanish. How I wished that the Indian tongue had already merged into the Spanish as it is sure to do in time! But this side of Coban the Indians only speak their own language, and answer "yes" to every question you may ask. Hitherto from Coban we could not have lost our way as there was but one path, but now where various tracks ran through the forest we particularly wanted a guide to tell us before starting which we were to take. Fortunately our porters were very good fellows, and gave us but little trouble, and before dark I was even thankful to José Maria for not having gone off with my gun.

That night I enjoyed the luxury of having a room—indeed a whole house—to myself. Opposite the large shed, in which Pascual and the Indians hung their hammocks, was a tiny hut which just admitted my camp-bed, and there I established myself. Very thankful indeed was I for this accommodation, although in the middle of the night I was awakened by water splashing in my face, and found a terrible rain storm in progress. It continued the whole of the next day so that we were unable to continue our journey, but as I was out of sound of the Indians' voices I was able to read comfortably and so pass the time. When an Indian speaks it is always in a high unmusical tone; the language is hideous and sounds like a person speaking without any roof to his mouth.

Through the poles of my cage I could also watch the humming-birds and brown honey-suckers* which, in great numbers and regardless of the rain, hovered over the large fuschia-like flowers of the trees that surrounded the clearing. All night long a species of night-jar, which is very plentiful thronghout Central America, kept up its monotonous cry. Many and many a night both before and after this time have I been kept awake the entire night by these annoying birds. Their notes are exactly as if you said, " oh will you," through the teeth, putting great emphasis on the second word, and this they repeat three or four times.

At dawn the "chachas "†—the noisiest birds in the country—commenced to scream and fly about, and as the rain had nearly ceased we prepared to start again. A chacha is about the size of a pheasant, and has white plumage underneath. It frequents the trees of the dense forests, and it is said builds its nest in the branches like a small bird; the flesh is good but it does not equal that of the curassow.

Before we left Candelaria the native postman—a wild gaunt Indian—passed through on his way to Espiritu Santo, and I was thus enabled to send a message regarding the deserter. At this place the mail carrier to Peten branches off through the forest by a path which takes him in three days to the Paso de Sacluk on the Pasion river.

Our course to Concuen took an easterly curve, and though longer, yet I had been assured was the better

* Phætornis longirostris. † Ortalida Vetula.

of the two. But I think it was a case of "take either one, and you will wish you had taken the other before you have gone half way." The character of the country through which we passed was the same as before, and the road was, if possible, muddier and more swampy. But sometimes the higher grades led us along a dryer path under walls of limestone on which grew lovely ferns, begonias, and rich yellow orchids. These rocky heights are the favourite resorts of the howling monkeys—alüates—and here we heard them for the first time in our journey. When once heard, the hideous cries of these animals will not easily be forgotten. The sound is something between the howl of a wolf and an engine letting off steam; commencing with a low melancholy blowing, it increases until the forest is filled with the most unearthly roar. The peculiar noise is caused by the formation of the throat, which has a large pouch containing fleshy rattles.

At the end of one of the rock-lined paths the river which we had just crossed near Espiritu Santo reappeared on our left, but speedily disappeared into a broad-mouthed cavern. This tributary of the Pasion river is here about fifty feet broad, and enters the cave in a swift clear stream, after a previous course of miniature falls and gently graduated rapids. The scene was very pretty; on the left and across the river was a thick jungle of palms, ceibas and large-leaved plants, the green wooded hills being just visible beyond. On the right, our path, which lay above the river, was bordered by a fern-covered rocky wall that turned abruptly across the road in front, forming a perpendicular barrier about one hundred feet in height. Here was the beautifully arched cave into which the stream flowed. The height of the opening was perhaps forty feet, and was draped with hanging mosses, ferns, orchids, and pink and white begonias. In the very centre of the arch, in the midst of a tangled skein of drooping vines and ferns was a lovely little nest, in and out of which flew its disturbed proprietor—one of my crimson-capped friends. The interior of the cavern was lofty and winding, though not of any great extent. Immense forest trees crowned the outside wall, and these with their accompanying creepers and parasites which shaded the grey rock gave a picturesque finish to the picture. In Vera Paz streams are constantly disappearing and coming forth again from rocky openings, and at Lanquin, on the road to Cajabon, there is a celebrated cave in which a river takes its rise.

When we resumed our journey the road once more became almost impassable; narrow ravines continually intersected it, and it was no easy matter to descend their perpendicular banks iuto a sea of mud, in an upright position.

Having walked ahead of the slow travelling Indians we here lost our way by taking a wrong path, and after some hours wandering through the forest, arrived at a lonely hut. By signs and by continually mentioning the name of the place—San Antonio—where we wanted to go, we at length made the old Indian who lived there understand our wishes, and the offer of a real induced him to act as our guide. Before starting he made us sit down and partake of some food. His wife made some fresh tortillas, which were very acceptable, bnt the meat—which was monkey—I could not manage after the first mouthful, although Pascual declared it was better than beef.

Attached to the house was the usual shed, containing a fine new shrine and saint, before whom were some very beautiful lilies and a long raceme of lilac wistaria. I afterwards heard that this place was called San Domingo. It was fortunate for us that we found it, as we were far out of our course, and it was some hours before we reached San Antonio, where the porters had arrived long before us.

Our last league had been through a low swampy district, with no other trees than palms. These were magnificent specimens of their kind, their enormous fronds branching out directly from their base for a length of fifty or sixty feet. Often the green plumes met overhead, forming an avenue of perpetual shade that extended for a long distance. San Antonio—as it is called after the saint who honoured our sleeping shed—is situated on a high eminence surrounded by valleys, which are crossed at the north by the last ridge of mountains, beyond which lies the river Pasion. Curious strata of slate rock ran diagonally across our hill in such symmetrical lines that they looked like the foundations of buildings, but the only houses near were a few native ones, whose owners declined politely but firmly to furnish us with either eggs or tortillas.

Before we started next morning one of the porters informed me by signs that he wished to return, and at the same time introduced me to the native who was willing to take his place. Similar transfers had been made at Espiritu Santo, and it was curious with what little trouble the exchange was effected. The Indians themselves simply said they were tired, and if I was willing they had men to replace them. There was no question of pay raised, no dispute as to the weight of the load, and no trouble of any sort; in fact, had it not been mentioned to me, I do not think I should have known that they were not the same men who started from Coban.

As San Antonio was only five leagues from Concuen, and we had not accomplished more than four on the previous day, I determined to make a one day's march of it instead of two, as the porters wished. We therefore started early in a drizzling rain, and after descending the hill, entered marshy palm groves similar to those of yesterday. When we reached the mountain range we had before noticed, it was an agreeable surprise to find that the path ran through it instead of over it. Forest trees once more mixed with the palms, and the path became drier and more pleasant. The vegetation was very varied; here was the pepper myrtle, known by its white curly bark; a small palm,* with bunches of red or yellow beans on high red stalks; the orange-yellow strelitzia and the alocassia. There were also some fine orchids† of a bright orange colour,

* Malortica gracilis. † Stanhopea.

with fleshy lips, like a slipper handsomely worked with purple spots.

Shortly after crossing the dry and rocky bed of a river, we looked round and saw that the mountains of Chama were behind us. In front was an immense expanse of level forest and jungle. At Talpemix—another shrine—we had another monkey luncheon, and after two leagues of dry forest path arrived at Concuen.

Some years ago an ex-officer of the army of the Emperor Maximilian, who was fond of exploring and anxious to make his fortune, found himself in this neighbourhood. Knowing the wealth of this region in dye woods, india-rubber, sarsaparilla, &c., he determined to make it his home, and as he was acquainted with the Indian language soon obtained labourers, and in time made a large clearing of the forest and built a small house. His dwelling and those of his workmen constitute "Concuen," which is the Indian word for "Pasion." Mr. Sarg had given me a letter of introduction to this gentleman—Don Ramon—and from him I received a most hospitable welcome.

CHAPTER XXI.

EL RIO DE LA PASION—DON OACLOS—WILD COCOA—TREES—DYE
WOODS—BIRDS—A CANOE—START FOR EL PASO—IGUANAS—A
USEFUL FIRE-ARM—JAGUAR—CURASSOW—HANGING NESTS—
FISHING BY TORCHLIGHT—SCORPION AND COCKCHAFER—INDIAN
ENCAMPMENT—LACANDONES—ARRIVAL AT EL PASO DE SACLUK.

T the foot of the hill on which the house of Don Ramon was situated, flows the Pasion, a broad, swift, and deep river, which is visible for some distance as it winds through the wooded lowland. This river forms the boundary between Vera Paz and Peten. It rises in a small lake in the latter Department, under the name of Santa Isabel, when it becomes the Pasion, and flows with a thousand twists and turns tending to all the points of the compass towards Tenosigue, before reaching which it takes the name of Usumacinta. From Tenosigue, after an equally tortuous course, it empties itself out by several mouths into the Gulf of Mexico.

Besides the river and the clearing, nothing is to be

seen from the house as far as the eye can reach but virgin forest, whose depths conceal innumerable ruins both small and great. Hardly a league away on the opposite side of the river, are the remains of a very extensive city, to which Don Ramon has cut a path through the wood; but so thick is the jungle and so overgrown with great trees are the stone walls, that it is difficult to trace the form or meaning of any of the massive fragments.

The forest was full of beautiful birds, and as I had to pass three or four days at Concuen waiting for a canoe, there was plenty of opportunity to add to my collection of skins. My companion on these shooting expeditions was Don Ramon's overseer, a fine-looking intelligent young Spaniard—Don Carlos by name—who, by the way, bore a striking resemblance to his more illustrious namesake. He afterwards took the place of Pascual, and remained with me until my departure from Peten, and a more obliging and useful companion I could not have found. He was intensely fond of shooting, and as I wanted some monkey skins we started one morning on an alüate hunt.

These creatures retire during the day into the deep recesses of the forest, but at night they surround the house, and howl as if a thousand pigs were being killed. Don Ramon declares positively that they have regular hours for howling; viz., at eight p.m., at midnight, and at four a.m. When I was there, I fancied the concert was kept up nearly all night.

It was a fresh and glorious morning when we

started, but the heavy dew not having yet dispersed, every tree and bush gave us a moist greeting. At every step there was something new—to me at least—in flower, bird, or shrub. Here was a small tree about fifteen feet in height, with tapering leaves and large oblong pods attached to the branches without any stem. This was the wild cocoa. In Coban and other parts of Guatemala, where there are no small coins, the seeds of this plant—from which cocoa is prepared—take their place. There was a much taller tree, with its trunk gashed and scarred in a zig-zag fashion to obtain the milk which flowed from its wounds. This was the india-rubber tree*—ule—which yields many gallons every two years. In an outhouse at Don Ramon's I had seen several splendid slabs of prepared caoutchouc, seven or eight inches think and of excellent quality.

The process of preparing the india-rubber is very simple. A pail full of the milk is cured by the heat and smoke produced from a slow fire in which a handful of palm-nuts has been dropped, through a funnel-shaped earthenware jar without bottom which covers it. The milk is then poured into a large basin, in which a wooden spaddle is revolved by hand in the smoke until the layer is dried. This process is repeated until the slab has gained the required thickness, and the pure rubber is then exposed for a few days in the sun. Sometimes the Indians allow the milk to flow into a large hole dug at the base of the

* Castillio elastica.

tree, merely adding the juice of certain plants to assist in the coagulation. Near these milk-giving trees were others, whose bark was immediately stained blood-red after the smallest incision. As Carlos slashed away at them with his machete—I suppose for my edification—I thought of Dante's suffering trees, that bled red drops when pierced, and asked so mournfully, "Why dost thou wound me? why break me? hast thou no pity?"* Then there were pepper and cinchona trees, and others with a curly red bark almost as bitter as that of the latter.

This region has a wealth of dye woods and medicinal shrubs, and is probably the richest in Guatemala, but at present it is utterly neglected and almost unknown, and will remain so until roads are made, or even a single road has in some measure opened up the country.

We had hardly been out ten minutes before we had a shot at a splendid curassow, or "panjil," as it is usually called. Sending an Indian back with it to the house for dinner we strolled on, sometimes bagging a large yellow-breasted toucan, a mot-mot, or a crimson-backed tanager.† The country people call this bird the "alcalde;" the cardinal red-bird they call the "corregidor." The waxwing, which is also found in Vera Paz, they have named "alguazil," as its plumage is is not so gaudy as that of the others.

* El tronco suo gridò: " Perchè mi schiante ?
Da che fatto fu poi di sangue bruno ;
Ricomincio a gridar: Perchè mi scerpi,
Non hai tu spirto di pietate alcuno ?"
† Ramphocelus sanguinolentus.

A Monkey Hunt.

As we approached the monkey rocks we gave up shooting, and with noiseless steps ascended their fortress, but it was deserted. Hardly had we descended, when from another direction we heard the well-known howling, and then through bush and brier, over rocks and streams, we hurried to the rendezvous. Gradually the sounds grew louder and louder, until it seemed as if the forest was full of demons; then it suddenly stopped. The animals had seen or heard us, and already were racing quietly but with great speed over the tree tops.

The ground was free from brush, so we were enabled to follow in full cry. The shaking leaves and the occasional spring through the air of a large black body betrayed their course. On we went, tripping and stumbling over tough lianes and fallen trees, while the nimble creatures overhead silently but surely widened the distance between us. At last, when we had almost given up the chase, a wider gulf than ordinary separated the trees; this we speedily reached, and high up among the branches of a lofty ironwood tree we could discern a dozen reddish-black apes, chattering and grinning at us in an agony of rage.

Singling out two of the largest we toppled them over, but owing to what Mrs. Partington calls their "reprehensible tails," they swung head downwards far out of reach. Thinking that their hold would relax in time, we allowed the others to go without molestation, and sat down to await the result. An hour passed and still there were no signs of loosening, and the

Indian told Carlos that they frequently never fall at all, so firm is the knot that binds them to the branch. Rather than lose the skins, we determined to send the native back to the house for an axe to cut down the tree. We had not the least idea where we were, but the instinct of the Indian did not fail him, and he assured us he would soon return.

During his absence we searched for land shells, and found some very beautiful specimens. The raised bark of the dead tree trunks revealed many handsome beetles, some of metallic blue colour, others enamelled with green and gold. We heard, too, the note of a bird that sounded like a silver bell, but though we followed it as far as we thought prudent, we could never catch even a glimpse of it. Carlos knew it by some Indian name, but I could not recognise it from his description.

After some hours waiting our native returned, accompanied by two others, and they at once set to work vigorously to hew down the hard-wooded tree. It fell at last and we secured the monkeys, which were great ugly fellows with bushy beards and heavy fur. As we returned home we saw great numbers of small black monkeys with white throats and chests. These are called " micas," the large ones being " monos."

Thus my few days at Concuen passed very pleasantly, until it was time to start down the river to the Pasco de Sacluk, which we hoped to reach on the third day. Don Ramon had kindly lent me his large canoe —a capital one, hollowed out from the trunk of a mahogany tree—and had made it very comfortable with a small awning. It was not easy to stow away all the baggage and provisions, and still have room for two pair of long legs, but at last it was accomplished, and with four Indian paddlers in the bows, Carlos and the captain of the boat in the stern, and myself in the centre, we shot out into the stream and were soon out of sight of Concuen.

The scenery had very little variety, as the broad river flowed through a flat forest of grand trees and impenetrable jungle. Creepers with clusters of flowers like "lady's slippers," and a saponaceous tree bearing deep purple blossoms lined the low banks, which seldom attained a height of over twenty or thirty feet. Here and there, instead of the sloping river sides, natural stone walls arose, as smooth and regular as if built by hands, and topped by large trees; sometimes the white mud banks pushed themselves far out into the river, their upper parts clothed with bright green grass, rank and drooping, and contrasting with the more sombre green of the stately forest trees.

Had it not been for animal life the voyage would have been decidedly monotonous, but of that there was no want. Stretched out on almost every overhanging bough was a great iguana, which on our approach would raise its crest, extend its pouch, drop with a splash into the water and scramble to the shore. Basking on the mud banks were hideous alligators—lagartos—ten or twelve feet long; sometimes we got within shot of them, but oftener they glided quietly into the river, almost before we had distinguished them from logs of wood. To shoot these brutes, and also turkeys and curassows, I always used a "Smith and Wesson" revolver, with an adjustable wooden stock. It thus took the place of a rifle, and was infinitely more serviceable to an only moderate shot like myself, as it was as easy to use as a drawing-room rifle. In shooting birds it gave far more sport than a shot gun, as the turkey, &c., generally sat looking at you, or would simply hop higher and higher up the branches until lost in the foliage.

Besides these animals we saw several small turtles, some of which the Indians lassoed as they floated unthinkingly on the surface. Once when half asleep a voice whispered, " Señor, el tigre," and looking under the awning there was a large jaguar, or congar, crouched in the bamboos not ten yards from the canoe. Before I could grasp my revolver he knew we had perceived him, and sprang back into the thicket. Most likely he had been lying in wait for a turtle, of which those animals are very fond and catch very skilfully.

In the early morning, while the night vapours were still clinging to the branches and clouding the river with a film, commenced the harmonies of the forest; parrots screamed, monkeys howled, toucans croaked, orioles sang, and the chachas chattered as they scrambled over the tops of the trees.

To procure our daily rations of curassow, it was not necessary—indeed it would have been impossible—to enter the jungle, but by paddling quietly along the banks we obtained as many as we wanted, when they flew up from the water to the branches of a neighbouring tree. I never at any time saw these birds after seven o'clock in the morning, but from daylight up to that hour they were very plentiful. Sometimes a few wild ducks afforded amusement in stalking, but we rarely came up with them.

Some birds were with us all day, such as the great kingfisher,* a small blue heron called "padre santo," on account of its sanctimonious appearance, the snowy heron,† and a snake bird‡ with long tapering neck fringed with silver grey feathers. Now and then we saw a purple and green porphyrio, or a black and white spotted water-hen stepping demurely along the brink of the river under the shade of the brambles and rushes, and often the pretty gallina de monte ran hastily back from the water's edge, where it had come to drink.

In one spot a large tree, leafless and dead, stood by itself; from its bare branches depended more than a dozen nests of the same shape as the oriole's, but of greater depth. These belonged to a bird known as the "oro pendulo," which is of a rich chocolate colour, and has a bright golden tail. The note of this bird is peculiarly clear and loud.

Thus, there was plenty of interest in our trip, and as neither the days nor nights were oppressively hot, the time passed very pleasantly.

* Ceryle torquata. † Ardea candidissima.
‡ Ardea Agami

As the crew were not acquainted with this part of the river, and the nights were dark, and snags and sandbanks abounded, we used to draw up close under the bank in the evening. The Indians would then clear a space for sleeping, and after hanging their hammocks, fish by torchlight with hook and bait. We were, therefore, never without a variety of fish, flesh, and fowl, and when in the daytime we landed at some convenient spot for breakfast or dinner, our meals were almost too luxurious. Carlos and the captain were excellent cooks, and iguana baked in clay, fried fish and delicate curassow or turkey were every-day delicacies. To these were added fried bananas, coffee, and some very nice tortillas made into a kind of sandwich by the aid of cooked beans. These had been provided for me by Don Ramon, and when toasted on the embers, were extremely tempting.

At one of these resting-places, we witnessed a curious fight between a cockchafer and a scorpion. The latter was lying quite still when the cockchafer approached it, and spread one of its membranous wings over the venomous insect. The scorpion at once curled its tail, intending to sting its adversary, but of course merely pierced the thin web, and the sting entered its own back. Then the cockchafer withdrew, and the enraged scorpion kept on stinging itself, until it lay still, apparently dead. These insects look so wicked that one can believe almost any story about them, even that of the Indians, who declare that if a mother scorpion neglects to provide food for her young, they set to work and devour her.

The only signs of human habitation that we saw were in an opening in the forest, where some cross-poles and the remains of a camp-fire indicated its recent occupation. Our Indians said it had been an encampment of Lacandones, who alone wander about these dismal forests. Of this almost extinct tribe little is known, although many stories are afloat concerning the ferocity and rude independence of its members.

In Peten I could hear nothing authentic about these Indians, but at Tenosique I was told that they sometimes appeared there in small parties to exchange vanilla, wild cocoa, and tobacco, for salt, cotton, and old fire-arms if they could obtain them. They never gave or received money, but differed in no other respect from other Indians, farther than being more shy and distant in their manners.

Towards the evening of the third day after leaving Concuen, we saw some canoes drawn up on the right bank of the river, and above them an open shed, in which was a man who informed us that we had arrived at the "Paso de Sacluk." Two of the boatmen were immediately despatched to the village of Sacluk—six leagues off—with a letter from Dr. Berendt to the alcalde, requesting him to send mules as soon as possible for our conveyance. We then took up our quarters in the shed, which was very dirty, and surrounded by the hot, damp forest.

CHAPTER XXII.

MAHOGANY CUTTERS—RAINY NIGHT—A TAPIR—A FEARFUL SPECTACLE—PASO NUEVO—TOUCAN—A BEAUTIFUL PIGEON—THE SAVANNAS—ARRIVAL AT SACLUK—NARANJA COTTAGE—SACLUK—OCCUPATION—NIGHT—EL REY ZOPILOTE—EN ROUTE TO FLORES A SAVANNA VILLAGE—SAN BENITO—PETEN-ITZA—CONQUEST OF THE ITZACS.

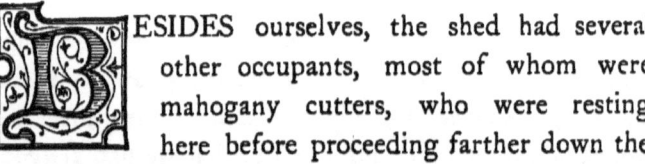ESIDES ourselves, the shed had several other occupants, most of whom were mahogany cutters, who were resting here before proceeding farther down the river. They were all jet black negroes, and one of them who came from Belize had lately been rescued from the wild Indians, who had kept him a prisoner for six months until found and released by a Spanish priest. He said he had been treated very kindly in the small village where he had been confined, but beyond that information was very reticent and did not know —or pretended not to know—who his captors were, or where the village was situated.

The shed had such an uninviting appearance, and was so full of "niguas" and "garrapatas" that I determined to sleep in my canoe. In the middle of the night a tremendous storm broke overhead, and drenched me almost before I was awake. In a few minutes Carlos came sliding down the muddy bank, and gathering up the rugs assisted me in my return to the then welcome roof. It was not a pleasant night, as in addition to other insects there was a large supply of mosquitoes, and the negroes cooked something every hour. Across the river there was a large swamp, and malaria must have loaded every breath of wind that swept through the damp hut.

The next day, while waiting for the mules, I crossed the river, and amused myself by searching for land and water shells. Many of the latter I found in the swamp, and also some small land-tortoises. In my pursuit of one of these I laid my gun in a dry place, and by the help of some logs was working my way across a very treacherous piece of marsh.

Suddenly I heard a patter of feet, and through the bushes on the other side I saw a fine tapir moving along. Every now and then it stopped, and sniffed with its long snout as if scenting danger, and when at last it came out into the open and saw me standing not twenty yards off it showed hardly any surprise, but quietly retreated into the thick cover. In size it was bigger than a large hog, but its pig-like appearance was redeemed by its large soft eyes, its proboscis and the texture of its mouse-coloured coat.

On returning to the shed I was greeted with a most revolting spectacle. A large fire had been made outside, and in front of it were four bodies hanging by their necks to some cross bars. Had we been in a cannibal country I should have thought that they were the mahogany cutters roasting before a slow fire. They proved, however, to be large monkeys that the negroes had shot for food. The hair had been singed off, and they were now waiting to be cooked. I was told that the flesh of these large monkeys—*monos*—was much more sweet and tender than that of the small ones—*micos*; but I declined to test the quality of either.

As the mules did not appear, another wretched night had to be passed, and it was not until noon on the following day that we left the unhealthy "Paso." The first part of the road was through forest, varied by a few stretches of open grass-land, until we reached the Subim river which flows into the Pasion a little below El Paso. This point is called "El Nuevo Paso," and canoes can reach it from the Pasion river, but at the time of our visit the water over the bar was too shallow to admit of entrance.

After crossing the stream, the muddy road continued through the forest for two leagues. Here we shot two or three varieties of toucans; one of which we had not before seen. The breast of this species[*] is variegated, and the bill very much indented. I also obtained a very beautiful pigeon with chocolate wings, and with the breast and neck of clouded brown feathers edged with brilliant purple; the bill and iris crimson, and the feet bright red.

[*] Pteroglossus torquatus.

Magnificent trees—mahagony, ceibas, &c.—bordered our swampy path, and their great roots threw as many impediments as possible in the way of progression. The road was level, but the pack mules obstinately refused the middle of it which was too muddy for their tastes; and it was most amusing to watch with what determination they would force their way between narrow trunks and prickly bushes, totally regardless of the baggage on their backs. Once we met a mule team, one of which headed for the same narrow passage that one of ours did. Here they had a regular fight, until our opponent by sheer weight capsized the other upon his back in the mud. As this happened to be the mule which carried two rather weak boxes, the scene was not so amusing as I had at first imagined. Before we got out of the forest the usual afternoon storm came on, and with such vigour that, in spite of strong boots and leggings, I had to dismount and pour the water out when the rain had ceased.

At last we left the woods, and the savannas lay stretched before us. These savannas form the most striking features in the scenery of Peten, and consist of vast stretches of prairie land dotted over with countless small conical hills. Thickly wooded and varying in circumference at the base from a couple of hundred yards to even half a mile, the curious hills rise suddenly from the grassy plain like huge extinguishers. No rivers water the plains, but here and there a few shallow ponds are dotted about, affording a scanty drinking supply to the herds of cattle. Where there is most water, there lie the pretty savanna villages, and it was to these that our path led us after leaving the forest. The track through the deep grass was hardly visible as it ran in a narrow line, or rounded the bases of the hills, but our animals knew it well enough, and after three leagues we saw the small white church and the houses of Sacluk.

At the entrance to the village we were received by the alcalde, Don Antonio, who at once conducted us to the house which had been prepared for our reception. This was an oval two-roomed building, thatched and with white-washed walls, that had been built by Dr. Berendt during his visit to Peten, and which Don Antonio had caused to be swept and garnished, and made ready for us. As Sacluk was to be our headquarters, the alcalde undertook to provide us with food, and we were soon established in the comfortable cottage, which I christened "Naranja," on account of the beautiful orange trees that overshadowed it.

The chief part of the village formed a square, enclosing a large, uneven, closely-cropped green, and behind each of the surrounding houses were others dotted about promiscuously and forming the outskirts. Most of them had gardens surrounding three sides, but the front invariably opened directly upon the flat grassy plain. The dwellings were of a very simple nature, and consisted of white-washed mud walls and a thatched roof, but they looked picturesque on account of the number of trees in which they were embowered. There were mango, orange, sapote, custard-apple, and a variety of other fruit-trees, mixed with banana, dracœna, and similar large-leafed plants. On the north, south and east sides the conical hill chains approached to within a few hundred yards, but on the west there was a vast extent of flat prairie.

The population amounted to between two hundred and three hundred, but a quieter and more dead-alive place could not be imagined. With the exception of the pigs, cattle, and poultry, which roamed at will all round the houses, there was little or no life to be seen. At certain periods of the day the women issued from their cottages with their heads swathed in blue shawls, and carrying pitchers, which they proceeded to fill from two neighbouring ponds. There they would chatter and gossip for a short time, and then return and disappear into their homes.

As for the male part of the inhabitants, I do not know exactly what their occupation was; some were said to own small farms at some distance away, but the majority of them did nothing except swing in their hammocks, and now and then herd cattle So lazy were they that they had never taken the trouble to fence in even one of the wretched ponds from which they obtained their drinking water; but instead, allowed the cows, pigs, and horses to bathe in them at their leisure. Of course this village, like all others, had its inner life, and to itself was a little world, of which the traveller could have but an imperfect knowledge.

It was certainly warm at Sacluk, as my thermometer

usually marked eighty-six degrees in the daytime, and seventy-eight at night, but there were no mosquitoes, and the air was so bright and clear, and there were so many lovely birds to collect that the few days we spent there passed very quickly and pleasantly. There were some brilliant humming-birds, among which I obtained rather a rare specimen, with its under part of a fine brown barred with white. But the most lovely as well as the most numerous were the species of fly-catchers. One of them had a blue back and breast with a black band round the neck, and black wings lined with yellow. The upper part of its head was of a light metallic green, and its little legs were bright pink. The other one* had plain brown wings, but the head, crest, and breast were of the most beautiful crimson, and as it darted through the air after insects, it looked like a ball of fire. The female of the same species was very dowdy-looking in comparison with her mate. Little ground doves—tortolitas—were very plentiful, and so tame, that they would hardly take the trouble to fly away when approached quite closely.

There was also a dull-coloured little fellow, but who possessed the mellowest voice possible; all day, and, unfortunately, for a greater part of the night, he sat up in an orange-tree calling "See here, what cheer, see here, what cheer," sun or rain, it was all the same to him, he would repeat his strange remark. In the daytime the notes sounded loud and true, but at night when it commenced its duet with the night-jar, it had

* Pyrocephalus mexicanus.

a maddening effect. "See here, what cheer!" sang one, "Oh, will you? oh, will you?" whistled the other, and this they would keep on repeating until despairing of sleep, I often rushed out exclaiming, "Yes, I will," and fired a shot in the direction of the delinquents.

I had much wanted to obtain a king vulture—one of the most brilliantly-coloured of the carrion-birds— and one day a villager ran in to inform us that "el rey sopilote," was feeding on a dead mule not far from the house. On going out, we could see numbers of the common buzzards standing in a circle at some little distance from the carcase, evidently waiting— according to their custom—for the king to finish his meal first. The chance of bagging his bird delighted Carlos, and taking the gun he commenced a careful stalk round the base of the wooded hills. As he drew near, the sopilotes edged off, but the white object was too busily occupied to notice anything outside the carcase, in which it was nearly hidden.

Cautiously and slowly Carlos crept up, until within easy distance, when "bang" went the gun, and with a loud howl out flew a gaunt village dog, which, with its tail between its legs and several grains of shot in its body, scampered back as fast as it could to its home. I shall never forget the subdued aspect of our sportsman, when he returned to the cottage, after an extended walk of a few miles.

After a few days we left Sacluk for Flores—the capital of Peten—which is situated about seven leagues to the north. The savanna over which we rode was covered with a little flower like a nemophila, but of a transparent white; there were others of a yellow colour, and a few purple petunias. The cone-shaped hills abounded in liquid amber trees, cedars and firs, whose dark green foliage was relieved by patches of crimson from a tall flowering shrub. Between the hills were orchards of trees something like the apple, but with dark glossy leaves. Occasionally, there was a stretch of shady wood, then prairie again. In one of these was a small savanna village, consisting of a miserable collection of dirty thatched cottages.

The houses were all shut up, and had it not been for the cattle, one would have imagined them to have been deserted. Here were numbers of a small brown bird,* with a yellow spot on its head, and two very long tail feathers, which hindered its flight in a very uncomfortable manner. Here also the crimson fly-catchers turned somersaults in the air, and the "uraca," a large, white-breasted bird uttered its noisy cry. Red-shouldered starlings, too, flew about in large flocks. At the edge of a small lagoon, a white crane walked solemnly along, and some small long-legged birds whistled and bowed to one another in a most comical manner.

After leaving the savanna, the road through the forest was very swampy, but level, and with a few intermittent spaces of rock and stone. Many beautiful orchids grew on the trees, but the bulbs were so wet that it would have been useless to have gathered them.

* Milvulus tyrannus.

Before we had half finished our ride, rain overtook us, and continued until we arrived at San Benito, a small village situated on a rocky slope, which ran down to the lake of Peten.

The historian Villagutierre states that the chief island in the Lake of Peten was first peopled by the Itzacs, a tribe who had migrated southwards from Yucatan about the year 1430. Hence its name, Peten-Itza.

At last the Spaniards determined on the conquest of Peten by peaceful means if possible, if not, by force of arms. Missionaries were sent, who after incredible hardships and sufferings arrived at the Lake only to be put to death. Then two successive expeditions were sent in 1695 and 1696, and both were driven out of the country. Other attempts were made to reach the Lake which failed signally. At last a gentleman of Merida, Don Martin Ursúa, who was anxious for notoriety, obtained permission to open a road from Yucatan to the Lake of Itza and to subdue the natives. After great preparations and much fruitless negotiation, General Ursúa embarked in a large galley with one hundred and six soldiers and two priests, leaving the rest of his men encamped on the shore of the Lake. When about half way to the island armed canoes appeared on all sides and formed a semi-circle around the galley, which continued its course to land, where it received volleys of arrows both from the canoes and from the shore.

The lofty "adoratorios" on the island appeared to

be crowned with batteries, and the shore had entrenchments of stone and spears. The Indians were quite demoralized by the musketry, and fled in all directions as the troops landed. None of the Spaniards were killed, but many of the Itzacs lost their lives, not only from wounds but also in their attempt to reach the main-land by swimming. Thus the conquest was accomplished on the 15th of March, 1697. The other islands and towns soon after hastened to offer their allegiance to the Spanish authorities, and Peten, although geographically and ethnologically belonging to Yucatan, has been politically united to Guatemala.

On the chief island were found twenty large temples —adoratorios—made of alabaster, and an immense number of idols of different materials and designs. Some of them were of jasper, and one female form was of emerald; this latter was taken possession of by Ursúa. Another resembled the sun, with rays of mother of pearl. There were also many statues of stone, wood and plaster, finely sculptured, but often fear-inspiring.

The dress of the natives was made from the thread of the agave. Among the various products was a superior quality of indigo, also vanilla, cocoa, cotton, wax, honey and grain. Such is a rough sketch of the downfall of the Itzacs, the site of whose ancient capital rose before us out of the Lake of Peten.

CHAPTER XXIII.

LAKE OF PETEN—FLORES—ISOLATION—GLAZED POTTERY—DRESS—
GEOGRAPHICAL KNOWLEDGE—CAVE OF JOBITZINAL—INTERIOR
OF CAVE—A CURIOUS BIRD—SHELLS—CORTES' HORSE—PETEN BY
MOONLIGHT—RUINS OF TICKAL—RETURN TO SACLUK—HIERO-
GLYPHICS—DESERTED CITIES.

THE general absence of knowledge regarding the region of Peten, and its inaccessibility, invest it with a charm that the unknown always possesses. The mysterious lake that had been sought in vain for months by armed expeditions was tinged with a romance that was peculiarly attractive, and now standing on its banks, the wildness and strangeness of the scene impressed me more even than I had anticipated.

The entire length of the Lake of Peten—which is only about five hundred feet above sea-level—is about nine leagues, and its broadest part is about three leagues. It is divided almost in two by a large peninsula, which approaches within half a league of the mainland. Here is situated the principal island, on which

Flores—the capital of the Department—stands. The hills which rise immediately from the opposite shore are wooded, with here and there a few acres of cultivated ground and a cottage at their base. Far away across the deep water, on the slopes of the hills towards the north-west, lie the white villages of San Andres and San José. The lake here sweeps round in a north-easterly direction, then forms an ill-shaped horseshoe with the Island of Flores as its first nail.

The southern shore—on which we were standing—is flat, but covered with forest, whose intense green forms a lovely setting to the water, which rivals the sky in its clear blue. In contrast to the bright colouring is the island capital, which stands out in white and stony barrenness. From the very edge of the water to the rocky summit nothing is to be seen but houses, clustering together so closely that the eye passes over the plantain leaves and palms that are sparsely scattered over the stony soil. The houses are mostly thatched, only a few of the more modern being tiled; all have white-washed mud walls, which are frequently so close to one another that the eaves of different buildings touch. They rise in terraces one above the other up to the narrow summit, which is crowned by a white church, the government buildings, and the sloping-roofed cottage of the Jefe Politico. The population is said to number about two thousand, which is, as may be imagined, far too great for an island, every part of which may be visited in less than half-an-hour.

From San Benito we crossed over in a canoe, and

were soon lodged in a new one-roomed cottage, which we reached by a double flight of steps. The owner informed us that his old cottage had been burnt, and that he had been hitherto unable to obtain furniture for his new one. He seemed surprised that I had never heard of the celebrated fire that had destroyed half the town, and when I asked him if it was of recent occurrence, he replied, " Yes, a little less than four years ago." After that I was more than ever impressed with the remoteness of Peten. Owing to the hospitality of the neighbours our room soon became habitable, as one sent a table, another some chairs, and a third a hammock.

On account of the small dimensions of the island, and the fact that whatever space is not covered with houses is occupied by pigs, the best way of enjoying Flores is from a distance, and as the population is strictly nautical, canoeing affords many delights. Nevertheless, on the island itself there was much of interest, more especially in the vast quantity of idol remains which are continually being dug up. When it was known that I wished to obtain some of these curiosities, our house was literally besieged by men, women, and children, all anxious to dispose of some fragment of stone or pottery. It was very seldom that an entire piece was offered, but rudely carved heads, hands, feet, and broken figures abounded. Some of the pottery was finely glazed, but the workmanship was in most cases superior to the design. Nearly all of the glazed figures contained pellets used as rattles or whistles. A mask that was offered to me, and which was about half the natural size, was extremely good, but the price asked was so exorbitant that I declined it. A stone jar shaped like a macaw—guacamayo—was also well carved. Besides these images they brought me some of the "small change" of the country, which consisted of oblong pieces of obsidian, each piece having a stated value according to its size and shape. No large remains were to be seen on the island, with the exception of a half-buried stone on which the inscriptions were almost worn away.

The dress of the women of Flores was much gayer than that of their sisters of Sacluk, and consisted of a bright-coloured, high-waisted wrapper, which made up for its late commencement by its flowing length. Their dark hair was adorned with a broad gold—or gilt—coronet, which invested them somewhat with the air of tragedy queens.

I do not think anyone had ever been farther than Sacluk, consequently their geographical knowledge was limited. Once, after I had said that I lived in Great Britain, which was also an island, I was asked whether it was larger than Flores!

Opposite the town, and at about a league and a half from San Benito, there is the celebrated cave of Jobitsinal. I was anxious to pay it a visit, as I had heard many stories about it. Some said that its extent was unknown, that it had been traversed for three days without any outlet being found; others that it ran under the lake, and the exit was believed to be on the other side. As the path to it was entirely overgrown the alcalde ordered it to be cleared, and one day, well provided with guides, provisions, rope and candles, we made the expedition.

On our way we saw many strange trees and plants, some of which are used as medicines. One of these trees is called "Oshoo," and its pith is eaten for certain complaints; another has a fruit like a custard apple, which when opened revealed a kernel covered with a beautiful silvery sheen like floss silk. The nut had a pleasant sweet flavour. There were also "fever trees," —kope—whose orange-red blossoms are collected and made into a decoction said to be beneficial in cases of fever. The thick bush was tangled with yellow creepers, and the branches of the forest trees were looped with many grenadillas, whose purple and white passion flowers mingled with the fleshy blossoms of the vanilla.

The entrance to the cave was in the side of a low range of limestone hills, and through it we descended into a small chamber, which led by a narrow opening into a larger one. This vault was vast and lofty, but the floor was hilly and strewn with rocks. Sparkling stalactites encrusted the roof and walls, but no stalagmites arose from the stony base. From this chamber many small apertures conducted into other galleries, and so numerous were the grottoes that the use of the rope was necessary to avoid the chance of being lost.

The torches lit up the crystal caverns with splendid effect, but revealed nothing extraordinary and but little novelty in this much-vaunted cave. In one place red drops oozed from the falling cones and sharp aigrettes, but beyond this phenomenon, which was probably due to some crimson lichen, the glittering walls showed nought but what is expected in every well-regulated grotto. That the cave does not extend under the lake was evident, as it follows the course of the hills which run parallel with it.

After an inspection of three or four hours, during which we examined all the chambers—as far as we could judge—we returned to Flores. I could not help thinking that had the inhabitants ever seen or heard of the Mammoth Cave of Kentucky, or the Alabaster Cave near Auburn, in the United States, they would not be so boastful of their own.

Among the strange birds of Peten is a curious rail or "parra," which is very plentiful on the lake shores. Its wings and body are chocolate-red, the feathers under the wing being bright yellow, the head and neck black, the legs and long needle-like toes green. Its peculiarity consists in a yellow shield, which rises from the bill, and in a sharp bony spur which issues from the shoulder of each wing. The natives say that the birds use this spur for fighting, but it is difficult to imagine with what effect.

In the lake, besides some brilliant coloured fish, there are some fine shells—caracolas—and also rare mussels with teeth. In the deep water near San Andres, it is a popular belief that the stone image of a horse which belonged to Cortes may be seen. The boatman who conducted us to the spot declared that he could see it distinctly, but I must say that I could distinguish no signs of any animal. Its appearance there is accounted for in the following manner. When Cortes passed through Peten, on his march to Honduras, he left a horse behind him. As the Itzacs had never seen anything larger than a tapir, they thought that the white horse was a sacred monster, and consequently was too holy to eat common food. They therefore strewed flowers and poultry before it, and not unnaturally the poor beast died of starvation. Then they reproduced it in stone, but unfortunately whilst they were once removing it from one island to another it fell overboard, and now lies at the bottom of the lake.

Of the different aspects under which one can appreciate the scenery of this region, whether it be at sunrise, when pink vapours reach to the horizon, or at sunset, when the transparent atmosphere renders the coloured outlines more distinct, or in a storm, when the angry waters beat in storm waves against the shores below San Andres, I think Peten by moonlight is the most beautiful. From the water the view then is especially lovely; it has no grandeur; but a quiet pathos that is not soon forgotten. The sun has long since disappeared, and a filmy haze gathers over the scene, tranquilly absorbing the darkening shadows. Suddenly over the brow of the distant hills there is a softening of the darkness, until a broad luminous space lightens the summit. The clouds show a silver lining and gleam in fanciful shapes, then settle back into gloom; even the bar of light is overshadowed, and a black velvet curtain enshrouds the mountain top; but only momentarily, and as it lifts a clear background is revealed which opens out as the glorious moon slowly rises from behind the cliff. A silver lustre spreads over the landscape, touching the tall cocoa palms and the white strips of sand, and bringing into strong relief the dark promontories and the low wooded islands that rise from the golden ripple.

Flores, like a great white ghost, seems to float above the water, and not a living or moving thing is to be seen. The distant note of a marimba occasionlly breaks the silence, but that is all; no other sound, unless it be true that you really hear the twinkle of the stars, as they hang so big and glittering, and apparently so close. Stars everywhere, above and below, their brilliance not at all abashed by the pale Queen as she sails among them, but rather heightened by the contrast of her soft rays with their sharp clear sparkle. No wonder the little Swedish girl, when asked why she regarded the stars so attentively, replied, "I was thinking if the wrong side of heaven is so glorious, what must the right side be?"

Concerning the antiquities of the surrounding country, I was informed that the only ruins worth visiting were those of Tickal, which are situated twelve leagues north of Las Playas, which is the most northerly point of the lake. From a man who had seen them I gained some information. He said that they were a league in extent, and evidently the remains

Curious Panels. 301

of a large city, as several houses were standing and in a perfect condition. These buildings were three and four stories high, entirely built of stone, and almost all unopened.

The opportunity of unearthing old Indian treasures was too good to be neglected, and as Carlos was willing I resolved—a resolve which was never executed—to visit Tickal. The journey thither was simple, viz., by canoe to Las Playas, and then on foot through the forest to the ruins, near which was an Indian village, to whose alcalde I received a letter from the Jefe Politico. As the expedition would probably involve a stay at Tickal of three or four weeks—the digging out of the tree-encumbered ruins being no light undertaking— we returned to Sacluk where the baggage was left, in order to make a few preparations.

On arriving there I found, that if I did not then avail myself of the mules I had engaged to take me to Tenosique, I should have great difficulty in procuring others hereafter. Not wishing to remain in Peten during May, when the thermometer rose over one hundred degrees—it was already ninety degrees—and the water even worse than at present, I reluctantly gave up my visit to Tickal.

At Flores I had obtained two wooden panels,* that had been taken from a lower room in one of the opened houses at Tickal. These panels were of very

---

* These two wooden panels, with ancient hieroglyphic carvings, have, since this work was written, been presented by the author to the Collection in South Kensington.

hard wood, from a tree known as the "small sapote," and were covered with carved hieroglyphics. As no other relics of any kind had been found, I consoled myself with the idea that probably the unopened houses contained no curiosities. It certainly seems probable that when the inhabitants abandoned their city they would take their household goods with them. Then, on the other hand, comes the question, why did they laboriously stone up their houses when they left them? why, too, did they leave them? and where did they go to? All is wrapped in mystery regarding these strange beings. The present race of Indians can throw no light on the subject, and look with superstitious reverence on the deserted buildings, which they dread to enter as much as they do the hill caverns and gloomy haunts of the surrounding country.

On an intensely hot morning we bade farewell to Sacluk, Carlos to return to Concuen as best he might, and I, with a guide and two muleteers, on the way to Tenosique. This with the slow pack-mule was a journey of five or six days, through a flat, unbroken forest.

CHAPTER XXIV.

COMMUNICATION WITH FLORES—SAVANA—SAN PABLO—SHEDS FOR TRAVELLERS—SAN DIEGO—NEST OF PAVO—BIRD CRY—MAHOGANY TREE—RONDELETTA—PALMETTO—GANAPATAS—THE PETEN TURKEY—JAGUAR STORIES—ENTER MEXICO—NO WATER—STORM IN FOREST—RIVER SAJAB—LAKE COPAR—HOLY GHOST ORCHID—ARRIVAL AT TENOSIQUE.

FLORES is connected with the outer world by four lines of communication. The shortest route is that to Belize, which lies due east, and is reached by the river of the same name after a journey of between thirty and forty leagues. The northern road to Merida in Yucatan is more open than the other, but very scarce of water. The southern road to Guatemala of about one hundred and thirty leagues, I have already described, and that to the west, of about one hundred and twenty leagues, we are about to traverse.

The three leagues of savanna over which we rode, before reaching the forest, presented new features. Here were sunken pits full of palm trees and luxuriant grasses; the oval hills were wooded, but instead of the rich soil of which they are usually composed, we only saw a covering of stones, as if all the stones and rocks had been collected from the prairie and heaped together. Thickets of mimosa and lilac-flowered plants intersected our path before entering the forest, which at length we gladly welcomed on account of the shade.

Our first day's journey was very short, but water is so scarce in these regions that the different halting places have to suit the localities in which it is found. It was called San Pablo, and consisted of two sheds made of cross sticks, with palm leaves, leaning against them. The muleteers quickly built fresh huts as the old ones were by no means inviting, and throughout the journey we enjoyed similar accommodation, except in two or three instances where the government had erected two or three well-thatched sheds for the accommodation of travellers.

Here I first became acquainted with "ramon" a tall shrub, with laurel like leaves which mules and other animals are extremely fond of, and which is the only provender they obtain in these journeys. The first thing muleteers do on arriving at their camping place is to disappear into the woods and cut branches of ramon for their animals. Fortunately it is generally plentiful, but there are spots where it is not found, consequently a knowledge of the localities of this plant is as necessary as that for water.

Our second night's lodging was in one of the government sheds—San Diego—near a large lake the water of which was worse I think than that obtained from the mud hole on the preceding day. Here I found a ground nest containing four eggs of a splendid blue colour, which the arrieros said belonged to the mountain pheasant, but which from their size I should say were those of a curassow. The cry of the former bird is most distressing, on account of its resemblance to that of a human being in distress. Ever since leaving Coban I had constantly heard the pleading notes—two short ones and a long—and frequently I had stopped, thinking I had lost my way and that somebody was calling me from a distance.

The forest between Peten and Tenosique is by no means a jungle; here and there are swamps and thickets, but as a rule the dry and sometimes rocky ground is shaded by enormous trees under whose branches the shrubs and bushes attain no very great luxuriance. One of the finest trees is the mahogany—caoba— whose tall straight trunk shoots up to a great height before the branches spread. Its fruit is a large pod containing numerous seeds, the kernel of which is exceedingly bitter. The natives say that it is as effective as quinine in cases of fever, and if so it appears to me that a valuable trade has been long neglected, as I do not think mahogany cutters either collect the pods or attach the slightest value to them.

Besides these trees there are palms, pepper trees, india-rubber, dye-woods, and sapotes; the fruit of the latter was scattered over the ground (probably by monkeys) but was quite hard and unripe, much to the

x

disgust of the mules who would turn it over with their noses and give a snort of disapprobation.

One tree is very conspicuous, on account of its bright red pods like gigantic capsicums. In some places the air is scented with the fragrant rondeletia—a shrub which bears brilliant crimson flowers with yellow centres. Pink jessamines and a few other sweet smelling flowers are also met with. A small palmetto too, whose young shoots are woven into hats, is very common. The great drawback to enjoyment in this forest is the immense quantity of garrapatas; they hang on every bush, and as frequently the path is so narrow that you have to force your way through it is impossible to avoid being covered with them.

At dark when you have arrived at your halting place you might rid yourself of these disgusting creatures, but all night you knew they were dropping from the palm leaves and clutching you with their crab-like embrace. Without experience, it is impossible for anyone to conceive the annoyance caused by these insects. I look upon them as a blot in an otherwise pleasant journey. Happily there were no mosquitoes, as the rainy season had not yet set in. With the exception of the "Paso de Sacluk," I had not been troubled with mosquitoes at any place in Guatemala.

At night our shed was always illuminated by the most brilliant fire-flies, or rather fire-beetles, which have two globes of light behind the head and another under the tail. So strong and clear was this light that when two or three were placed in an impromptu shade of twisted paper it was perfectly easy to read by them, and the shed seemed hung with Chinese lanterns.

In the day time we saw many handsome butterflies, and in chasing one of these beauties, whose wings were lavender trimmed with orange, I nearly got lost in the forest; but after a few hours' wandering where I was, I came out on the path only a few yards from where my mule was standing waiting for me. Another fine butterfly had beautiful violet wings lined with chocolate and with two large white eyes at the inner base. In the way of sport there were always some curassows to be obtained in the early morning, and in addition to these there was the beautiful Peten turkey,* which has a wonderful bronze sheen on its plumage, and is marked on its tail with eyes like those of the Argus pheasant. In April and May these birds abound in the neighbourhood of Sacluk, and at a hacienda there I had seen a tame brood of them strutting about very contentedly. There was also the common " pavo del monte," and the mountain-partridge, and a singing quail that pipes very sweetly in the morning. Afterwards at Tenosique I saw and heard two of these quails that were in confinement, and their notes were as musical as those of a thrush. The other birds that we noticed comprised trogons, macaws, toucans, parrots, pigeons, woodpeckers, a few harpy-eagles, humming birds, tree-creepers, and the claret-coloured pheasant known as "montezumas."

Of four-footed animals, besides monkeys, we saw but few; now and then a wild pig or a badger crossed our

* Meleagris ocellata.

path, and one night we heard a jaguar roaming round our sheds, but we never got a shot at it. Jaguars seldom attack men, although they have been known to follow a trail for days, waiting for a good opportunity to spring. It was through these woods, too, that two young Americans once attempted to penetrate into the Lacandone country. After a day's journey they found that some necessary had been left behind, and so one of them returned for it, his companion in the meantime continuing his course, and marking the trees as he went. Presently, the one who had gone back found on his return that these marks ceased, and soon discovered the dead body of his companion, and a sheet of paper describing how he had been attacked from behind by a jaguar, which he had beaten off, but he felt himself dying, owing to the severe wounds at the back of his neck, which were aggravated by the festering insects. The survivor returned.

The following event, most extraordinary if true, is said to have occurred in this forest to a mahogany-cutter who had been out marking trees. As he was returning to his hut, he suddenly felt a soft body pressing against him, and on looking down saw a congar, which, with tail erect, and purring like a cat, twisted itself in and out of his legs, and glided round him, turning up its fierce eyes as if with laughter. Horror-stricken and with faltering steps he kept on, and the terrible animal still circled about, now rolling over and now touching him with a paw like a cat playing with a mouse. At last the suspense became too great, and with a loud shout he struck desperately at the creature with his axe. It bounded on one side, and crouched snarling and showing its teeth. Just as it was about to spring, the man's companion's, who had heard his call, appeared in the distance, and with a growl the beast vanished into the thick bushes. The strain had been so intense that for days the man's life was despaired of, and when he recovered, he gave up mahogany cutting and quitted the forest for ever.

On the fourth day after leaving Sacluk, we crossed the almost dried up bed of the Yatchilan river—a tributary of the San Pedro—and two leagues from it we entered Mexico. The so-called boundary is marked by three crosses, which have been erected on a small ridge, but it is a doubtful point whether the real Mexican boundary is here or at Tenosique. At any rate the change was for the worse, as the path was narrower, there were more swamps, no more large sheds, and mosquitoes began to be troublesome. Fallen trees continually barricaded the overgrown track, and round these it was necessary to struggle through the thorny shrubs, for no traveller would dream of cutting through the prostrate trunk, as that would facilitate the progress of the next comer.

After a night's rest at a halting-place called La Pita, where there was a small pool of stagnant water, we went to our next watering spot and found the holes quite dry. There were no bromelias either, from whose cup-like leaves we had sometimes been able to extract a small quantity of clear water.

It was too late to continue our journey in the hope of finding water, and we had made up our minds to pass a thirsty night when there were sudden indications of a storm brewing. A low moaning wind arose, and the heavens were transformed from a serene to an angry and menacing aspect. Before the sun had disappeared in the west, black clouds made it as dark almost as night. Then came a deafening roll of thunder, followed by crash after crash, and the profound blackness of the sky only found expression when relieved by the glare of lightning as it flashed across the horizon.

The wind by this time had increased to a hurricane, and our rude sheds were quickly prostrated, and we had to sit, Marius-like, among the ruins to prevent them from flying away. The storm increased in violence, and at one moment, just as the last ray of light betokened sunset, a rent in the black clouds discovered the moon peering down at us. Thus we had rain, wind, thunder, lightning, sun and moon all at the same time. The light lasted but a second, and the rain fell as if the heavens were dropping. Fortunately, the greatest force of the hurricane passed above our hollow, but the crashing of the falling trees sounded terribly near, and made us cast anxious glances at our own partial protectors. The rain, though heavy, did not last long, and the wind, after a passionate climax gradually subsided. Then we quenched our thirst, rebuilt our huts, and went to bed.

Next morning, as usual, we had to rise at three, in

order to be ready to start at daylight, but were delayed for some time on account of one of our Indians who had an attack of fever. We made but a short journey that day, passing on the way some broad cuttings in the forest, where woodmen had dragged their mahogany logs down to the San Pedro river which flowed at some distance on our right. By this time the sleepless "garrapata" nights had so worn me out that I determined to push on to Tenosique the following day, and leave the pack mules to follow.

The first part of the last day's journey was through a bad swamp, in which our own mules were up to their girths in mud, and I congratulated myself in not having to witness the struggles of the pack animals. Then after four leagues we crossed the river Sajab, which is nine leagues from Tenosique. After this the path was drier, until we passed the large lake of Copar. This was a picturesque but gloomy expanse of water, without even a bird to enliven its utter solitude. Here for the first time I saw the curious Holy Ghost orchid*—Espiritu Santo—so called on account of the yellow dove-like form that stands in the centre of the white globular flower.

The trail soon after was so overgrown that it was difficult to pass, and in many places necessitated a long delay whilst being cut through. At last we came to a stream in which were fish like trout, but with tails of a bright red. This stream we had to cross over on a slippery trunk, and the mules reached the other side by

* Peristeria elata.

plunging through mud and water that almost submerged them.

The sun was just setting when we issued from the forest, and the air of the savanna seemed deliciously fresh, after the damp woods in which we had been shut up. A ride of a league over the prairie land, which differed from that of Peten in having flat, irregular clumps of trees, brought us to Tenosique. As my guide, Juliano, lived here, we dismounted at his cottage, and the welcome we received from his wife and family was only excelled by that of the mosquitoes. The night was by no means of unmixed enjoyment, as all through it these aggravating insects sang a soft accompaniment to the music of an infant, aged six months.

CHAPTER XXV.

THE USUMACINTA—TENOSIQUE—PRETENSIONS—SOCIETY—ADVAN-
TAGE OF POVERTY OVER RICHES—SPITE—TO-MORROW—A TWIST-
ING STREAM—ANECDOTE OF SPANISH INDOLENCE—DEPARTURE
FROM TENOSIQUE—PHILODENDRONS—CROSSING THE RIVER—
RARE SWALLOWS—RIVER CHACAMAS—LOST IN THE PRAIRIE—A
WET NIGHT—A LAKE SCENE—ARRIVAL AT MONTECRISTO.

T Tenosique I found an old acquaintance in the Pasion river, which here takes the name of Usumacinta—Sacred Ape. This river, after describing a semicircle through the vast wooded solitudes of the Lacandone country, breaks through the mountain chain in a series of rapids above Tenosique, and flows past the town in a broad and swift stream.

The town, or rather village, is situated on the high banks on the right of the river, but on the opposite side are also many houses and haciendas, some overlooking the water, others lying far back in groves of fruit trees and bananas. On the north side the forest approaches close to the village, and indeed there is little else to be seen all around but wood. There is, however, a good deal of cultivation—chiefly of tobacco and sugar-cane—carried on in the neighbourhood, and many herds of cattle feed on the intersecting prairie lands. Most of the houses are mere mud-plastered and thatched huts, but a few, and naturally the coolest, consist of thin upright poles which admit of free ventilation. In one of these latter, which was surrounded by a good sized garden, I was established by a gentleman named Don Felipe Romero, to whom I had a letter of introduction. He himself lived on the opposite side of the river, and I was very glad to have the house to myself.

There is little to be said about Tenosique, and certainly nothing in its favour. Its pretensions are quite out of proportion to its size. It has a customhouse, whose officials make up for the usual dull business by the strictest investigation of baggage when the occasion presents itself. It also possesses a Jefe Politico and a commandante, the latter of whom kept a small grocery, who was so annoyed at my refusal to hire a horse from him for my journey, that one entire night I was prevented from sleeping by a patrol of soldiers, who walked about my verandah under the pretence of looking after my property. I afterwards found out that he was at daggers drawn with Don Felipe, and was angry that the latter should reap the benefit of furnishing me with horse and canoes, &c., for my journey to Palenque.

The green in the centre of the village was used as a

parade ground for a few soldiers, who sometimes drill as cavalry and sometimes as infantry. When they were not there, it was occupied by the horse of the commandante, and by some snipe-billed hogs, who were so thin that they almost became invisible when running away from you. In the same plaza stands a large ugly church, closed and unused because no priest lives in the place.

For so small a town the number of feuds and petty quarrels was very great, and it was difficult to hear a good word of anybody.

At a small sort of restaurant where I used sometimes to breakfast, I constantly met an old lady indulging in chocolate. She was very garrulous and amusing, and prided herself on her ancient pedigree. She was not as rich as formerly, she said, but still had never gone without her "desayans," *i.e.*, her early morning cup of chocolate. Her family plate consisted of a "jicaro," or silver-mounted cocoa-nut bowl, and this she always carried with her, the silver ring which formed a stand for it being a constant source of admiration.

"Ah!" she exclaimed one day, "for the good old times when nobody was rich and there were no mosquitoes."

As I did not see the connection between poverty and mosquitoes, I asked her to explain. She said that when nobody had any money there was no moving from place to place, now even the Indians were well off, and whenever they travelled they carried mosquitoes with them. She assured me that she remembered when there were no mosquitoes at Tenosique. " And now," she added, with a gesture of disgust, " bah !"

Two days before our arrival the town had been thrown into great excitement by a murder. The owner of a small general store, which faced the plaza, had been shot dead, as he was writing at the counter, by a man who jumped on his horse and escaped. The affair was wrapped in mystery, as no robbery was committed, and the murderer was an utter stranger. The widow and her family were in sad distress, but never seemed to tire of showing the shot marks in the adjoining plaster wall, and the spot where the poor man was sitting. Some of the soldiers and inhabitants were out searching the country, but up to the time of my departure the villain had not been caught.

The heat here was excessive, my thermometer seldom showing less than ninety-eight degrees in the daytime and ninety-two degrees at night; in the early morn a cold wind used to sweep through my house, which, though refreshing at the time, brought fever and rheumatism in its train. I was therefore very anxious to continue my journey, but day after day it had to be postponed. Two or three times all was ready, but on the morning of departure the boatmen—soldiers—who had been engaged by Don Felipe, were placed on some trifling duty by the orders of the friendly commandante, who thus vented his spite on both of us at the same time.

Here, as in other parts of Spanish America, everything is to be done " mañana," and no one knows how much aggravation is concentrated in that one word "to-morrow."

"Do nothing to-day which by any possible means yon can put off until to-morrow," is here the application of the old adage.

At last the preparations were actually completed, and the canoe with two boatmen and my horse and guide were ready.

My reason for travelling by land to Monte Cristo—from which place I could reach Palenque—was because, although it is only distant from Tenosique about fourteen leagues, yet by river, on account of the many windings, it requires over three days to complete the journey. The canoe with my baggage was therefore to await my return from Palenque at Monte Cristo.

Some of the bends taken by the Usumacinta river are so great that a ride of a few hours across country will bring you to the same spot, to reach which a canoe will take two days. In any other country short canals would long ago have facilitated traffic.

An amusing story was told me at Coban by a gentleman who was once travelling on this river, which illustrates Spanish American indolence, as well as the ease with which canals might be made. At the village of Cabecera, near Tenosique, he was asked by a deputation of the inhabitants who had heard of his skill as a surveyor whether he thought a canal could be made from their village to Povecue which would save a very long river journey. He visited the district and found that by taking advantage of two small streams a canal of about a league would be all that was necessary. They were delighted at this, and begged him to write an official letter to the government on their behalf, asking for permission to commence the work at once. Ten years afterwards he was again at Cabecera, and the first question asked him was, "Do you not think a canal could be made from this village to Povecue?" On informing them that he had been asked the same question ten years previously, and had taken some trouble about the matter, the chief spokesman replied that on account of politics and the death of his father, &c., &c., the government letter had probably been overlooked. Search was made and the letter was found, when once more all was excitement and nothing was spoken of but the canal.

Some years elapsed before my informant was there again, and immediately on his arrival a deputation entered his room. "Do you not think a canal—" but the speaker got no farther, and together with the deputation was kicked off the premises.

It was with no feelings of regret that I looked my last on Tenosique, and with my guide Pedro started for Monte Cristo. We were to cross the river at Cabecera, and our road thither lay through wood-land and savanna. The noisy cries of chachas, parrots, and uracas echoed on all sides, and the trees were garlanded with yellow and red creepers.

One portion of a wood, past which we were riding, glowed so brilliantly with a crimson flush that I went to see the cause. It proved to be a number of splendid orchids whose flowers graduated in colour from a pale pink to a bright spotted crimson, the inner cup being pink and white. The blossoms grew on a long spike, one of which I measured, being over five feet in length, and having on it more than one hundred flowers.

Afterwards I saw many trees laden with them, but all near Tenosique and none on the other side of the river. Twisting around the trunks of the trees that bore these unfamiliar flowers, were the large leaves of a philodendron whose open spathes showed the well remembered "lords and ladies" of our own woods.

At Cabecera where there were several picturesque cottages, but as dirty and uncomfortable as usual, we crossed the Usumacinta in a canoe, our animals swimming behind. On the other side we entered a thick forest, which we traversed for many leagues until we reached a small cluster of huts overlooking a low swampy extent of country. Skirting a marsh, we presently entered a more open district on the far side of which was a village. Near here we saw a large and very rare species of swallow with a white throat; it was evident that a pair of them had their nest in a solitary dead tree, as we watched them flying in and out of its hollows for some time. These birds would have been a very valuable acquisition to my collection, but—irrespective of the nest—my preserving materials were all in the canoe, so they were left in peace.

The country now was varied with wood and plain, and occasionally we passed a small village. At one of these I began to entertain suspicions that my guide was ignorant of the road, as he was very anxious to pass the night here and predicted a coming storm. It certainly was getting late, but as he—Pedro—had been the cause of our late start from Tenosique, I did not feel inclined to gratify him, and moreover did not wish to lose a whole day which would be entailed by a halt at the proposed spot.

We rode on until we arrived at a deep river—the Chacamas—which had to be crossed in the same manner as the Usumacinta, into which it flowed at a short distance on our right. By the time we had re-saddled and were ready to start again it was almost dark, but Monte Cristo was only two leagues farther on, and Pedro said the road was easy.

After a short piece of woodland we entered a large stretch of undulating prairie, diversified with clumps of trees and reedy marshes. The foot-path was so narrow and the rank grass so high that frequently I lost sight of Pedro altogether. At length, after continuing for about an hour along this unpromising trail, he stopped, and looked about him with the air of a man who did not know where he was. I then accused him of being ignorant of the road, but he assured me it was all right and we should soon reach Monte Cristo. He then at once turned off into quite another direction to that we had previously been following, and I was satisfied we had lost our way.

I will not recount our various wanderings, it will be sufficient to say that for hours we wandered in the dark backwards and forwards, and around that prairie labyrinth. The provoking part was that the lying guide would not allow that he had lost his way, but would point out some distant spot, which when we reached he would stop at, and point again to some other landmark in the direction we had come.

What the object of his extraordinary proceedings was I could not imagine, but at last I became so angry that drawing my revolver I ordered him to force his way through the thick bushes to a large tree.

Before it had grown quite dark, we had visited that very spot in our peregrinations, and I had fancied that at some little distance off I could distinguish houses. The guide, however, stated positively that there could be no houses in that direction, and we had wandered off somewhere else. When we reached the tree, nothing was to be seen, as it was pitch dark, it being nearly midnight and a heavy rain falling. All we could do was to take advantage of the slight shelter, and pass the night there. Dismounting, we searched for some dry sticks to make a fire, and as I was trying to kindle it I told Pedro to secure the horses.

As he approached mine, it moved off, and in a moment was lost in the darkness. Thinking it would soon return, we turned our attentions to the fire which, owing to the damp, steadily refused to burn. An hour passed, and as the animal did not return, I rolled myself in my rugs, which I had fortunately removed from his back and tried to sleep. But sleep was out of the question, not only on account of the mosquitoes, but because of my anxiety regarding the horse, that had gone off with my revolver, which was in the holster, and my saddle-bags, which contained papers, notes, orchid bulbs, and a variety of other things including my money.

At the first streak of dawn we set out to return to the river we had crossed the previous evening, thinking that perhaps my animal had made its way back there. On looking round before we left, there, at a distance of about a quarter of a mile, but across a swamp, were the houses I had thought I had seen. After this Pedro had nothing more to say, and acknowledged he had lost the road, and did not know what village it could be.

It was no easy matter to trace our course through the high, soaking grass and tangled thickets; numerous cattle paths intersected the prairie, and large swamps intervened between the brush-covered undulations. The sight of one of these swamps repaid me for the bad night's lodging. High reeds, rushes, and mimosa bushes concealed a small lake from which every now and then large birds arose. Pushing my way to a small eminence overlooking it, I gazed down on the most wonderful collection of water-birds I had ever seen. On a little island in the middle were snowy herons, blue herons, and white ibises,* with long red beaks and legs. Wading about or standing at the edges were great white birds† with bare black necks and long turned-down bills; large as these were they had their superiors in enormous fellows with brownish

* Ibis alba.   † Tantalus loculator.

white plumage of the most ragged description. These birds* had also bare black necks, and immense beaks that seemed capable of crushing a turtle. As a contrast to these were numerous little bitterns,† which ran nimbly about and twisted in and out among the reeds, as if in ridicule of the stately walk of their big friends.

The predominant white colour was relieved by some roseate spoon-bills, and now and then a metallic green jacamar would skim swiftly across the water. Then there were some purple gallinules, and the same species of "spur-wing" that I had seen at Peten. Occasionally, with a harsh croak, one of the long-legged birds would take wing, and there would be a commotion as if danger were near, then quiet would again reign.

In the surrounding willows and bushes were many songsters and pretty-plumaged birds; there were crimson-headed fly-catchers, orioles and clarineros, whose clear notes sounded joyfully in the still morning air. As the sun rose, most of the feathered tribe left the lake and wended their flight towards the neighbouring river.

At Chacamas, which we reached after some trouble, we could neither hear nor see anything of my animal, and so with an Indian guide we proceeded to Monte Cristo. There we were kindly received by the alcalde, whose countenance fell when he heard that my money was with the missing horse, but brightened again when I told him that there was more in the expected canoe. He at once sent out a searching party, and late that

* Mycteria americana.   † Ardetta exilis.

evening the animal was brought back with the saddle and revolver all right, but without the saddle-bags. I had strong suspicions that these had been stolen, but as it was possible they might have been shaken off, I had no alternative but to submit to the loss.

It was extremely fortunate that I had divided my money into two bags, taking half with me and sending the rest with my baggage in the canoe, or I doubt whether I should have obtained a horse and guide to take me to Palenque. The authorities of these villages are very civil when they think there is anything to be made by it, but without money they will do nothing. With the understanding, therefore, that payment should be made on the arrival of my canoe, the alcalde promised to procure me a horse and guide to start next morning for the ruins of Palenque.

CHAPTER XXVI.

TO-MORROW—MONTE CRISTO—START FOR PALENQUE—HORSE-FLIES
—SAN MIGUEL—DON DAVID—CUEVA DE DON JUAN—GHOST
STORIES—SANTO DOMINGO DEL PALENQUE—START FOR RUINS—
THICK FOREST—THE PALACE—ANCIENT NAME OF PALENQUE—
GENERAL ASPECT—ANCIENT INHABITANTS—HIGH TOWER—
RELICS—CROSSES—PYRAMIDS—EXTENT OF RUINS.

FTER a sleepless night in a hammock
—which though pleasant enough to
lounge in during the daytime, makes a
very poor substitute for even the most
indifferent bed, especially where mosquitoes abound—
I rose betimes so as to be ready for the long ride of
about thirteen leagues.

For a couple of hours I waited in anxious expectation
of my horse and guide, and then, as I might have
expected, my host informed me that he had been
unable to procure a guide, but that "mañana" I should
start. The poor man had been unable to resist the
prospect of payment for another day's board and
lodging. An idle day at Monte Cristo was a penalty
I had not anticipated. The village consisted of between

seventy and eighty houses, perched on the high left bank of the Usumacinta, and possessed no interest whatever. Its only redeeming feature was its quiet; some people perhaps might have thought it too quiet, as the very cows which browsed along the main street, would stop chewing their cud, and gaze in wondering awe at the sight of a stranger. The houses were like those of other villages in this part of the country, consisting merely of mud-plastered walls, forming a room with an uneven mud floor and a thatched roof.

The furniture usually comprised a table, a bench, a hammock, and perhaps two chairs. In some cases a mud partition divided the room into two unequal parts, the smaller of which was used by the family as a sleeping apartment, the larger one being a public resort for anybody who might choose to stroll in. No attempt is ever made at comfort or convenience, and cleanliness ranks nowhere. I really do not remember ever having seen a ladino wash his hands or face during my travels in Central America.

I found Monte Cristo far hotter even than Tenosique, my thermometer invariably marking over one hundred degrees in the shade; therefore, when at night the shutters were carefully closed under the pretence of keeping out the mosquitoes, the temperature of the room was almost suffocating.

It was evidently the intention of my host to detain me a second day, as, though my horse appeared, there was no guide. At last I mounted, and said it did not matter I would go alone—which, by the way, would have been impossible—then a man emerged from a neighbouring doorway and offered his services. I afterwards found out that he had all along been engaged to go with me.

For the first five leagues we rode through a wooded country—montana—following a narrow, obscure path, over which vines and creepers interlaced, and across which colossal fallen trees offered serious obstacles. Then in the hot noon we came out on to the grassy savanna, with its groves of trees and shady clumps. Near a small stream we startled some deer, and shortly afterwards were ourselves startled by the attacks of enormous horseflies, which sadly irritated our poor animals, already suffering from the great heat of the sun.

For seven leagues the monotonous savanna continued, and then we approached the mountains of Palenque. Here an occasional hacienda gave a little life to the scene, and the landscape became more varied. When within two leagues of Santo Domingo del Palenque, we turned off to the right, as I wished to visit a German gentleman who owned a farm— San Miguel—about three leagues further on, and who was well acquainted with the ruins.

After passing some groves of splendid mango trees, and winding across a low range of hills, where we saw some of the wildest looking Indians, we rode through a very pretty wood, and emerged on the small plateau on which stood the house we were seeking. The owner—Herr Schener, or Don David, as he was always called—was delighted to see a stranger, and although my letter to him was in my lost saddle-bags, received us most hospitably, and at once agreed to accompany us to the ruins on the following day. Years ago he had settled with his family in this solitary spot, to engage in cattle raising, and since his arrival here hardly ever met a European. Perhaps once a year a visitor to the ruins passed his door on his way from Las Playas, and then Don David gladly assisted him in his researches.

Opposite his house, on the other side of a valley, were the mountains in which are situated the ruins of Palenque. High up in the sierra our host pointed out a white rock in which is a cavern known as the " Cueva de Don Juan." The Indians regard it as a shrine, and declare that much wealth is concealed within it. Some years ago two white men determined to explore it; but on arriving at the mouth of the cave found that a landslip had blocked up the entrance.

The Indians still pray there; but no attempt has been made to remove the obstruction. Of course, these wonderful ruins of Palenque have innumerable ghost stories attached to them, and the tales related of human beings who have vanished for ever whilst trying to discover buried treasures, of walls which have been rebuilt in a night, and of mysterious voices that have been heard issuing from the dark vaults, would fill a chapter.

Before daylight we were in the saddle, and some

distance on the road toward Santo Domingo, near which village are the ruins we were going to visit. After crossing a stream, a broad grassy sweep, bounded by woodland, brought us to the village which is prettily situated on undulating ground, and abounding with mango and other fruit trees. The highest point is occupied by a new church which overlooks the valley. In the front walls of the unfinished edifice, two bas-reliefs, from the ruins, have been inserted. The figures, which compose these bas-reliefs, face each other, one on each side of the main entrance, and very strange enigmatical personages they are. One of them wears an extraordinary head-dress of leaves and flowers, and in its mouth is a tube from which issues fire and smoke. From the shoulders hangs a leopard skin, which is ornamented with a snake, bird, and other devices. Anklets and armlets complete the costume.

Remembering a few of the Mexican symbols of cosmogony, I could not help fancying that this figure was intended to represent one of the great natural forces, viz.: heat. The other figure has an equally complicated head-dress, but composed of feathers, and of the sacred bird—el gavilan—holding a fish in its beak. The rest of the embellishments include a tiger's head, a grotesque figure, and other quaintly carved subjects.

Over both figures are several hieroglyphics. From the eminence on which the church stands, the view of the surrounding country is picturesque. The diversity of wood and plain, the broad green lanes, a glimpse of water, the cattle feeding, and the pretty (at a distance) thatched cottages, form a pleasant scene.

As for the inhabitants of this pleasant nook, they simply exist. Their occupations are a little cock-fighting, a little gambling, and talking a great deal of scandal.

After a visit to the ruins, one feels that modern life here is a sorry burlesque on that ancient Indian civilization which lies buried in the thick forest on the other side of the green valley. Leaving our small packs at a house in the village where we intended to sleep, we started for the ruins which are situated three leagues away. The trail we followed was so overgrown that the Indians who accompanied us had plenty of occupation in clearing the way for us. In the high trees were numerous large green parrots with yellow heads, and now and then a trogon or a mot-mot flew past. I was glad to hear that garrapatas were not very troublesome in the forest, but was told that on the savannas they were so numerous that in April of each year the Indians were accustomed to burn large tracts of land in order to destroy them.

Several muddy gullies had to be crossed, and before ascending the steep forest-hill on whose side stand the ruins, we forded a beautiful stream of sparkling water. Soon after this, we passed fragments of stone walls and a few carved blocks, and then dismounted near the foot of an elevation on

Palace of Palenque.

which stands the principal ruin, *i. e.*, the Palace of Palenque.

So dense was the forest that I did not, at first, perceive any signs of the great building above us, but a front view disclosed a stone edifice with a long corridor supported by pillars.

The walls were stuccoed and ornamented with curious designs, and as well as the projecting eaves were in a wonderful state of preservation. Ascending the elevation over the débris of what had once been stone steps, we entered the corridor, which was over two hundred feet in length. The most curious part of this was the formation of the ceiling, which was made by the inclination of the walls to each other after a certain height, and then connected by a horizontal layer of stones.

From the corridor we entered a large quadrangle, surrounded by a stone gallery. The court-yard was thickly overgrown with shrubs and bushes, and strewn with a great quantity of shells and fossils. The proper name of Palenque is Nascham,* *i. e.*, House of Serpents, and a few wriggling creatures we saw in the underbrush justified its title. Half-hidden, also, by the vegetation were huge stone idols indifferently sculptured; but which, together with the flights of steps, the large galleries, the ornamented stucco, the towers, and the numerous chambers, gave an idea of the rude grandeur of their mysterious architects.

Dotted about on lofty eminences were other edifices,

* Casa de culebras.

some large, some small, and some of two and three stories. Most of the houses had some distinguishing feature, such as a tablet of hieroglyphics or a symbolical bas-relief. In these the sculpture varied greatly, from the poorest outline to the well-finished and symmetrical design. The solidity and boldness of the structures, which are all built on lofty pyramidal bases, inspire wonder and surprise rather than admiration, and the small rooms and generally complicated arrangement of the interiors excite curiosity rather than enthusiasm.

Nearly all the chambers possess a striking peculiarity in numerous solid handles let into the walls at intervals. Neither Don David nor myself could fathom their object, as they were all at uncertain heights, and in different situations. Some of them were in the doorways, as if intended to act as hinges, others in the centre of the walls, as if they might be used for slinging hammocks; but others again were so high up as to be useless for such a purpose. Another peculiarity is that, wherever the steps are entire, the distance between them is so great that giants alone could ascend them with ease, whereas most of the chambers themselves are so small that they seem intended for dwarfs.

Everywhere great trees had thrown done the stonework, rendering the steep ascent to the edifice a matter of much climbing, and creeping plants and bushes have spread wherever they can twine and twist themselves. The sight of the ruined temples and houses perched on their sheltered elevations, and buried in the silent forest, leaves a wondering and solemn impression on the mind of the spectator.

Picture the city as it must have been ; the massive houses painted and covered with ornaments, the temple altars decked for sacrifice, the terraces and steps crowded with the plumed and fantastically dressed people, and the streets thronged with busy life. Look at it as it is ; a series of shattered hulls lost in a forest ocean. Masses of tree-encumbered stones rise on all sides ; human skill has fought against nature and has succumbed ; not entirely, so as to leave no trace, but so drowned, so overshadowed that the poor stony ghosts look more sad and mournful in their green graves than if standing in a sandy desert.

> "Here in green ruins, in the desolate walls
> Of antique palaces where man hath been,
> Though the dun fox or wild hyæna calls,
> And owls that flit continually between
> Shriek to the echo, and the low winds moan ;
> Here the true silence is self-conscious and alone."

And concerning the strange race of beings who inhabited the city how little is known ! who they were and whence they came is mere conjecture, whither they went when they quitted their homes is wrapped in mystery. They disappeared as completely as did the blind Œdipus, when he wandered into the sacred woods of the Eumenides and was never heard of or seen again.

We lunched on the banks of a stream that issued from an aqueduct below the palace. This aqueduct is by no means the least interesting of the Palenque remains. It is well built of stone and high enough to admit of ingress, and runs a long distance underground. How far is not known, as stones and rubbish prevent a thorough investigation; nor has the source of the stream been discovered.

Afterwards I ascended a high tower, whose summit had to be reached from the outside by means of branches and the broken walls. The tower was of three stories, and although each story could be traversed yet there were no means of reaching them from the interior.

The view was one of tree-tops, and I could see nothing of the waters of Las Playas, which are said to be visible from that elevation, and the village of Santo Domingo was the sole inhabited spot that met the eye. In another house, we saw some lime that had recently been found in a stone jar, which was walled up in the building. The lime was as white and soft as if of yesterday's manufacture.

It is strange that more relics have not been found, as during the hot season it is the custom for some of the families from the village to spend a few days in these cooler regions. The only building that has been discovered very lately contains a beautiful bas-relief of a Cross ornamented with wreaths. The workmanship of this is much more delicate than on that which is known as the "Stone of the Cross," which lies neglected on the hill-side, gradually being effaced. That this symbol which is revered throughout Christendom cannot fix the date of Palenque, is evident, when we remember that the cross was worshipped throughout the primeval world ages before Christianity. It is found among the Chinese, the Mexicans, the Celts; in India, Egypt, and Etruria, and even in the South Pacific. Probably it derived its sacred character from the starry effigy that the old sun-worshippers nightly saw in the sky above them.

Astronomy was the soul of their religious system, and each planet that was supposed to contain a portion of the eternal fire that circulated throughout the universe had its own special temple or pyramid. The pyramid form was chosen as being the fittest to represent the rays of the sun, and the best way in which flame could be depicted.

An ancient philosopher, describing the geometrical figures that compose each of the elements, assigns that of the pyramid to fire.

"The equilateral triangle," he says, "enters into the composition of the pyramid, for it has four sides and four equal angles, which constitute the nature of fire, that most subtle and moving of the elements. It is not without good reason, then, this figure has been to monuments for the worship of the sun and moon ; for it appears that nature herself has traced the drawing." It is vaguely hinted by the inhabitants of Santo Domingo that the ruins of Palenque extend at intervals for miles along the mountain-side in the direction of Tenosique, but as the Indians who travel about the forest profess to know nothing about them, their existence may be doubted. Perhaps the still standing monuments were the temples and public buildings of a people who themselves live in frail houses. If so, the materials would long ago have perished, and the stone edifices remain the only connecting links between the present and the far distant past.

Turning from these grand old memorials of a lost race, we felt that we were leaving a strange land whose atmosphere breathed of a buried secret that would never be unfolded.

CHAPTER XXVII.

BANKS OF THE USUMACINTA—INGA PODS—LAGARTOS—RIO CHICO
—LAS PLAYAS—ROUTE TO PALENQUE—SAN GERONIMO—GUACO
— DYE WOODS — PALIZADO — MODERN CIVILIZATION — TOWN
LIMITS—LOGWOOD—ON THE RIVER—LAS CRUCES—BOCA CHICA
—LAGUNA DE TERMINOS.

N our return to Monte Cristo I was delighted to find that the canoe had arrived, and lost no time in embarking for our journey down the Usumacinta. The banks of this river are here even flatter than at Concuen, but clothed with trailing bamboos and trees decked with pink, yellow and violet blossoms.* From one species of tree hung enormous pods two and three feet long, and about three inches in breadth. Hideous alligators of a larger size than those we had previously seen were stretched motionless on the mud banks, and once more we saw and heard the great iguanas flopping hastily into the water from the overhanging branches. Among the bamboos and willows we also noticed a

* Inga spectabilis.

beautiful little bird of crimson and yellow plumage, with a delicately striped head.

At intervals we passed wattled and palm-leafed cottages standing singly or in groups, all surrounded with fruit-trees, and many of them bright with garden flowers. But there was an absence of industrial life that deprived the quiet river scene of a great charm, and in the leagues of fertile land there was hardly one cultivated field.

Before long we passed on our left the Rio Chico, which with a few more creeks of the Usumacinta runs down in a southerly direction towards Palenque, near which place the head of the navigation terminates in Las Playas de Catasaja. In the wet season the plain becomes a large circular lake, owing to the rising of the waters, and the village of Las Playas is then entirely surrounded, except at the point where lies the road to Palenque. It is usually by this line of travel down the Rio Chico that visitors to the ruins reach their destination.

At length we had to leave the broad Usumacinta, and two leagues before reaching the village of Jonuta turned into a branch of the great river which is called the Rio Palizada. Floating down the river was pleasant in the day-time, as there was usually an agreeable breeze, but at sunset the wind died away and mosquitoes came out in myriads. A low leaf-thatching covered half the canoe as a protection against sun and rain, but at night the heat was too great to allow one to creep under it. After patiently enduring the attacks of the mosquitoes for a few hours during the first night, I ordered the boat to be run ashore, determining in future only to travel by day. In a canoe, mosquito-netting is a delusion, as if it is of fine material it at once gets torn, and if of coarse, the heat is insupportable. In the cottages, where we sought our night's lodging, it was easier to escape from our persecutors than in the narrow canoe. On land you can attack a mosquito with some chance of success and in the proper way, that is, by never aiming at him in the position where you imagine him to be. If, for instance, you feel him settling on the right cheek, immediately deal a heavy blow on the left. If he appears to be buzzing over your head, at once swing the pillow violently against the floor. You are not likely to hit him in any case, but you must do your best. In a canoe, where a vigorous motion is likely to capsize it and empty its contents into the expectant jaws of an alligator, the pursuit of a mosquito is necessarily very confined.

Before visiting the Usumacinta I thought I was well acquainted with these torments, but certainly I had never seen such numbers, or such large ones. I think it must have been on the banks of this river where the farmer lived who, on hearing a great noise among his chickens, rushed out one evening thinking that thieves were robbing his hen-roost. He saw nobody, and on counting his fowls, instead of any being missing, he found six more than belonged to him. His eyesight being a little defective, he did not discover until the next morning that he had counted six sturdy mosquitoes that had accidentally been fastened in the coop with his hens. "I thought they were too big for chickens when I counted them," he afterwards remarked.

At San Geronimo, where we slept one night, our host said that the following month was the best for mosquitoes, at present there were none worth mentioning. At one of the landing-places where we stopped for breakfast, one of the boatmen killed a nunyuca, which is said to be a very dangerous snake. This incident reminded me how very few snakes I had seen during my journey through what is usually considered a snake country. The few that I had seen I had killed and bottled, one or two being very prettily marked. The prettiest was a rattlesnake—cola de hueso; then there was also a yellow one called "corabilla," and a grey named "mano de piedra." The only large one bore the title of " bejuquilla," called so, I suppose, on account of its golden links.

From Guatemala I had always carried a piece of the root of the "guaco" plant, which is said, and on good authority, to be an efficacious remedy for snake-bites; I had no opportunity of proving its merits, but that I did not regret. The region of the Palizada abounds with dye-wood—palo de tinte—and the cutting of it forms the chief industry of this part of the republic. The tree is neither planted nor cultivated, but produces itself spontaneously in the damp soil of the lowlands, which are annually overflowed by the lagoons and rivers interspersed throughout the forests of Tabasco and Yucatan. Unfortunately log-wood cutting appears to necessitate " forced labour," and the condition of the "mozos sirvientes," as these unfortunate labouring classes of Indians are called, is much to be deplored. With a gradually increasing debt to their proprietors, these ignorant slaves become inoculated with the idea of perpetual servitude, without any hope in the future and without the least enjoyment of life. Death alone puts an end to their sufferings. The same system that originated sixty years ago exists to-day.

As we descended the river the absence of monkeys, which hitherto we had seen gambolling about the trees in the early morning, indicated an approach to human habitations, and at nine leagues from the Usumacinta we reached the town of Palizada. Quite a large place it seemed, with houses on both sides of the river, flags, shops, a boat-building establishment, and amid a flotilla of large and small canoes there was a steam tug. Here was civilization at last! no more travelling by mule, no more canoeing and alas! no more monkeys.

On landing, I heard that the tug would not leave for three or four days, but as my canoe was only engaged as far as here I disembarked my luggage, and after some difficulty found an empty room in which I established myself. It was not a luxurious apartment, as its door—it had no window—opened directly on the street, the refuse of which from time immemorial must have been swept into my chamber. However, as I could not get no other I had to be satisfied. Palizada possesses no attraction except to the log-wood merchant. The limits of the town are circumscribed by the forest, and by a tributary of the main river. A path along the river's bank certainly presents an opportunity for a walk, but in the day time the heat is so great, and in the evening the mosquitoes are so abundant that the pleasure becomes a pain.

The only public building, except the church, was a wooden structure called the "Galera publica," which was divided into a market prison and townhall. A remarkable specimen of art-coloring was in the plaza, where a blue and white striped lamp-post was surrounded with red and white brick seats, forming a grand circle in the centre of the square. The church, too, was painted in red and white stripes, and outshone the lamp-post in spite of the coloured seats. Facing the river were a few comfortable looking houses, but the inhabitants seemed as dull and as devoid of hospitality as a raft of their beloved log-wood. Business was dull they said, especially in log-wood. In fact everything was log-wood, you saw it on the river, you found specimens in the stores; I believe the people drank a decoction of it, and they certainly talked log-wood. After three days of Palizada you dream of log-wood.

On the evening of the third day I received information that the little tug would start for Carmen early on the following morning. I took very good care not to be late, and was grateful for the opportunity to accomplish the twenty leagues in a few hours instead of being obliged to travel by canoe. There were three or four passengers besides myself, and thus together with our luggage all the available space was occupied. Our run down the river was delightful, especially when we met the large heavy sailing canoes in full sail, making about twenty yards in the same number of minutes, even when aided by the strenuous exertions of their crews who pushed against the bank with long poles. Great alligators lay on the banks, but we flew past them too quickly to allow of a shot even when they stood their ground at our approach; fish hawks screamed at us from the trees; pelicans and long-legged water birds rose lazily from the adjoining lagoons, and the numberless twists and curves of the river continually presented fresh scenes and interesting objects of animal life.

After leaving Palizada a few huts and cottages were passed, but soon nothing was to be seen but the river and its forest-lined banks. The farther we proceeded the wilder became the scene, until the river opened out into three large lagoons, called Las Cruces.* Here land and water were so confused that it seemed a difficult matter to find the right passages. Sand banks, trunks of trees, mangrove swamps, islets, all formed an intricate water-way, the whole being surrounded in the distance by low lying forest, fringed with the coyol palm and papaya. Birds of all descriptions peopled the wide lakes and perched on the bare branches that stretched above the floating trunks. White cranes and graceful egrets rose from the rank grass, and the grave "padre santo" solemnly wagged his head at us as we passed under his drooping bough.

* Lagunas de Puerto Rico, de Atasta y del Pom.

344 *Across Central America.*

Leaving the lakes we entered the dangerous pass of the Boca Chica, and then emerged into the great Laguna de Terminos. This laguna, which takes its name from its situation between the provinces of Tabasco and Yucatan, is about fourteen leagues in length and seven in breadth. It is connected with the Gulf of Mexico by two mouths, between which lies the island of Carmen. The town of the same name is situated at the south-west extremity of the island, and, as we approached, the long line of trees, which was all the land we could at first see, rose higher and higher from the water, and gradually the shore and white houses of the old city expanded before us. We ran alongside a large wharf which, in spite of dull times, looked very lively after Palizada, and in a few minutes stepped on shore.

CHAPTER XXVIII.

ISLAND OF CARMEN—ITS DISCOVERY—DEPARTMENT OF CARMEN —TOWN—LIGHTHOUSE—MALINCHE—TRAFFIC BY WATER—SHIPPING—A TRAVELLING COMPANION—SOCIETY—WAITING FOR A BREEZE—A STAB IN THE DARK—LEAVE CARMEN—FRONTERA—A COLONY OF ALLIGATORS—THE MANATEE—THE BAR—WRECKERS —AT SEA.

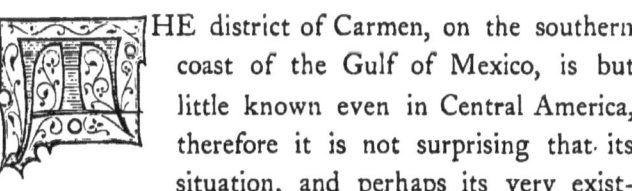HE district of Carmen, on the southern coast of the Gulf of Mexico, is but little known even in Central America, therefore it is not surprising that its situation, and perhaps its very existence, is unknown to many who are uninterested in dye-woods, which form its chief and almost only export. History says that the island was discovered in 1518 by Juan de Grijalva—one of Cortes' generals—and that it became the head-quarters of the old filibusters, who were eventually driven out by the Spanish government in 1716. During the occupation of the island by the filibusters, they made raids into the interior, established posts, whose remains are still to be seen, and by a system of robbery and extortion drove the

aborigines into the neighbouring provinces of Tabasco and Yucatan.

After the Spanish colonial government had obtained jurisdiction over the island, a Mexican ordinance defined the limits of the department, and Carmen was ruled by its own president. Later on it was added to the state of Yucatan; then in 1853 it was created a distinct department, and after four years was again incorporated with Yucatan.

When in 1857 Campeachy separated itself from the rest of Yucatan, Carmen followed her example, and is now the richest and most productive part of that State. The island is only seven leagues in length and two in breadth, its sandy soil being well covered with fruit trees and woods. The town is clean and well built, the tower of Atalaya forming a very picturesque object from the water. The government building, too, in which are concentrated all the public offices, is a very handsome edifice. Barracks, a prison, a hospital, a school, and a "Galera publica," are the most conspicuous of the remaining public buildings.

Opposite the town of Carmen and on the coast of Jicalango is a fine lighthouse with a revolving light. This was erected in 1866, and its great utility on this dangerous coast cannot be over-estimated. Near this spot is said to he the birthplace of Malinche, the favourite of Cortes; but as this celebrated woman has several more birthplaces—a plethora of which in addition to other relics is the usual penalty for greatness—much reliance cannot be attached to the statement.

On this coast likewise are some sugar plantations, but very little more is raised than is necessary for home consumption. On account of the limited extent of the island, and the constant inundations on the main land, all traffic is carried on by water, the navigation of which is divided between two classes of vessels. One of these consists of small canoes and piraguas, which are entirely occupied with the navigation of the lagoons and rivers; the other class is made up of large sailing canoes— from twenty to sixty tons burden—which carry to the port the products of the interior.

Besides the native shipping, the port is enlivened by several vessels, and once or twice a month by a small steamer that touches here on her way to Campeachy, to meet foreign-bound steamers from Vera Cruz. I had just missed this connecting link by a few hours on arriving from Palizada, and rather than wait two or three weeks in hot Carmen, had determined to take the first opportunity of going to Frontera, a town further down the Gulf, where I heard there would be a chance of finding a steamer for Vera Cruz. The only accommodation I had been able to find, was a small room in what was called an inn, but which in reality was a gambling-house. As the table was never spread with anything but cards, I had to seek my meals elsewhere.

By chance I found a very comfortable boarding-house, kept by one of that ubiquitous class—widows in reduced circumstances—and there I met an American gentleman, from Mexico, and his wife. We soon became acquainted, and as he was also going to Frontera on business, we agreed to travel together in one of the large canoes which was to leave as soon as the wind was favourable. As my new friends knew nearly everybody in the town, the few days we had to wait passed quickly. The inhabitants were a kind hospitable people much given to visiting, which they carried on in the true Spanish American style, by the aid of two long rows of chairs in which the visitors and the visited sat facing one another.

When the sun went down, society drove to the Alameda in old-fashioned chariots that would have done credit to a Lord Mayor's show. In the evening, there was usually a general gathering at some house, where music and dancing were indulged in to a not very late hour. Carmen is well supplied with shops, stores, restaurants, &c., but in the whole town I was unable to find a watchmaker who could repair my watch, which had been injured whilst travelling. Afterwards I congratulated myself that I had not found one, as a friend told me that in a town larger than Carmen, in Mexico, he had once taken a valuable watch, by a well-known English maker, to a jeweller for some slight repairs. In a few days, he received his watch and an envelope, which the man handed to him, saying, "Inside are a few wheels which I have removed, finding them to be superfluous."

Orders had been given to the captain of the canoe to send word to us immediately when he considered the wind suitable for carrying his vessel over the bar

Dispute with a Washer-woman. 349

into the Gulf. For four nights—the breeze only springs up in the night, or early morning—we had anxiously expected a messenger with the information; but not till the fifth morning did we receive the desired intelligence. Then hurrying down in the dark to the landing-place, we embarked and were soon cleaving the waters on our way to the ocean. It was a relief to get off at last, as it is not agreeable to lie awake night after night with the expectation of being summoned at any minute to rise and embark.

My slumbers would probably have been more disturbed than they were, had I known, as I afterwards found out, that for two or three nights a copper-coloured scoundrel had been waiting outside my door with a long knife for my especial benefit. His enmity to me had been caused by the following facts. When I arrived at Carmen, I sent for a washer-woman, who promised to return my clothes on the following day. After waiting for four days, I was afraid I might be summoned to leave suddenly, and therefore ordered them to be returned at once, whether washed or not. The old woman brought them back untouched, as she said that all the days she had kept them were saints' days, and, therefore, she could not wash. Nevertheless, she demanded full payment, and on my refusing it— but giving her something for her trouble—she left. Her husband then, breathing vengeance, lay in wait for me, until discovered by my landlord, who quickly brought a policeman, but after the rascal had disappeared. As, on account of the great heat, I always slept with my door—which opened directly on the street—half open, it is probable that my kindly-intentioned friend would have walked in had he meant anything more than mere bluster.

After a long day's sail we arrived at the mouth of the Tabasco river, and a pilot came on board to conduct us over the bar. Then the wind dropped, and to avoid a mosquito night on the river we took the pilot's boat and pulled for Frontera, which is situated some miles from the mouth on the right bank of the river. There I learnt that a steamer had left that morning for Vera Cruz, and nobody knew when another would arrive.

The town consists of a number of miserable cottages, most of which surround a large green square, and the principal street runs parallel with the river from which it is separated by a narrow road. A duller and more uninteresting place cannot be imagined; if you leave the main road you tumble into the river on one side, or into a swamp on the other, and often the main road itself is under water. Yet it contains a custom-house, new barracks, two inns, and a German and American consulate.

My American friend soon departed for Tabasco, an equally interesting town situated farther up the river. Before he went he introduced me to the chief of the custom-house, who proved to be an invaluable acquaintance. He would not hear of my remaining at the hot uncomfortable inn, but from his own house furnished an upper room for me in the unoccupied barracks. As these were on the river-bank, and the rooms opened on every side, they caught every passing breeze, and for coolness my quarters were unequalled in Frontera. Their only drawback was that they were liable to be seized at any moment by the rebels—pronunciados—who were daily expected; but that was of very slight importance in comparison with the comfort the airy barracks afforded.

It seemed to me I was always meeting with kind people and enjoying luxuries when I ought properly to have been roughing it. As the "pronunciados" did not appear during my visit I had even to be grateful to them. Their neglect could hardly have been caused by the strength of the garrison. The river here is very broad, as a few miles above the town the waters of the Usumacinta and of the Tabasco meet and flow together to the Gulf.

A trip in a canoe to the opposite shore reveals a strange sight. Here may be seen hundreds of huge "lagartos" basking on the mud banks, and floating like logs on the brown water. In such numbers do the monsters congregate, that in some places they may be seen lying like pigs in a pen, with their horrid jaws resting on each other's backs, and only waiting for somebody or something to " come in out of the wet," as the shark said when he swallowed a bag.

In these lagoons and quiet rivers is also found the

great pig-like "manatee," whose full length sometimes reaches twelve or fourteen feet. The flesh of this creature is esteemed a great delicacy, and many young ones fall victims to the epicurean taste of their neighbours, the alligators.

The departure of a visitor from Frontera depends entirely upon the wind. When a "norther" blows the accumulation of sand on the bar is so great that no steamer can cross. This bar has much to answer for, as not only are ships lost on it accidentally, but every year numerous vessels are loaded with worthless wood and wrecked intentionally by their unscrupulous owners. From what I heard, it seemed extraordinary that anyone could be found willing to insure vessels or cargo from this region.

After many days waiting for a steamer, one at last appeared from Vera Cruz whither it was about to return in two or three days. Up to the last minute I was afraid we should suffer a long delay, as on the morning for starting a "norther" set in, and the pilot refused to take the vessel over the bar. But the captain was anxious to get back as soon as possible, as his vessel was employed by the Mexican government to convey troops to the disaffected ports, and so he determined to cross the bar without the pilot. This he accomplished successfully, and with a wave of triumph in the direction of the pilot who was watching us through his telescope, we left the shallows behind and our ship ploughed her way through the deep ocean.

Adios.

And here I must lay down my pen; these seldom visited regions are fading from view, and will soon be replaced by others that have been more often described.. To those who in thought have accompanied me in my journey across the continent, I bid the Spaniard's kind farewell—Adios.

THE END.

www.ingramcontent.com/pod-product-compliance
Lightning Source LLC
Chambersburg PA
CBHW031423230426
43668CB00007B/417